Sources of
World Societies

Volume 2: Since 1450

Sources of
World Societies

Volume 2: Since 1450

Third Edition

THE COMPANION READER FOR
A HISTORY OF WORLD SOCIETIES

ELEVENTH EDITION

Merry E. Wiesner-Hanks
Patricia Buckley Ebrey
Roger B. Beck
Jerry Dávila
Clare Haru Crowston
John P. McKay

 bedford/st.martin's
Macmillan Learning

Boston | New York

For Bedford/St. Martin's

Vice President, Editorial, Macmillan Learning Humanities: Edwin Hill
Program Director for History: Michael Rosenberg
Senior Program Manager for History: William J. Lombardo
History Marketing Manager: Melissa Rodriguez
Director of Content Development: Jane Knetzger
Developmental Editor: Tess Fletcher
Senior Content Project Manager: Christina M. Horn
Senior Workflow Manager: Jennifer Wetzel
Production Assistant: Brianna Lester
Senior Media Project Manager: Michelle Camisa
Editorial Services: Lumina Datamatics Inc.
Composition: Lumina Datamatics Inc.
Photo Editor: Christine Buese
Cover Design: William Boardman
Cover Art: Dama de Blanco (White Lady), 1928 (oil on panel), Frida Kahlo (1907–1954)/
    CHRISTIES IMAGES/Private Collection/Bridgeman Images. © 2017 Banco de México
    Diego Rivera Frida Kahlo Museums Trust, Mexico, D.F./Artists Rights Society (ARS),
    New York
Printing and Binding: LSC Communications

Manufactured in the United States of America.

2   1   0   9   8   7
f   e   d   c   b

For information, write: Bedford/St. Martin's, 75 Arlington Street, Boston, MA 02116

ISBN 978-1-319-07040-3

Acknowledgments

PREFACE

The primary sources contained in *Sources of World Societies* span prehistory to the present, capturing the voices of individuals within the context of their times and ways of life, while enriching the cross-cultural fabric of history as a whole. Now with more visual sources and an emphasis on developing historical thinking skills, *Sources* draws from the records of rulers and subjects alike — from men and women, philosophers, revolutionaries, economists, laborers, and artists, among others, to present a textured view of the past. With a parallel chapter structure and documents handpicked to extend the textbook, this reader is designed to complement *A History of World Societies*, Eleventh Edition. *Sources of World Societies* animates the past for students, providing resonant accounts of the people and events that changed the face of world history, from myths of creation to accounts of hardship and conflict, from a local to a global scale.

With input from the textbook authors, as well as from current instructors of the world history survey course, we have compiled these documents with one goal foremost in mind: to make history's most classic and compelling voices accessible to students, from the most well-known thinkers and documentarians of their times to the galvanized or introspective commoner. While students have access to formative documents of each era, lesser-heard voices reveal life as the great majority of people lived it. In Chapter 30, for example, students can juxtapose President Truman's press release on the bombing of Hiroshima with the firsthand account of a Japanese survivor of the atomic bomb drop.

We have stepped back from drawing conclusions and instead provide just enough background to enable students' own analysis of the sources at hand. Chapter-opening paragraphs briefly review the major events of the time and place relevant to the documents that follow, within the framework of the corresponding textbook chapter. A concise headnote for each document provides context about the author and the circumstances surrounding the document's creation, while gloss notes supply clarification to aid comprehension of unfamiliar terms and references. Each document is followed by Reading and Discussion Questions that spur student analysis of the material, while chapter-concluding Comparative Questions encourage students to contemplate the relationships among the sources within and, when called for, between the chapters. All of the questions in *Sources* aim to form a dynamic connection for students that bridges the events of the past with their own evolving understandings of power and its abuses, of the ripple effects of human agency, and of the material conditions of life. The excerpts range in length to allow for a variety of class assignments.

CONTENTS

Sources of
World Societies

Volume 2: Since 1450

16

The Acceleration of Global Contact
1450–1600

Although long-standing trade routes meant that many of the world's civilizations were in contact with one another before 1500, this interaction accelerated drastically in the sixteenth century when Europe became a much larger player in world trade. Europe began establishing trade routes to the newly discovered Americas and sent Christian missionaries to all corners of the globe. The sources in this chapter examine the impact of Europe's entrance into the global community and address the continued importance of the civilizations that had established earlier trade routes in the Indian Ocean.

16-1 | The World as Europeans Knew It in 1502
World Map (1502)

Created in 1502, this map shows the world as Europeans knew it ten years after the voyages of Christopher Columbus. The African coastline is rendered in extraordinarily accurate detail. Trading destinations in India and Southeast Asia are also clearly indicated. The Americas, however, remain a rough sketch, a largely imagined place, not a known one. Nonetheless, the map offers a glimpse of the future. In 1494, Spain and Portugal signed the Treaty of Tordesillas, which established a line of demarcation running north-south (the blue line on the left side of the map running through modern-day Brazil). All non-European territories to the west of the line were to be Spanish. All those to the east were to be Portuguese. As you examine the map, think about what it reveals about the European age of expansion. How does it tell the story of the previous century of exploration? What does it suggest about the course of conquests yet to come?

READING AND DISCUSSION QUESTIONS

1. How would you explain the prominence of Africa on the map? How did Europeans develop such an accurate sense of its coastline?

2. What were the larger implications of the Treaty of Tordesillas? What does it tell you about the importance the Spanish and Portuguese attached to the discoveries and achievements of the fifteenth century?

VIEWPOINTS

The Motives of Columbus and His Patrons

The year 1492 was a momentous one in Spanish history. With the fall of the Muslim state of Granada, Ferdinand of Aragon and Isabella of Castile completed the Christian *reconquista* (reconquest) of the Iberian Peninsula. Having driven the "infidels" from their last Iberian stronghold, they turned to the "enemy within," issuing a proclamation expelling all Jews from their lands. It was at this moment, fired with a crusading spirit and eager to gain access to the wealth of Asia, that Ferdinand and Isabella chose to sponsor the exploratory westward voyage of Christopher Columbus. Keep this larger context in mind as you read the documents included in this feature. How does this history help explain the motives and expectations of Columbus and his patrons?

16-2 | Columbus Defends His Accomplishments
CHRISTOPHER COLUMBUS, *Letter from the Third Voyage* (1493)

When King Ferdinand and Queen Isabella decided to fund Columbus's expeditions, they were not engaging in an act of charity. They were making an investment. This is not to say that their motives were strictly material. Both were devout Catholics and were committed to spreading the faith. Nonetheless, Columbus claimed that he knew a faster route to Asia, and to late-fifteenth-century Europeans, Asia meant, first and foremost, a highly profitable trade in luxury goods. Thus when Columbus failed to deliver on his implied promise to deliver fabulous wealth, he knew he would have to explain himself. As you read the letter, think about Columbus's intended audience. How did he seek to refute his critics? Why did he feel he had to?

Cecil Jane, ed. and trans., *Select Documents Illustrating the Four Voyages of Columbus.* Published by Haklut Society, 1967.

Most serene and most high and most powerful princes, the king and queen, our sovereigns: The Holy Trinity moved Your Highnesses to this enterprise of the Indies, and of His infinite goodness, He made me the messenger thereof, so that, being moved thereunto, I came with the mission to your royal presence, as being the most exalted of Christian princes and so ardently devoted to the Faith and to its increase. The persons who should have occupied themselves with the matter held it to be impossible, for they made of gifts of chance their riches and on them placed their trust.

On this matter I spent six or seven years of deep anxiety, expounding, as well as I could, how great service might in this be rendered to the Lord, by proclaiming abroad His holy name and His faith to so many peoples, which was all a thing of so great excellence and for the fair fame of great princes and for a notable memorial for them. It was needful also to speak of the temporal gain therein, foreshadowed in the writings of so many wise men, worthy of credence, who wrote histories and related how in these parts there are great riches. And it was likewise necessary to bring forward in this matter that which had been said and thought by those who have written of the world and who have described it. Finally, Your Highnesses determined that this enterprise should be undertaken.

Here you displayed that lofty spirit which you have always shown in every great affair, for all those who had been engaged on the matter and who had heard the proposal, one and all laughed it to scorn, save two friars who were ever constant.

I, although I suffered weariness, was very sure that this would not come to nothing, and I am still, for it is true that all will pass away, save the Word of God, and all that He has said will be fulfilled. And He spake so clearly of these lands by the mouth of Isaiah, in many places of his Book, affirming that from Spain His holy name should be proclaimed to them.

And I set forth in the name of the Holy Trinity, and I returned very speedily, with evidence of all, as much as I had said, in my hand. Your highnesses undertook to send me again, and in a little while I say that, . . . by the grace of God, I discovered three hundred and thirty-three leagues of Tierra Firme,[1] the end of the East, and seven hundred islands of importance, over and above that which I discovered on the first voyage, and I circumnavigated the island of Española, which in circumference is greater than all Spain, wherein are people innumerable, all of whom should pay tribute.

Then was born the defaming and disparagement of the undertaking which had been begun there, because I had not immediately sent caravels laden with gold, no thought being taken of the brevity of the time and the other many obstacles which I mentioned. And on this account, for my sins or, as I believe that it will be, for my salvation, I was held in abhorrence and was opposed in whatever I said and asked.

---

[1] **Tierra Firme:** The mainland.

For this cause, I decided to come to Your Highnesses, and to cause you to wonder at everything, and to show you the reason that I had for all. And I told you of the peoples whom I had seen, among whom or from whom many souls may be saved. And I brought to you the service of the people of the island of Española, how they were bound to pay tribute and how they held you as their sovereigns and lords. And I brought to you abundant evidence of gold, and that there are mines and very great nuggets, and likewise of copper. And I brought to you many kinds of spices, of which it would be wearisome to write, and I told you of the great amount of brazil[2] and of other things, innumerable.

READING AND DISCUSSION QUESTIONS

1. What religious implications did Columbus attach to his voyages? Why do you think he chose to highlight the opportunity his discoveries created for the spread of Catholicism?

2. What material advantages did Columbus claim would result from his discoveries? How might his readers have responded to his claims?

16-3 | Spanish Ambitions in the New World

THEODORE DE BRY, *Columbus at Hispaniola* (ca. 1590)

In his letters to King Ferdinand and Queen Isabella, Columbus told his side of the story, describing his voyages in ways that were meant both to please his patrons and to emphasize his personal accomplishments. His was not the last word, however. In the decades following Columbus's death, the motives behind his expeditions and the subsequent Spanish colonization of the Americas became matters of considerable debate. For example, this late-sixteenth-century engraving by the Protestant artist and engraver Theodore de Bry contains all of the motives mentioned by Columbus (see Document 16-2) but presents them in a way that *offers* an implicit rebuke to the Genoese explorer. As you examine it, think about its intended message. What did the artist see as the primary motives behind Spanish exploration and colonization? How did he want his viewers to feel about the scenes he included in this engraving?

---

[2] **brazil:** Brazilwood, a very expensive wood that was much sought after in Europe.

Private Collection/Bridgeman Images.

READING AND DISCUSSION QUESTIONS

1. Which motive did de Bry portray as most important? How did he indicate this?

2. What importance should we attach to the fact that the cross on the left is being erected by a small group of soldiers? What does the scene tell us about de Bry's views on Spanish missionary work in the Americas?

3. What should we make of the Native Americans fleeing the Spanish ships on the right side of the engraving? What are they afraid of? Did de Bry believe their fears were justified?

VIEWPOINTS COMPARATIVE QUESTIONS

1. What common elements are included in both Columbus's letter and de Bry's engraving? How do those elements combine in each document to tell the story of Columbus's voyages?

2. Why might Europeans have seen Columbus's voyages differently at the beginning of the sixteenth century than they did at the end? What intervening events, both in the Americas and in Europe, might have reshaped European perspectives?

16-4 | Cross-Cultural Communications and Conquest
BERNAL DÍAZ DEL CASTILLO, From *The True History of the Conquest of New Spain* (1568)

Initial Spanish occupation of the New World focused on exploiting native labor in the Caribbean. When the natives began to die off in large numbers because of disease and harsh treatment, some Spanish explorers (known as conquistadors) sought the conquest of new lands. One, Hernán Cortés, left his settlement at Cuba and landed in Central America in 1518. By 1519, he had collected a number of native tribes as allies and marched on the largest city in Mexico, Tenochtitlan, taking control of the entire area by 1521. This expedition is described by Bernal Díaz del Castillo, an eyewitness to the invasion. He wrote fifty years after participating in the conquest and named his work *The True History* to distinguish it from earlier accounts that were not written by eyewitnesses.

As Xicotenga was bad tempered and obstinate and proud, he decided to send forty Indians with food, poultry, bread and fruit and four miserable looking old Indian women, and much copal and many parrots' feathers. From their appearance we thought that the Indians who brought this present came with peaceful intentions, and when they reached our camp they fumigated Cortés with incense without doing him reverence, as was usually their custom. They said: "The Captain Xicotenga sends you all this so that you can eat. If you are savage Teules,[3] as the Cempoalans[4] say you are, and if you wish for a sacrifice, take these four women and sacrifice them and you can eat their flesh and hearts, but as we do not know your manner of doing it, we have not sacrificed them now before you; but if you are men, eat the poultry and the bread and fruit, and if you are tame

---

Bernal Díaz del Castillo, *The True History of the Conquest of New Spain*, trans. Alfred Percival Maudslay (London: Bedford Press, 1908), 257–263.

[3] **Teules:** A series of divinities from Central America. Occasionally they are considered wicked. Later, "Teules" virtually became a synonym for the Spanish.

[4] **Cempoalans:** A tribe in Central America.

Teules we have brought you copal (which I have already said is a sort of incense) and parrots' feathers; make your sacrifice with that."

Cortés answered through our interpreters that he had already sent to them to say that he desired peace and had not come to make war, but had come to entreat them and make clear to them on behalf of our Lord Jesus Christ, whom we believe in and worship, and of the Emperor Don Carlos, whose vassals we are, that they should not kill or sacrifice anyone as was their custom to do. That we were all men of bone and flesh just as they were, and not Teules but Christians, and that it was not our custom to kill anyone; that had we wished to kill people, many opportunities of perpetrating cruelties had occurred during the frequent attacks they had made on us, both by day and night. That for the food they had brought he gave them thanks, and that they were not to be as foolish as they had been, but should now make peace.

It seems that these Indians whom Xicotenga had sent with the food were spies sent to examine our huts and ranchos, and horses and artillery and [to report] how many of us there were in each hut, our comings and goings, and everything else that could be seen in the camp. They remained there that day and the following night, and some of them went with messages to Xicotenga and others arrived. Our friends whom we had brought with us from Cempoala looked on and bethought them that it was not a customary thing for our enemies to stay in the camp day and night without any purpose, and it was clear to them that they were spies, and they were the more suspicious of them in that when we went on the expedition to the little town of Tzumpantzingo, two old men of that town had told the Cempoalans that Xicotenga was all ready with a large number of warriors to attack our camp by night, in such a way that their approach would not be detected, and the Cempoalans at that time took it for a joke or bravado, and not believing it they had said nothing to Cortés; but Doña Marina[5] heard of it at once and she repeated it to Cortés.

So as to learn the truth, Cortés had two of the most honest looking of the Tlaxcalans taken apart from the others, and they confessed that they were spies; then two others were taken and they also confessed that they were spies from Xicotenga and the reason why they had come. Cortés ordered them to be released, and we took two more of them and they confessed that they were neither more nor less than spies, but added that their Captain Xicotenga was awaiting their report to attack us that night with all his companies. When Cortés heard this he let it be known throughout the camp that we were to keep on the alert, believing that they would attack as had been arranged. Then he had seventeen of those spies captured and cut off the hands of some and the thumbs of others and sent them to the Captain Xicotenga to tell him that he had had them thus punished for daring to come in such a way, and to tell him that he might come when he chose by day or by night, for we should await him here two days, and that if

---

[5] **Doña Marina:** A native woman who learned Spanish. She served as a translator for Cortés and became his lover, giving birth to a son.

he did not come within those two days that we would go and look for him in his camp, and that we would already have gone to attack them and kill them, were it not for the liking we had for them, and that now they should quit their foolishness and make peace.

They say that it was at the very moment that those Indians set out with their hands and thumbs cut off, that Xicotenga wished to set out from his camp with all his forces to attack us by night as had been arranged; but when he saw his spies returning in this manner he wondered greatly and asked the reason of it, and they told him all that had happened, and from this time forward he lost his courage and pride, and in addition to this one of his commanders with whom he had wrangles and disagreements during the battles which had been fought, had left the camp with all his men.

Let us get on with our story. . . .

* * *

While we were in camp not knowing that they would come in peace, as we had so greatly desired, and were busy polishing our arms and making arrows, each one of us doing what was necessary to prepare for battle, at that moment one of our scouts came hurrying in to say that many Indian men and women with loads were coming along the high road from Tlaxcala, and without leaving the road were making for our camp. . . . Cortés and all of us were delighted at this news, for we believed that it meant peace, as in fact it did, and Cortés ordered us to make no display of alarm and not to show any concern, but to stay hidden in our huts. Then, from out of all those people who came bearing loads, the four chieftains advanced who were charged to treat for peace, according to the instructions given by the old Caciques.[6] Making signs of peace by bowing the head, they came straight to the hut where Cortés was lodging and placed one hand on the ground and kissed the earth and three times made obeisance and burnt copal, and said that all the Caciques of Tlaxcala and their allies and vassals, friends and confederates, were come to place themselves under the friendship and peace of Cortés and of his brethren the Teules who accompanied him. They asked his pardon for not having met us peacefully, and for the war which they had waged on us, for they had believed and held for certain that we were friends of Montezuma and his Mexicans, who have been their mortal enemies from times long past, for they saw that many of his vassals who paid him tribute had come in our company, and they believed that they were endeavoring to gain an entry into their country by guile and treachery, as was their custom to do, so as to rob them of their women and children; and this was the reason why they did not believe the messengers whom we had sent to them. In addition to this they said that the Indians who had first gone forth to make war on us as we entered their country had done it without their orders or advice, but by that of the Chuntales Estomies [barbarous Otomís], who were wild people and very stupid, and that when they saw that we were so few in number, they

---

[6] **Caciques:** Leaders.

thought to capture us and carry us off as prisoners to their lords and gain thanks for so doing; that now they came to beg pardon for their audacity, and had brought us food, and that every day they would bring more and trusted that we would receive it with the friendly feeling with which it was sent; that within two days the captain Xicotenga would come with other Caciques and give a further account of the sincere wish of all Tlaxcala to enjoy our friendship.

As soon as they had finished their discourse they bowed their heads and placed their hands on the ground and kissed the earth. Then Cortés spoke to them through our interpreters very seriously, pretending he was angry, and said that there were reasons why we should not listen to them and should reject their friendship, for as soon as we had entered their country we sent to them offering peace and had told them that we wished to assist them against their enemies, the Mexicans, and they would not believe it and wished to kill our ambassadors; and not content with that, they had attacked us three times both by day and by night, and had spied on us and held us under observation; and in the attacks which they made on us we might have killed many of their vassals, but he would not, and he grieved for those who were killed; but it was their own fault and he had made up his mind to go to the place where the old chiefs were living and to attack them; but as they had now sought peace in the name of that province, he would receive them in the name of our lord the King and thank them for the food they had brought. He told them to go at once to their chieftains and tell them to come or send to treat for peace with fuller powers, and that if they did not come we would go to their town and attack them.

He ordered them to be given some blue beads to be handed to their Caciques as a sign of peace, and he warned them that when they came to our camp it should be by day and not by night, lest we should kill them.

Then those four messengers departed, and left in some Indian houses a little apart from our camp, the Indian women whom they had brought to make bread, some poultry, and all the necessaries for service, and twenty Indians to bring wood and water. From now on they brought us plenty to eat, and when we saw this and believed that peace was a reality, we gave great thanks to God for it. It had come in the nick of time, for we were already lean and worn out and discontented with the war, not knowing or being able to forecast what would be the end of it. . . .

I will leave off here and will go on to tell what took place later, about some messengers sent by the great Montezuma.

READING AND DISCUSSION QUESTIONS

1. How does this source describe the various Mexican tribes? What does Castillo's description of these people reveal about how Europeans viewed the natives of Central America?

2. How are the Europeans, especially Cortés, able to converse with the Mexica?

3. Describe the meeting between Cortés and the native tribes. What kind of agreement is struck between them? How do the natives interact with Cortés?

16-5 | Scenes from the Spanish Conquest of the Mexica
From *The Florentine Codex* (ca. 1577–1580)

A member of the Franciscan order, the Spaniard Bernardino de Sahagún (1499–1590) was one of the earliest missionaries to arrive in Mexico. Although committed to converting the native population of Mexico to Christianity, Sahagún learned the Aztec language of Nahuatl and helped compile an extensive study of Aztec culture and religious beliefs. This work raised concern among Sahagún's superiors for its sympathetic portrayal of the Aztec people. For this reason, his works were lost for more than two hundred years until their eventual discovery in a library in Florence. The manuscript contains writing in Nahuatl, occasionally with a Spanish translation, in addition to numerous illustrations made by native artists. Even though the text was influenced by European ideas—for example, the Mexica gods are called devils—it is one of the few sources written in a native language about the conquest. The illustration here shows the beginning of the conflict between the Spanish and the Mexica, when King Moctezuma was captured and put in chains.

DE AGOSTINI EDITORE/Bridgeman Images.

READING AND DISCUSSION QUESTIONS

1. How are the natives and the Spanish portrayed in this image, and does it suggest any bias? Explain your answer.

2. Judging from the drawings, why might the Spanish have had a military advantage over the natives?

■ COMPARATIVE QUESTIONS ■

1. Compare and contrast the descriptions of Native Americans offered by Columbus and by Castillo. How would you explain the differences you note?

2. Taken together, what do the documents included in this chapter tell you about the motives and goals behind Spanish exploration and colonization in the New World?

3. Compare and contrast de Bry's engraving of Columbus at Hispaniola and the images from *The Florentine Codex*. How did each deal with the issue of violence between Europeans and Native Americans?

17

The Islamic World Powers
1300–1800

With the decline of the Mongol Empire in the late thirteenth and fourteenth centuries, power shifted to a number of Turkish territories. By the sixteenth century, three areas had developed into major Islamic empires: the Safavid in Persia, the Ottoman in Anatolia, and the Mughal in India. Their collective territories stretched from eastern Europe and West Africa through present-day Bangladesh. As each state flourished, it made significant political, economic, intellectual, and artistic contributions. Islamic culture was enriched by the states' interactions with one another and with the increasingly mobile peoples of Christian Europe. However, the impressive extent of Islamic society and culture represented by the three states belies the sharp and often violent differences among them and the internal tensions in each society. The following documents reveal the splendor and troubled nature of the Ottoman, Safavid, and Mughal Empires, as well as their increasing interactions with western Europeans.

17-1 | An Ottoman Sultan Threatens the Shah of Persia
SULTAN SELIM I, *From a Letter to Shah Ismail of Persia* (1514)

Sultan Selim I (r. 1512–1520) presided over a massive territorial expansion of the Ottoman Empire, conquering much of the Middle East, including the holy cities of Mecca and Medina. After defeating the Mamluk Dynasty in Egypt in 1517, Selim assumed the title of caliph—a political and religious successor to Muhammad—thereby declaring Sunni Ottoman leadership of the Muslim world. The excerpt that follows is from Selim's letter to Shah Ismail of Persia, the young founder of the Shi'ite Safavid Empire and a growing threat to Selim's power.

John J. Saunders, ed. and trans., *The Muslim World on the Eve of Europe's Expansion* (Englewood Cliffs, N.J.: Prentice-Hall, 1966), 41–43. Copyright © 1966 by Prentice-Hall, Inc. All rights reserved.

The ensuing conflict in 1514 marked an important moment in Sunni–Shi'ite power struggles in the Islamic world.

The Supreme Being who is at once the sovereign arbiter of the destinies of men and the source of all light and knowledge, declares in the holy book [the Qur'an] that the true faith is that of the Muslims, and that whoever professes another religion, far from being hearkened to and saved, will on the contrary be cast out among the rejected on the great day of the Last Judgment; He says further, this God of truth, that His designs and decrees are unalterable, that all human acts are perforce reported to Him, and that he who abandons the good way will be condemned to hell-fire and eternal torments. Place yourself, O Prince, among the true believers, those who walk in the path of salvation, and who turn aside with care from vice and infidelity. . . .

I, sovereign chief of the Ottomans, master of the heroes of the age; . . . I, the exterminator of idolaters, destroyer of the enemies of the true faith, the terror of the tyrants and pharaohs of the age; I, before whom proud and unjust kings have humbled themselves, and whose hand breaks the strongest scepters; I, the great Sultan-Khan, son of Sultan Bayezid-Khan, son of Sultan Muhammad-Khan, son of Sultan Murad-Khan, I address myself graciously to you, Emir Ismail, chief of the troops of Persia, comparable in tyranny to Sohak and Afrasiab [legendary Asian kings], and predestined to perish . . . in order to make known to you that the works emanating from the Almighty are not the fragile products of caprice or folly, but make up an infinity of mysteries impenetrable to the human mind. The Lord Himself says in his holy book: "We have not created the heavens and the earth in order to play a game" [Qur'an, 21:16]. Man, who is the noblest of the creatures and the summary of the marvels of God, is in consequence on earth the living image of the Creator. It is He who has set up Caliphs on earth, because, joining faculties of soul with perfection of body, man is the only being who can comprehend the attributes of the divinity and adore its sublime beauties; but he possesses this rare intelligence, he attains this divine knowledge only in our religion and by observing the precepts of the prince of prophets . . . the right arm of the God of Mercy [Muhammad]; it is then only by practicing the true religion that man will prosper in this world and merit eternal life in the other. As to you, Emir Ismail, such a recompense will not be your lot; because you have denied the sanctity of the divine laws; because you have deserted the path of salvation and the sacred commandments; because you have impaired the purity of the dogmas of Islam; because you have dishonored, soiled, and destroyed the altars of the Lord, usurped the scepter of the East by unlawful and tyrannical means; because coming forth from the dust, you have raised yourself by odious devices to a place shining with splendor and magnificence; because you have opened to Muslims the gates of tyranny and oppression; because you have joined iniquity, perjury, and blasphemy to your sectarian impiety; because under the cloak of the hypocrite, you have sowed everywhere trouble and sedition; because you have raised the standard of irreligion and heresy; because yielding to the impulse of your evil passions, and giving yourself up without rein to the most infamous disorders, you have dared to throw off the control of Muslim laws and to permit lust and rape, the massacre of the most virtuous and respectable men, the destruction of pulpits and temples, the profanation of tombs, the ill-treatment of the ulama,[1] the doctors [teachers] and emirs [military commanders and princes] descended from the Prophet, the repudiation of the Quran, the cursing of the legitimate Caliphs.[2] Now as the first duty of a Muslim and above all of a pious prince is to obey the commandment, "O, you faithful who believe, be the executors of the decrees of God!" the ulama and our doctors have pronounced sentence of death against you, perjurer and blasphemer, and have imposed on every Muslim the sacred obligation to arm in defense of religion and destroy heresy and impiety in your person and that of all your partisans.

Animated by the spirit of this fatwa [religious decree], conforming to the Quran, the code of divine laws, and wishing on one side to strengthen Islam, on the other to liberate the lands and peoples who writhe under your yoke, we have resolved to lay aside our imperial robes in order to put on the shield and coat of mail [armor], to raise our ever victorious banner, to assemble our invincible armies, to take up the gauntlet of the avenger, to march with our soldiers, whose sword strikes mortal blows, and whose point will pierce the enemy even to the constellation of Sagittarius. In pursuit of this noble resolution, we have entered upon the campaign, and guided by the hand of the Almighty, we hope soon to strike down your tyrannous arm, blow away the clouds of glory and grandeur which trouble your head and cause your fatal blindness, release from your despotism your trembling subjects, smother you in the end in the very mass of flames which your infernal jinn [supernatural spirit] raises everywhere along your passage, accomplishing in this way on you the maxim which says: "He who sows discord can only reap evils and afflictions." However, anxious to conform to the spirit of the law of the Prophet, we come, before commencing war, to set out before you the words of the Quran, in place of the sword, and to exhort you to embrace the true faith; this is why we address this letter to you. . . .

We urge you to look into yourself, to renounce your errors, and to march towards the good with a firm and courageous step; we ask further that you give up possession of the territory violently seized from our state and to which you have only illegitimate pretensions, that you deliver it back into the hands of our lieutenants and officers; and if you value your safety and repose, this should be done without delay.

But if, to your misfortune, you persist in your past conduct, puffed up with the idea of your power and your foolish bravado, you wish to pursue the course

---

[1] **ulama:** Religious teachers and interpreters of the Qur'an and Muslim law.

[2] **the legitimate Caliphs:** Shi'ites broke with mainstream Islam over a dispute about the early caliphate. They believe that Muhammad's cousin and son-in-law Ali (the fourth caliph) should have been the first caliph. Shi'ites thus believe that the first three caliphs are illegitimate.

of your iniquities, you will see in a few days your plains covered with our tents and inundated with our battalions. Then prodigies of valor will be done, and we shall see the decrees of the Almighty, Who is the God of Armies, and sovereign judge of the actions of men, accomplished. For the rest, victory to him who follows the path of salvation!

READING AND DISCUSSION QUESTIONS

1. What is Selim's principal complaint against Ismail? How does he state it?

2. Where in the letter does Selim use the rhetoric of religion against Ismail, and where does he accuse Ismail of political failings? How do the two arguments work together?

3. What do you think Selim's real purpose was in writing this letter: to give Ismail an opportunity to repent, to provoke Ismail into declaring war, or to justify his own decision to attack Ismail?

17-2 | Akbar's Court as Seen by a Portuguese Jesuit

ANTONIO MONSERRATE, From *The Commentary of Father Monserrate: On Mughal India* (ca. 1580)

In 1580, Portuguese Jesuit missionary Antonio Monserrate (1536–1600) arrived in Mughal India. At the request of the sovereign, Akbar, who had a keen interest in other religions, Monserrate had been sent from Portuguese Goa with illustrated Bibles and other religious materials. He was appointed as a tutor to Akbar's son Murad, and he remained with Akbar for some years, accompanying him on military ventures and engaging with the sovereign in theological debate. Monserrate's *Commentary*, commissioned by his Jesuit superior, was never delivered and only resurfaced in the early 1900s in Calcutta. It offers invaluable insight into early modern European contact with Mughal India, demonstrating both the zeal of Jesuit missionaries and the tolerant nature of Akbar's rule.

The wives of the Brahmans — a famous class of nobly-born Hindus — are accustomed, in accordance with an ancient tradition of their religion, to burn themselves on the same pyres as their dead husbands. The King ordered the priests to be summoned to see an instance of this. They went in ignorance of what was to take place; but when they found out, they plainly indicated by their saddened faces how cruel and savage they felt that crime to be. Finally Rudolf [a Jesuit] publicly reprimanded the King for showing openly by his presence there that he approved of such a revolting crime, and for supporting it by his weighty judgment and explicit approbation, (for he was heard to say that such fortitude could only come from God). Such was Zelaldinus' [Akbar's] kindness

The Commentary of Father Monserrate, S.J., on His Journey to the Court of Akbar (London: Oxford University Press, 1922), 61–63.

and favor towards the priests that he showed no resentment; and a certain chief, a great favorite of his, a Brahman by birth, who held the office of Superintendent of sacred observances, could no longer persuade him to attend such spectacles. The wretched women are rendered quite insensible by means of certain drugs, in order that they may feel no pain. For this purpose opium is used, or a soporific herb named bang, or — more usually — the herb "duturo," which is known to the Indians, although entirely unfamiliar alike to modern Europeans and to the ancients. Sometimes they are half-drugged: and, before they lose their resolution, are hurried to the pyre with warnings, prayers, and promises of eternal fame. On arriving there they cast themselves into the flames. If they hesitate, the wretched creatures are driven on to the pyre: and if they try to leap off again, are held down with poles and hooks. The nobles who were present were highly incensed at the Fathers' interference. They did not dare to gainsay the King; but they grumbled loudly amongst themselves, saying, "Away with you, black-clothed Franks." The whole city was filled with praise and admiration when news was brought that the Franks had dared to rebuke the King regarding this affair.

On one occasion, the Fathers met a crowd of worthless profligates [male prostitutes], some of those who dress and adorn themselves like women. The priests were rightly disgusted at this, and took the first opportunity of privately complaining to the King (since he was so favorable to them) about this disgraceful matter. They declared with the greatest emphasis that they were astonished at his permitting such a class of men to live in his kingdom, let alone in his city, and almost under his eyes. They must be banished, as though they were a deadly plague, to his most distant territories; even better, let them be burnt up by devouring flames. They never would have believed that such men could be found in the court itself and in the royal city, where lived a king of such piety, integrity, and prudence. Therefore let him give orders that these libertines should never again be seen in Fattepurum, seeing that his remarkable prophet [Muhammad] had guaranteed that good men should never suffer for their good actions. The King laughed at this piece of sarcasm and retired, saying that he would attend to the matter.

READING AND DISCUSSION QUESTIONS

1. How do you explain Monserrate's decision to create an implicit contrast between the forced suicide of widows and the tolerance of male prostitutes? What point might he have been trying to make?

2. What is Monserrate's opinion of Akbar? What should we make of the apparent contradiction between his abhorrence of some of Akbar's policies and his description of Akbar as a king possessed of "piety, integrity, and prudence"?

3. Based on Monserrate's account, what is the status of Catholic priests in Akbar's court? How did he present their relationship with Akbar? How might Akbar have seen that relationship?

Building an Islamic Palace

The palaces built by the great Islamic rulers played an important role in both stimulating and shaping the cultural flowering of the Islamic world. Drawing on their enormous resources and the incredible skills of Islamic architects, artists, and artisans, Islamic rulers fashioned palaces that reflected their power, their ambitions, and their values. Once built, such palaces served a variety of functions. As a political setting, they helped sultans, shahs, and emperors display their exalted status to visiting diplomats, courtiers, and dignitaries. Islamic rulers were great patrons of the arts, and thus palaces became cultural centers inhabited by a host of talented and creative individuals. Finally, palaces served as engines of economic and urban growth, gathering people from far and wide to serve the needs of the palace and its inhabitants. The two paintings included in this feature reveal the important role Islamic rulers played in the planning and construction of their own palaces. As you examine the paintings, ask yourself why rulers might have felt it important to play such an active role in this process. What connections might they have made between their palaces and the success of their reigns?

17-3 | A Mughal Emperor Plans a Persian Garden
Babur and His Architect Plan the Bagh-i-Wafu (ca. 1590)

Babur (r. 1483–1530), the founder of the Mughal Dynasty, played a key role in bringing Persian gardens to India. Babur's interest in gardens predated his invasion of India. The Persian miniature included here shows Babur and his architect working on Babur's very first garden, the Bagh-i-Wafu (Garden of Fidelity) in Kabul, Afghanistan. The Bagh-i-Wafu was a *charbagh*, a Persian-style garden in which the garden is divided into four quadrants by paths that intersect at the center. The rigid geometry of such gardens was meant to evoke man's mastery over nature and, from the point of view of the garden's creator, the ruler's mastery over his realm. The paths that gave the garden its distinctive look often contained channels that served as artificial streams, recalling the rivers Muslims believe flow through Paradise and providing a handy source of water for the garden. Thus, such gardens were both beautiful and highly symbolic.

READING AND DISCUSSION QUESTIONS

1. What practical purposes might such gardens have served? What clues are offered in this image?

2. Why might Mughal rulers have wanted to be seen as the primary creators of their gardens? What political purposes might such associations have served?

3. What does this garden suggest about Islamic ideas about nature? About natural beauty?

17-4 | A Capital Fit for an Emperor

TULSI THE ELDER AND MADHU THE YOUNGER, *Akbar Inspects the Construction of Fatehpur-Sikri* (ca. 1590–1598)

In 1569, the Mughal emperor Akbar (r. 1556–1605) decided to build a new capital for his empire. Built on a site a little more than twenty miles from the existing capital of Agra, Fatehpur-Sikri would be a walled complex of palaces, mosques, and pleasure gardens. It is believed that Akbar took a direct hand in designing the complex and that he kept a close eye on the project over the course of the fifteen years needed to complete its construction. While the basic style and design were Persian, Indian influences can be seen in many of the buildings. The illustration from the *Akbarnama* (Memoirs of Akbar) included here shows Akbar supervising the construction of his new capital. As you examine it, think about what it reveals about carrying out such a building project in sixteenth-century India. What resources, both human and material, went into the creation of Fatehpur-Sikri?

STAPLETON COLLECTION/Victoria & Albert Museum, London, UK/Bridgeman Images.

READING AND DISCUSSION QUESTIONS

1. What does the image suggest about the Mughals' knowledge of architecture and engineering?

2. What were the sources of that knowledge?

3. What kinds of workers contributed to the construction of the city? What importance should we attach to the fact that Akbar is shown in conversation with a humble artisan?

VIEWPOINTS COMPARATIVE QUESTIONS

1. What do these documents tell us about the importance of palaces to Islamic rulers?

2. What do Mughal palaces and gardens reveal about cross-cultural sharing in the Islamic world?

17-5 | A Mughal Emperor Describes His Life and Rule

NURUDDIN SALIM JAHANGIR, From the *Memoirs of Jahangir* (ca. 1580–1600)

Akbar's third son, Prince Salim (1569–1628), succeeded his father as the Mughal sovereign in 1605 and took the name Jahangir, or "World Conqueror." During his reign, he continued many of his father's policies, including (limited) religious tolerance and wars of territorial expansion. Jahangir found himself locked in a familiar pattern of Mughal succession when his son Khurram rebelled in 1622, just as Jahangir rebelled against his own father. The passages here are taken from Jahangir's autobiography. In the first section, he presents measures to promote justice and social welfare in the realm. In the second, he describes a hunting trip with his favorite wife, Nūr-Jahān Begam.

After my accession, the first order that I gave was for the fastening up of the Chain of Justice, so that if those engaged in the administration of justice should delay or practice hypocrisy in the matter of those seeking justice, the oppressed might come to this chain and shake it so that its noise might attract attention. Its fashion was this: I ordered them to make a chain of pure gold, 30 gaz in length and containing 60 bells. Its weight was 4 Indian maunds, equal to 42 'Irāqī maunds. One end of it they made fast to the battlements of the Shāh Burj of the

The *Tūzuk-i-Jahangīrī* or *Memoirs of Jahangir*, ed. Alexander Rogers and Henry Beveridge (London: Royal Asiatic Society, 1909–1914), 2, 105.

fort at Agra and the other to a stone post fixed on the bank of the river. I also gave twelve orders to be observed as rules of conduct in all my dominions—

1. Forbidding the levy of cesses [taxes] under the names of tamghā and mīr bah·rī [river tolls], and other burdens which the jāgīrdārs[3] of every province and district had imposed for their own profit.
2. On roads where thefts and robberies took place, which roads might be at a little distance from habitations, the jāgīrdārs of the neighborhood should build sarā'īs [public rest houses], mosques, and dig wells, which might stimulate population, and people might settle down in those sarā'īs. If these should be near a <u>kh</u>ālisa estate,[4] the administrator of that place should execute the work.
3. The bales of merchants should not be opened on the roads without informing them and obtaining their leave.
4. In my dominions if anyone, whether unbeliever or Musalman, should die, his property and effects should be left for his heirs, and no one should interfere with them. If he should have no heir, they should appoint inspectors and separate guardians to guard the property, so that its value might be expended in lawful expenditure, such as the building of mosques and sarā'īs, the repair of broken bridges, and the digging of tanks and wells.
5. They should not make wine or rice-spirit or any kind of intoxicating drug, or sell them; although I myself drink wine, and from the age of 18 years up till now, when I am 38, have persisted in it. When I first took a liking to drinking I sometimes took as much as twenty cups of double-distilled spirit; when by degrees it acquired a great influence over me I endeavored to lessen the quantity, and in the period of seven years I have brought myself from fifteen cups to five or six. My times for drinking were varied; sometimes when three or four sidereal hours of the day remained I would begin to drink, and sometimes at night and partly by day. This went on till I was 30 years old. After that I took to drinking always at night. Now I drink only to digest my food.
6. They should not take possession of any person's house.
7. I forbade the cutting off the nose or ears of any person, and I myself made a vow by the throne of God that I would not blemish anyone by this punishment.
8. I gave an order that the officials of the Crown lands and the jāgīrdārs should not forcibly take the ryots' [farmers'] lands and cultivate them on their own account.
9. A government collector or a jāgīrdār should not without permission intermarry with the people of the pargana [district] in which he might be.

---

[3] **jāgīrdārs:** Regional rulers whose income came primarily from taxes imposed within their districts.

[4] <u>kh</u>ālisa estate: Land controlled by the state.

10. They should found hospitals in the great cities, and appoint physicians for the healing of the sick; whatever the expenditure might be, should be given from the khālisa establishment.

11. In accordance with the regulations of my revered father, I ordered that each year from the 18th of Rabī'u-l-awwal, which is my birthday, for a number of days corresponding to the years of my life, they should not slaughter animals [for food]. Two days in each week were also forbidden, one of them Thursday, the day of my accession, and the other Sunday, the day of my father's birth. He held this day in great esteem on this account, and because it was dedicated to the Sun, and also because it was the day on which the Creation began. Therefore it was one of the days on which there was no killing in his dominions.

12. I gave a general order that the offices and jāgīrs [land plots] of my father's servants should remain as they were. Later, the mans.abs [ranks or offices] were increased according to each one's circumstances by not less than 20 percent to 300 or 400 percent. The subsistence money of the ah.adīs was increased by 50 percent, and I raised the pay of all domestics by 20 percent. I increased the allowances of all the veiled ladies of my father's harem from 20 percent to 100 percent, according to their condition and relationship. By one stroke of the pen I confirmed the subsistence lands of the holders of aimas [charity lands] within the dominions, who form the army of prayer, according to the deeds in their possession. I gave an order to Mīrān Sadr Jahān, who is one of the genuine Sayyids of India [descendants of Muhammad], and who for a long time held the high office of s.adr [ecclesiastical officer] under my father, that he should every day produce before me deserving people [worthy of charity]. I released all criminals who had been confined and imprisoned for a long time in the forts and prisons. . . .

On the 25th the contingent of I'timādu-d-daulah passed before me in review on the plain under the jharoka.[5] There were 2,000 cavalry well horsed, most of whom were Moghuls, 500 foot [soldiers] armed with bows and guns, and fourteen elephants. The bakhshis reckoned them up and reported that this force was fully equipped and according to rule. On the 26th a tigress was killed. On Thursday, the 1st Urdībihisht, a diamond that Muqarrab Khān had sent by runners was laid before me; it weighed 23 surkh, and the jewellers valued it at 30,000 rupees. It was a diamond of the first water, and was much approved. I ordered them to make a ring of it. On the 3rd the mansab [military rank] of Yūsuf Khān was, at the request of Bābā Khurram, fixed at 1,000 with 1,500 horses, and in the same way the mansabs of several of the Amirs [nobles] and mansabdars [office holders] were increased at his suggestion.[6] On the 7th, as the huntsmen had

---

[5] **jharoka:** Balcony used for architectural ornamentation and for spying.
[6] **fixed at 1,000 . . . suggestion:** A system of military ranking that also determined compensation. High-ranking commanders were in one of three classes according to the proportion of horsemen in their unit.

marked down four tigers, when two watches and three gharis [a length of time] had passed I went out to hunt them with my ladies. When the tigers came in sight Nūr-Jahān Begam submitted that if I would order her she herself would kill the tigers with her gun. I said, "Let it be so." She shot two tigers with one shot each and knocked over the two others with four shots. In the twinkling of an eye she deprived of life the bodies of these four tigers. Until now such shooting was never seen, that from the top of an elephant and inside of a howdah [carriage atop an elephant] six shots should be made and not one miss, so that the four beasts found no opportunity to spring or move. As a reward for this good shooting I gave her a pair of bracelets of diamonds worth 100,000 rupees and scattered 1,000 ashrafis [over her].

READING AND DISCUSSION QUESTIONS

1. What is the purpose of Jahangir's Chain of Justice? What impression does it create of the sovereign?

2. Jahangir's twelve orders deal with a variety of issues. How would you categorize them? Which order is most striking to you, and why?

3. What is the effect of Jahangir's frequent references to gold and jewels in both of these excerpts? What image does that create of him and his realm?

4. In the second excerpt, Jahangir describes both military forces and a hunting expedition with his wives. How would you compare the tone of this passage with his comments about justice and social order?

■ COMPARATIVE QUESTIONS ■

1. What do the documents included in this chapter reveal about the role of religion in Islamic imperial government? How was religion used to justify policy? How was it used to legitimize authority?

2. Compare and contrast Selim's letter to Ismail and the excerpts from the *Memoirs of Jahangir*. What did each author see as a ruler's primary duty? How did each go about fulfilling that duty?

3. Compare the Mughal building projects described in this chapter with Justinian's building projects in sixth-century Constantinople (Document 8-4). What similarities and differences do you note?

4. How would you characterize Monserrate's interactions with Akbar? How do they compare with those of the Spanish and the Mexica in roughly the same period (Document 16-4)?

18

European Power and Expansion
1500–1750

The seventeenth century was a time of deep crisis for Europe. The commercial and agricultural sectors suffered from prolonged economic stagnation, and many nations found themselves locked in expensive and devastating internal and external wars. In an effort to cope with these difficulties, European states instituted increased government growth and extended control over their populations through new forms of taxation, the military, and the state bureaucracy. The following documents reveal the different ways in which European governments engaged with the challenges of the seventeenth century. In countries like England, a system of constitutionalism envisioned political power as a careful balance of many forces. In France and eastern European states, the doctrine of absolutism stressed the divine and total power of the monarch. Despite their differences, both systems represented careful attempts to establish centralized states that claimed sovereignty over their territories and peoples.

VIEWPOINTS

The Sources of Government Authority

At the heart of the debate between absolutists and constitutionalists were differences of opinion on the ultimate source of government authority. For absolutists, the answer was clear. All authority was in the hands of divinely appointed monarchs, and their laws and decisions were to be viewed as direct commandments from God. Moreover, the monarch was the head of a divinely ordered society in which each person played an assigned part in carrying out God's plan. In sharp contrast, constitutionalists saw governments and societies as essentially voluntary associations, at least in their initial formation. Their starting point was not God, but the inherent rights of the individual. Society and government existed to protect those rights by providing law and order. In forming governments and entering society, individuals agreed to abide by the rule of law, but only so that freedom could be guaranteed. The documents included in this feature offer an opportunity to compare the ideas of the seventeenth century's leading theorist of absolutism, Jacques-Benigne Bossuet, with those of the century's leading theorist of constitutionalism, John Locke. As you read the excerpts from their work, pay particular attention to the way in which their central assumptions about the nature of authority shape their views on government, law, and society. How did each believe that government and society came into existence? How did their beliefs about the origins of government and society shape their views on its nature and functions?

18-1 | God's Lieutenants on Earth

JACQUES-BENIGNE BOSSUET, *On Divine Right* (ca. 1675–1680)

French absolutism developed in the seventeenth century as a response to a number of crises, including the French Wars of Religion (ca. 1562–1598) and a civil war known as the Fronde (1648–1653). A bishop in the French Catholic Church and tutor to the son of Louis XIV, Jacques-Benigne Bossuet (1627–1704) was an important architect of French absolutism. Drawing on biblical sources, Bossuet argued in his treatises that monarchs' authority came directly from God. This concept of the divine right of kings implied that any challenge to royal authority was tantamount to sacrilege.

We have already seen that all power is of God. The ruler, adds St. Paul, "is the minister of God to thee for good. But if thou do that which is evil, be afraid; for he beareth not the sword in vain: for he is the minister of God, a revenger to execute wrath upon him that doeth evil" [Rom. 13:1–7]. Rulers then act as the ministers of God and as his lieutenants on earth. It is through them that God exercises his empire. Think ye "to withstand the kingdom of the Lord in the hand of the sons of David" [2 Chron. 13:8]? Consequently, as we have seen, the royal throne is not the throne of a man, but the throne of God himself. . . .

J. H. Robinson, ed., *Readings in European History*, 2 vols. (Boston: Ginn, 1906), 2:273–277.

Moreover, that no one may assume that the Israelites were peculiar in having kings over them who were established by God, note what is said in Ecclesiasticus: "God has given to every people its ruler, and Israel is manifestly reserved to him" [Eccles. 17:14–15]. He therefore governs all peoples and gives them their kings, although he governed Israel in a more intimate and obvious manner.

It appears from all this that the person of the king is sacred, and that to attack him in any way is sacrilege. God has the kings anointed by his prophets with the holy unction in like manner as he has bishops and altars anointed. But even without the external application in thus being anointed, they are by their very office the representatives of the divine majesty deputed by Providence for the execution of his purposes. . . . Kings should be guarded as holy things, and whosoever neglects to protect them is worthy of death. . . .

But kings, although their power comes from on high, as has been said, should not regard themselves as masters of that power to use it at their pleasure; . . . they must employ it with fear and self-restraint, as a thing coming from God and of which God will demand an account. "Hear, O kings, and take heed, understand, judges of the earth, lend your ears, ye who hold the peoples under your sway, and delight to see the multitude that surround you. It is God who gives you the power. Your strength comes from the Most High, who will question your works and penetrate the depths of your thoughts, for, being ministers of his kingdom, ye have not given righteous judgments nor have ye walked according to his will. He will straightway appear to you in a terrible manner, for to those who command is the heaviest punishment reserved. The humble and the weak shall receive mercy, but the mighty shall be mightily tormented. For God fears not the power of any one, because he made both great and small and he has care for both" [Ws. 6:2]. . . .

Kings should tremble then as they use the power God has granted them; and let them think how horrible is the sacrilege if they use for evil a power which comes from God. We behold kings seated upon the throne of the Lord, bearing in their hand the sword which God himself has given them. What profanation, what arrogance, for the unjust king to sit on God's throne to render decrees contrary to his laws and to use the sword which God has put in his hand for deeds of violence and to slay his children! . . .

The royal power is absolute. With the aim of making this truth hateful and insufferable, many writers have tried to confound absolute government with arbitrary government. But no two things could be more unlike, as we shall show when we come to speak of justice.

The prince need render account of his acts to no one. "I counsel thee to keep the king's commandment, and that in regard of the oath of God. Be not hasty to go out of his sight: stand not on an evil thing for he doeth whatsoever pleaseth him. Where the word of a king is, there is power: and who may say unto him, What doest thou? Whoso keepeth the commandment shall feel no evil thing" [Eccles. 8:2–5]. Without this absolute authority the king could neither do good nor repress evil. It is necessary that his power be such that no one can hope to escape him, and, finally, the only protection of individuals against the public authority should be their innocence. This conforms with the teaching of St. Paul: "Wilt thou then not be afraid of the power? do that which is good" [Rom. 13:3].

I do not call majesty that pomp which surrounds kings or that exterior magnificence which dazzles the vulgar. That is but the reflection of majesty and not majesty itself. Majesty is the image of the grandeur of God in the prince.

God is infinite, God is all. The prince, as prince, is not regarded as a private person: he is a public personage, all the state is in him; the will of all the people is included in his. As all perfection and all strength are united in God, so all the power of individuals is united in the person of the prince. What grandeur that a single man should embody so much!

The power of God makes itself felt in a moment from one extremity of the earth to another. Royal power works at the same time throughout all the realm. It holds all the realm in position, as God holds the earth. Should God withdraw his hand, the earth would fall to pieces; should the king's authority cease in the realm, all would be in confusion.

Look at the prince in his cabinet. Thence go out the orders which cause the magistrates and the captains, the citizens and the soldiers, the provinces and the armies on land and on sea, to work in concert. He is the image of God, who, seated on his throne high in the heavens, makes all nature move. . . .

Finally, let us put together the things so great and so august which we have said about royal authority. Behold an immense people united in a single person; behold this holy power, paternal and absolute; behold the secret cause which governs the whole body of the state, contained in a single head: you see the image of God in the king, and you have the idea of royal majesty. God is holiness itself, goodness itself, and power itself. In these things lies the majesty of God. In the image of these things lies the majesty of the prince.

So great is this majesty that it cannot reside in the prince as in its source; it is borrowed from God, who gives it to him for the good of the people, for whom it is good to be checked by a superior force. Something of divinity itself is attached to princes and inspires fear in the people. The king should not forget this. "I have said," — it is God who speaks, — "I have said, Ye are gods; and all of you are children of the Most High. But ye shall die like men, and fall like one of the princes" [Ps. 82:6–7]. "I have said, Ye are gods"; that is to say, you have in your authority, and you bear on your forehead, a divine imprint. "You are the children of the Most High"; it is he who has established your power for the good of mankind. But, O gods of flesh and blood, gods of clay and dust, "ye shall die like men, and fall like princes." Grandeur separates men for a little time, but a common fall makes them all equal at the end.

O kings, exercise your power then boldly, for it is divine and salutary for human kind, but exercise it with humility. You are endowed with it from without. At bottom it leaves you feeble, it leaves you mortal, it leaves you sinners, and charges you before God with a very heavy account.

READING AND DISCUSSION QUESTIONS

1. According to Bossuet, what is the nature of monarchical authority? What are its sources and purposes?

2. Why must a prince wield his absolute power carefully?

3. In Bossuet's view, are there any limits on what a king can do? Do all royal acts automatically receive divine sanction?

18-2 | Government and the State of Nature

JOHN LOCKE, From *Two Treatises of Government: Of the Ends of Political Society and Government* (1690)

John Locke (1632–1704) was a physician, philosopher, and teacher with ties to the pro-parliamentary faction of the English government. His writings on political theory provided an important foundation for the development of constitutionalism in England. Under suspicion of taking part in a plot to assassinate Charles II, he fled to Holland in 1683. His return to England coincided with the Glorious Revolution of 1688, and he claimed that his *Two Treatises* endorsed the ascension of William III to the English throne. The excerpt here from his second treatise shows Locke's interest in developing a philosophy of government through the careful investigation of human nature.

Sec. 123. If man in the state of nature be so free, as has been said; if he be absolute lord of his own person and possessions, equal to the greatest, and subject to no body, why will he part with his freedom? Why will he give up this empire, and subject himself to the dominion and control of any other power? To which it is obvious to answer, that though in the state of nature he hath such a right, yet the enjoyment of it is very uncertain, and constantly exposed to the invasion of others: for all being kings as much as he, every man his equal, and the greater part no strict observers of equity and justice, the enjoyment of the property he has in this state is very unsafe, very unsecure. This makes him willing to quit a condition, which, however free, is full of fears and continual dangers: and it is not without reason, that he seeks out, and is willing to join in society with others, who are already united, or have a mind to unite, for the mutual preservation of their lives, liberties, and estates, which I call by the general name, property.

Sec. 124. The great and chief end, therefore, of men's uniting into commonwealths, and putting themselves under government, is the preservation of their property. To which in the state of nature there are many things wanting.

First, There wants an established, settled, known law, received and allowed by common consent to be the standard of right and wrong, and the common measure to decide all controversies between them: for though the law of nature be plain and intelligible to all rational creatures; yet men being biassed by their

John Locke, *Two Treatises of Government* (London: A. Millar et al., 1764).

interest, as well as ignorant for want of study of it, are not apt to allow of it as a law binding to them in the application of it to their particular cases.

Sec. 125. Secondly, In the state of nature there wants a known and indifferent judge, with authority to determine all differences according to the established law: for every one in that state being both judge and executioner of the law of nature, men being partial to themselves, passion and revenge is very apt to carry them too far, and with too much heat, in their own cases; as well as negligence, and unconcernedness, to make them too remiss in other men's.

Sec. 126. Thirdly, In the state of nature there often wants power to back and support the sentence when right, and to give it due execution, They who by any injustice offended, will seldom fail, where they are able, by force to make good their injustice; such resistance many times makes the punishment dangerous, and frequently destructive, to those who attempt it.

Sec. 127. Thus mankind, notwithstanding all the privileges of the state of nature, being but in an ill condition, while they remain in it, are quickly driven into society. Hence it comes to pass, that we seldom find any number of men live any time together in this state. The inconveniencies that they are therein exposed to, by the irregular and uncertain exercise of the power every man has of punishing the transgressions of others, make them take sanctuary under the established laws of government, and therein seek the preservation of their property. It is this makes them so willingly give up every one his single power of punishing, to be exercised by such alone, as shall be appointed to it amongst them; and by such rules as the community, or those authorized by them to that purpose, shall agree on. And in this we have the original right and rise of both the legislative and executive power, as well as of the governments and societies themselves.

Sec. 128. For in the state of nature, to omit the liberty he has of innocent delights, a man has two powers.

The first is to do whatsoever he thinks fit for the preservation of himself, and others within the permission of the law of nature: by which law, common to them all, he and all the rest of mankind are one community, make up one society, distinct from all other creatures. And were it not for the corruption and viciousness of degenerate men, there would be no need of any other; no necessity that men should separate from this great and natural community, and by positive agreements combine into smaller and divided associations.

The other power a man has in the state of nature, is the power to punish the crimes committed against that law. Both these he gives up, when he joins in a private, if I may so call it, or particular politic society, and incorporates into any commonwealth, separate from the rest of mankind.

Sec. 129. The first power, viz. of doing whatsoever he thought for the preservation of himself, and the rest of mankind, he gives up to be regulated by laws made by the society, so far forth as the preservation of himself, and the rest of that society shall require; which laws of the society in many things confine the liberty he had by the law of nature.

Sec. 130. Secondly, The power of punishing he wholly gives up, and engages his natural force, (which he might before employ in the execution of the law of nature, by his own single authority, as he thought fit) to assist the executive power of the society, as the law thereof shall require: for being now in a new state, wherein he is to enjoy many conveniencies, from the labor, assistance, and society of others in the same community, as well as protection from its whole strength; he is to part also with as much of his natural liberty, in providing for himself, as the good, prosperity, and safety of the society shall require; which is not only necessary, but just, since the other members of the society do the like.

Sec. 131. But though men, when they enter into society, give up the equality, liberty, and executive power they had in the state of nature, into the hands of the society, to be so far disposed of by the legislative, as the good of the society shall require; yet it being only with an intention in every one the better to preserve himself, his liberty and property; (for no rational creature can be supposed to change his condition with an intention to be worse) the power of the society, or legislative constituted by them, can never be supposed to extend farther, than the common good; but is obliged to secure every one's property, by providing against those three defects above mentioned, that made the state of nature so unsafe and uneasy. And so whoever has the legislative or supreme power of any commonwealth, is bound to govern by established standing laws, promulgated and known to the people, and not by extemporary decrees; by indifferent and upright judges, who are to decide controversies by those laws; and to employ the force of the community at home, only in the execution of such laws, or abroad to prevent or redress foreign injuries, and secure the community from inroads and invasion. And all this to be directed to no other end, but the peace, safety, and public good of the people.

READING AND DISCUSSION QUESTIONS

1. According to Locke, what powers do individuals have in the state of nature? What are some of the inevitable difficulties that arise when living in the state of nature?

2. Once individuals agree to form a government, what powers does the government have? What are its primary obligations?

3. In what ways does the treatise challenge the absolutist tendencies of seventeenth-century English monarchs?

VIEWPOINTS COMPARATIVE QUESTIONS

1. According to each author, what is the ultimate source of political authority? How did each author's views on this subject shape his understanding of the nature of government?

2. What aspects of Locke's theory might Bossuet have found most objectionable? Why? What might Locke have been most critical of in Bossuet's argument? Why?

3. What did each author see as the purpose of government? On what, if anything, might they have agreed?

18-3 | The English Parliament Asserts Its Authority
The Bill of Rights (1689)

Almost a century of struggle between the forces of constitutionalism and absolutism in England culminated in the Bill of Rights. The Bill of Rights was an unequivocal statement that Parliament, not the monarch, was the source of English law, and that all Englishmen, including the monarch, were subject to the law. Acceptance of the Bill of Rights was a nonnegotiable condition of the ascendance of William and Mary to the English throne. Thus, the very first act of the new monarchs was an acknowledgment of the limits of their power. As you read this excerpt, think about the light it sheds on late-seventeenth-century notions of freedom and tyranny. What kinds of abuses of power did Parliament fear? What rights and liberties did it seek to protect?

Whereas the late King James the Second, by the assistance of divers evil counselors, judges and ministers employed by him, did endeavor to subvert and extirpate the Protestant religion and the laws and liberties of this kingdom;

By assuming and exercising a power of dispensing with and suspending of laws and the execution of laws without consent of Parliament;

By committing and prosecuting divers worthy prelates for humbly petitioning to be excused from concurring to the said assumed power;

By issuing and causing to be executed a commission under the great seal for erecting a court called the Court of Commissioners for Ecclesiastical Causes;

By levying money for and to the use of the Crown by pretense of prerogative for other time and in other manner than the same was granted by Parliament;

By raising and keeping a standing army within this kingdom in time of peace without consent of Parliament, and quartering soldiers contrary to law;

By causing several good subjects being Protestants to be disarmed at the same time when papists were both armed and employed contrary to law;

By violating the freedom of election of members to serve in Parliament;

By prosecutions in the Court of King's Bench for matters and causes cognizable only in Parliament, and by divers other arbitrary and illegal courses;

And whereas of late years partial corrupt and unqualified persons have been returned and served on juries in trials, and particularly divers jurors in trials for high treason which were not freeholders;

And excessive bail hath been required of persons committed in criminal cases to elude the benefit of the laws made for the liberty of the subjects;

And excessive fines have been imposed;

And illegal and cruel punishments inflicted;

And several grants and promises made of fines and forfeitures before any conviction or judgment against the persons upon whom the same were to be levied;

All which are utterly and directly contrary to the known laws and statutes and freedom of this realm;

Avalon Project, Yale Law School, http://avalon.law.yale.edu/.

And whereas the said late King James the Second having abdicated the government and the throne being thereby vacant, his Highness the prince of Orange (whom it hath pleased Almighty God to make the glorious instrument of delivering this kingdom from popery and arbitrary power) did (by the advice of the Lords Spiritual and Temporal and divers principal persons of the Commons) cause letters to be written to the Lords Spiritual and Temporal being Protestants, and other letters to the several counties, cities, universities, boroughs and cinque ports,[1] for the choosing of such persons to represent them as were of right to be sent to Parliament, to meet and sit at Westminster upon the two and twentieth day of January in this year one thousand six hundred eighty and eight [old-style date], in order to such an establishment as that their religion, laws and liberties might not again be in danger of being subverted, upon which letters elections having been accordingly made;

And thereupon the said Lords Spiritual and Temporal and Commons, pursuant to their respective letters and elections, being now assembled in a full and free representative of this nation, taking into their most serious consideration the best means for attaining the ends aforesaid, do in the first place (as their ancestors in like case have usually done) for the vindicating and asserting their ancient rights and liberties declare

That the pretended power of suspending the laws or the execution of laws by regal authority without consent of Parliament is illegal;

That the pretended power of dispensing with laws or the execution of laws by regal authority, as it hath been assumed and exercised of late, is illegal;

That the commission for erecting the late Court of Commissioners for Ecclesiastical Causes, and all other commissions and courts of like nature, are illegal and pernicious;

That levying money for or to the use of the Crown by pretense of prerogative, without grant of Parliament, for longer time, or in other manner than the same is or shall be granted, is illegal;

That it is the right of the subjects to petition the king, and all commitments and prosecutions for such petitioning are illegal;

That the raising or keeping a standing army within the kingdom in time of peace, unless it be with consent of Parliament, is against law;

That the subjects which are Protestants may have arms for their defense suitable to their conditions and as allowed by law;

That election of members of Parliament ought to be free;

That the freedom of speech and debates or proceedings in Parliament ought not to be impeached or questioned in any court or place out of Parliament;

That excessive bail ought not to be required, nor excessive fines imposed, nor cruel and unusual punishments inflicted;

That jurors ought to be duly impanelled and returned, and jurors which pass upon men in trials for high treason ought to be freeholders;

---

[1] **cinque ports:** Confederation of coastal towns in Kent and Sussex.

That all grants and promises of fines and forfeitures of particular persons before conviction are illegal and void;

And that for redress of all grievances, and for the amending, strengthening and preserving of the laws, Parliaments ought to be held frequently.

READING AND DISCUSSION QUESTIONS

1. According to the authors, in what ways did James II abuse his power?

2. What steps did the authors take to protect the power of Parliament? What did they do to ensure the impartial application of the law?

3. What restrictions did the Bill of Rights place on the rights of Catholics? How might the authors have justified their inclusion of discriminatory provisions in a law meant to protect the rights of the English people?

18-4 | A Courtier Sketches the Character of a King

DUC DE SAINT-SIMON, From *The Memoirs of Louis XIV: On the Early Life of Louis XIV* (ca. 1730–1755)

The Duc de Saint-Simon (1675–1755) was born Louis de Rouvroy in Paris. His father was a former page of Louis XIII, and his noble status gave the young de Rouvroy the opportunity to enter court life at Versailles after a brief military career. Incredibly, Saint-Simon's careful notes and the often scathing picture they paint of court life escaped the attention of his fellow courtiers, and they remained unpublished until well after his death. The writings excerpted here give an intimate portrait of the personal qualities of Louis XIV and, by extension, of absolutist rule in seventeenth-century Europe.

I shall pass over the stormy period of Louis XIV's minority. At twenty-three years of age he entered the great world as King, under the most favorable auspices. His ministers were the most skillful in all Europe; his generals the best; his Court was filled with illustrious and clever men, formed during the troubles which had followed the death of Louis XIII.

Louis XIV was made for a brilliant Court. In the midst of other men, his figure, his courage, his grace, his beauty, his grand mien, even the tone of his voice and the majestic and natural charm of all his person, distinguished him till his death as the King Bee, and showed that if he had only been born a simple private gentlemen, he would equally have excelled in fetes, pleasures, and gallantry, and would have had the greatest success in love. The intrigues and adventures which early in life he had been engaged in—when the Comtesse de Soissons lodged at the Tuileries, as superintendent of the Queen's household, and was the center figure of the Court group—had exercised an unfortunate influence

Duc de Saint-Simon, *The Memoirs of Louis XIV, His Court and the Regency*, trans. Bayle St. John, chap. 73, www.gutenberg.org/files/3875/3875-h/3875-h.htm#2HCH0073.

upon him: he received those impressions with which he could never after successfully struggle. From this time, intellect, education, nobility of sentiment, and high principle, in others, became objects of suspicion to him, and soon of hatred. The more he advanced in years the more this sentiment was confirmed in him. He wished to reign by himself. His jealousy on this point unceasingly became weakness. He reigned, indeed, in little things; the great he could never reach: even in the former, too, he was often governed. The superior ability of his early ministers and his early generals soon wearied him. He liked nobody to be in any way superior to him. Thus he chose his ministers, not for their knowledge, but for their ignorance; not for their capacity, but for their want of it. He liked to form them, as he said; liked to teach them even the most trifling things. It was the same with his generals. He took credit to himself for instructing them; wished it to be thought that from his cabinet he commanded and directed all his armies. Naturally fond of trifles, he unceasingly occupied himself with the most petty details of his troops, his household, his mansions; would even instruct his cooks, who received, like novices, lessons they had known by heart for years. This vanity, this unmeasured and unreasonable love of admiration, was his ruin. His ministers, his generals, his mistresses, his courtiers, soon perceived his weakness. They praised him with emulation and spoiled him. Praises, or to say truth, flattery, pleased him to such an extent, that the coarsest was well received, the vilest even better relished. It was the sole means by which you could approach him. Those whom he liked owed his affection for them to their untiring flatteries. This is what gave his ministers so much authority, and the opportunities they had for adulating him, of attributing everything to him, and of pretending to learn everything from him. Suppleness, meanness, an admiring, dependent, cringing manner—above all, an air of nothingness—were the sole means of pleasing him.

This poison spread. It spread, too, to an incredible extent, in a prince who, although of intellect beneath mediocrity, was not utterly without sense, and who had had some experience. Without voice or musical knowledge, he used to sing, in private, the passages of the opera prologues that were fullest of his praises.

He was drowned in vanity; and so deeply, that at his public suppers—all the Court present, musicians also—he would hum these self-same praises between his teeth, when the music they were set to was played!

And yet, it must be admitted, he might have done better. Though his intellect, as I have said, was beneath mediocrity, it was capable of being formed. He loved glory, was fond of order and regularity; was by disposition prudent, moderate, discreet, master of his movements and his tongue. Will it be believed? He was also by disposition good and just! God had sufficiently gifted him to enable him to be a good King; perhaps even a tolerably great King! All the evil came to him from elsewhere. His early education was so neglected that nobody dared approach his apartment. He has often been heard to speak of those times with bitterness, and even to relate that, one evening he was found in the basin of the Palais Royal garden fountain, into which he had fallen! He was scarcely taught how to read or write, and remained so ignorant, that the most familiar historical and other facts were utterly unknown to him! He fell, accordingly, and sometimes even in public, into the grossest absurdities.

READING AND DISCUSSION QUESTIONS

1. How does Saint-Simon's description of Louis XIV's personality relate to Louis's historical role as a model of absolutist rule?

2. How does Saint-Simon's own presence as a courtier of Louis XIV complicate his assessment of the king's intolerance?

3. Saint-Simon claims that Louis was by nature "good and just" and that evil "came to him from elsewhere." What do these claims imply about the nature of absolutist rule?

4. What is Saint-Simon's tone, and how do you interpret it?

18-5 | Catherine the Great Augments the Power of Estate Owners

CATHERINE II OF RUSSIA, *Two Decrees* (1762, 1765)

Catherine II, or Catherine the Great (1729–1796), led the Russian empire following the deposition of her husband, Peter III, in 1762. Born Sophia Augusta Frederica in Prussian-controlled Pomerania (in present-day Poland), Catherine converted to the Russian Orthodox Church and married the Russian *tsarevich*, or heir apparent, Peter in 1745. In 1762, her husband the tsar was deposed in a coup d'état and assassinated eight days later. Taking the throne in his stead, Catherine oversaw an impressive expansion of Russian territory and embraced Enlightenment ideals, but her harsh treatment of Russia's peasant population—evidenced here in two decrees—may reveal her dependence on the support of the Russian landowning nobility and the practical limits of absolutism.

Decree on Peasant Disturbances, July 3, 1762

Upon our accession to the imperial throne of all Russia, we learned, to our great displeasure, that the peasants of some landlords, seduced and deluded by false rumors spread by unscrupulous people, had departed from the obedience due to their landlords and had proceeded to commit many unruly and defiant acts. We are firmly convinced that such false rumors will presently die away by themselves; the deluded peasants will recognize that from thoughtlessness they have fallen into grievous crime and will forthwith repent,

A Source Book for Russian History from Early Times to 1917, 3 vols. (New Haven: Yale University Press, 1972), 2:449, 453. Copyright © 1972 Yale University. Reprinted by permission of Yale University Press.

endeavoring thereafter to earn forgiveness through mute submission to their masters. Nevertheless, in order to check the spread of such evil and to prevent any false rumors from being disseminated again and credulous peasants being corrupted thereby, we deem it right to make known herewith that . . . inasmuch as the welfare of the state, in accordance with divine and public laws, requires that each and every person be protected in the enjoyment of his well-earned property and his rights, and, conversely, that no one step beyond the bounds of his rank and office, we therefore intend to protect the landlords in their estates and possessions inviolably and to keep the peasants in their proper submission to them.

Decree on Forced Labor, January 17, 1765

To be announced for the information of the whole populace: In consequence of the confirmation given by Her Imperial Majesty, on the eighth of January [1765], to a report submitted by the Senate, it has been ordained that, should an estate owner desire to commit any of his people [i.e., serfs] who deserve just punishment for recalcitrance to penal servitude in Siberia, for the sake of stricter discipline, the College of the Admiralty shall take the same in charge and employ them at hard labor for as long as their estate owners wish; and during the time such people remain at hard labor they shall be provided with food and clothing from the treasury on the same basis as convicts; and whenever their estate owners desire to take them back, they shall be returned without argument, with the sole reservation that if such people during their stay have not worn their clothes and footwear for the full prescribed term, these shall be taken away from them and returned to the treasury.

READING AND DISCUSSION QUESTIONS

1. How might Catherine II have justified the harshness of these decrees? What do they reveal about the structure of Russian society?

2. These decrees give great power to estate owners and take power away from serfs. How might they have enhanced or decreased the power held by Catherine's own government?

■ COMPARATIVE QUESTIONS ■

1. Saint-Simon's indictment of Louis XIV's personality raises the question of human fallibility. How do the political theories of Bossuet and Locke, as presented in this chapter, deal with the question of human frailties? How does the element of fallibility strengthen or weaken their arguments?

2. The question of divinity is conspicuously absent in Locke's excerpt. How might Locke have interpreted Bossuet's theologically based arguments about sovereignty? Is there room for religion in Locke's state of nature?

3. In what ways do the texts in this chapter address political transformations away from the feudal system in the seventeenth century? How do the texts show the continuity between the old and new systems?

4. How would Bossuet and Locke analyze Catherine II's actions and policies? On what basis would they approve or disapprove of the decrees included here?

5. How are the ideas of John Locke reflected in the English Bill of Rights?

New Worldviews and Ways of Life
1540–1790

Beginning in the sixteenth century, western Europe saw its religion-based notions of the natural and social worlds countered by arguments grounded in reason and observation. Leaders of the Scientific Revolution (ca. 1540–1690) drew on earlier European, Greek, and Arab insights to support their theories and to challenge the church-dominated wisdom of the time. Advances in astronomy, physics, mathematics, and other fields were supported and promoted by the huge profits and increasing technological demands of growing European trade. Intellectuals in Europe and the United States next turned a critical eye toward society and politics. Those active in the period known as the Enlightenment, which stretched from the late seventeenth to the late eighteenth century, insisted on rational approaches to human relations, drawing on scientific arguments and existing critiques of organized religion in their calls for the reform of societies and governments.

Changing Ideas of Science

The insights and breakthroughs of the Scientific Revolution had little or no practical impact on the lives of ordinary people during the early modern era. Nor did most of the scientific thinkers of the age intend that they should. Indeed, they described themselves not as scientists but as natural philosophers, as individuals who sought to contribute to the branch of philosophy concerned with the workings of the universe. Nonetheless, from the late sixteenth century on, the idea that science might have implications for the nature and quality of human life began to gain currency. Francis Bacon, whose work is excerpted below, was an early proponent of the practical application of science. By the eighteenth century, rulers like Peter the Great of Russia, influenced by Enlightenment ideas about the connection between reason and progress, had begun to take active steps to put science in the service of society and the state. As you read the documents included in this feature, reflect on the purpose of scientific inquiry. How might Bacon have defined that purpose? What about Peter the Great?

19-1 | Science in the Service of Human Longevity

FRANCIS BACON, From *The Great Restoration: History of Life and Death* (1623)

Francis Bacon (1561–1626) was a champion of the empirical method. Instead of beginning with core assumptions and then using those assumptions to interpret observed phenomena, Bacon argued that scholars should begin by collecting data through observation and experimentation and then use those data to form generalizations. He lived in England, where his career as a politician ended in disgrace. He turned seriously to writing and produced a great number of works on philosophical, social, and natural topics. He died of pneumonia, which he may have contracted in the process of an experiment in preserving meat through freezing. The work excerpted here is an excellent example of both Bacon's keen interest in the social value of knowledge and his careful approach to inquiry and the creation of knowledge.

TO THE PRESENT AND FUTURE AGES,
GREETING.

Although in my six monthly designations I placed the History of Life and Death last in order;[1] yet the extreme profit and importance of the subject, wherein even the slightest loss of time should be accounted precious, has decided me to make an anticipation, and advance it into the second place. For it is my hope and desire that it will contribute to the common good; that through it the higher physicians will somewhat raise their thoughts, and not devote all their time to common cures, nor be honored for necessity only; but that they will become the instruments and dispensers of God's power and mercy in prolonging and

---

The Works of Francis Bacon, ed. James Spedding, Robert Leslie Ellis, and Douglas Denon Heath (New York: Hurd and Houghton, 1864), 5:215–222.

[1] **last in order:** May refer to the publishing history of the work.

renewing the life of man, the rather because it is effected by safe, convenient, and civil, though hitherto unattempted methods. For although we Christians ever aspire and pant after the land of promise,[2] yet meanwhile it will be a mark of God's favor if in our pilgrimage through the wilderness of this world, these our shoes and garments (I mean our frail bodies) are as little worn out as possible. . . .

There are . . . two subjects of inquiry; the one, the consumption or depredation of the human body; the other, the repair or refreshment thereof; with a view to the restraining of the one (as far as may be), and the strengthening and comforting the other. The first of these pertains principally to the spirits and external air, which cause the depredation; the second to the whole process of alimentation [eating and digesting], which supplies the renovation. With regard to the first part of the inquiry, touching consumption, it has many things in common with bodies inanimate. For whatever the native spirit (which exists in all tangible bodies whether with or without life) and the ambient or external air do to bodies inanimate, the same they try to do to bodies animate, though the presence of the vital spirit in part disturbs and restrains these operations, and in part intensifies and increases them exceedingly. For it is very evident that many inanimate bodies can last a very long time without repair, but animate bodies without aliment and repair at once collapse and die out like fire. The inquiry therefore should be twofold; regarding first the body of man as a thing inanimate and unrepaired by nourishment; and secondly as a thing animate and nourished. And with these prefatory remarks I now pass on to the Topics of Inquiry.

Particular Topics

Or, Articles of Inquiry Concerning Life and Death

1. Inquire into the Nature of Durable and Non-Durable inanimate bodies, and likewise in Vegetables; not in a full and regular inquiry, but briefly, summarily, and as it were only by the way.
2. Inquire more carefully touching the desiccation, arefaction [drying], and consumption of bodies inanimate and vegetable; of the ways and processes whereby they are effected, and withal the methods whereby they are prevented and retarded, and bodies are preserved in their own state. Also inquire touching the inteneration, softening, and renewal of bodies, after they have once commenced to become dry.

Neither however need this inquiry be perfect or exact; as these things should be drawn from the proper title of Nature Durable; and as they are not the principal questions in the present inquiry, but only shed a light on the

---

[2] **land of promise:** The Christian heaven; afterlife.

prolongation and restoration of life in animals; wherein, as has been observed before, the same things generally happen, though in their own manner. From the inquiry concerning inanimate and vegetable bodies pass on to the inquiry of animals, not including man.

3. Inquire into the length and shortness of life in animals, with the proper circumstances which seem to contribute to either of them.
4. Since the duration of bodies is of two kinds, the one in their simple identity, the other by repair; whereof the former takes place only in bodies inanimate, the latter in vegetables and living creatures, and is performed by alimentation; inquire likewise touching alimentation, with its ways and process; yet this not accurately (for it belongs to the titles of Assimilation and Alimentation) but as before, in passing only.

From the inquiry concerning animals and things supported by nourishment pass on to that concerning man. And having now come to the principal subject of inquiry, that inquiry should be more accurate and complete on all points.

5. Inquire into the length and shortness of men's lives, according to the times, countries, climates, and places in which they were born and lived.
6. Inquire into the length and shortness of men's lives, according to their parentage and family (as if it were a thing hereditary); and likewise according to their complexion, constitution, habit of body, stature, manners and time of growth, and the make and structure of their limbs.
7. Inquire into the length and shortness of men's lives according to the times of their nativity; but so as to omit for the present all astrological and horoscopical observations. Admit only the common and manifest observations (if there be any); as, whether the birth took place in the 7th, 8th, 9th, or 10th month, whether by night or by day, and in what month of the year.
8. Inquire into the length and shortness of men's lives according to their food, diet, manner of living, exercise, and the like. With regard to the air in which they live and dwell, I consider that ought to be inquired under the former article concerning their places of abode.
9. Inquire into the length and shortness of men's lives according to their studies, kinds of life, affections of the mind, and various accidents.
10. Inquire separately into the medicines which are supposed to prolong life.
11. Inquire into the signs and prognostics of a long and short life; not into those which betoken that death is close at hand (for they belong to the history of medicine); but into those which appear and are observed even in health, whether taken from physiognomy or otherwise.

So far the inquiry touching the length and shortness of life is instituted in an unscientific and confused manner; but I have thought it right to add a systematic inquiry, bearing on practice by means of Intentions; which are of three kinds. Their more particular distributions I will set forth when I come to the inquiry itself. The three general intentions are: the prevention of consumption; the perfection of repair, and the renovation of that which is old.

12. Inquire into the things which preserve and exempt the body of man from arefaction and consumption, or at least which check and retard the tendency thereto.
13. Inquire into the things which belong to the general process of alimentation (whereby the body of man is repaired), that it may be good and with as little loss as possible.
14. Inquire into the things which clear away the old matter and supply new; and likewise those which soften and moisten the parts that have become hard and dry.

But since it will be difficult to know the ways to death, unless the seat and house (or rather cave) of death be first examined and discovered; of this too should inquiry be made; not however of every kind of death, but of such only as are caused, not by violence, but by privation and want. For these alone relate to the decay of the body from age.

15. Inquire into the point of death and the porches[3] which on all sides lead to it; provided it be caused by want and not by violence.

Lastly, since it is convenient to know the character and form of old age; which will be done best by making a careful collection of all the differences in the state and functions of the body between youth and old age, that by them you may see what it is that branches out into so many effects; do not omit this inquiry.

16. Inquire carefully into the differences of the state and faculties of the body in youth and old age; and see whether there be anything that remains unimpaired in old age.

READING AND DISCUSSION QUESTIONS

1. How does Bacon justify his investigation of life and death?
2. How does Bacon's scientific approach to life and death incorporate ideas of religion and church doctrine?
3. Bacon lays out a number of basic inquiries here. What is the relationship between them? Why does he proceed from inanimate objects through animals to people?

---

[3] **the porches:** Probably referring to transitional states; thresholds, gates (from the Latin *porta*).

19-2 | Science in the Service of the State

PETER THE GREAT AND GOTTFRIED LEIBNIZ,
On the Improvement of Arts and Sciences in Russia (ca. 1712–1718)

Peter the Great (1672–1725), tsar of Russia, transformed his country from a minor state to a major European power. Peter traveled incognito throughout Europe early in his reign, studying a range of subjects. Upon his return to Russia, he implemented dramatic reforms ranging from the speech and appearance of his citizens to the founding of a new modern capital, St. Petersburg. Deeply concerned with what he perceived to be the ignorance of Russians, he enlisted the help of the great German mathematician and philosopher Gottfried Leibniz (1646–1716). Excerpted here is Peter's appointment of Leibniz, Leibniz's recommendation to Peter for the edification of his people, and Peter's explanation of the scientific value of specimens such as the ones that he himself collected and displayed at his Kunstkamera, or "chamber of curiosities."

Decree on the Acceptance of Gottfried Leibniz into Russian Service, November 1, 1712

We, Peter I, tsar and autocrat of all Russia, etcetera, etcetera, etcetera.

We have most graciously judged it right that Gottfried Wilhelm von Leibniz, privy councillor in the judicature of the elector and duke of Brunswick-Lueneburg, be also appointed and confirmed as our privy councillor in the judicature, on account of his outstanding good qualities which have been praised to us and which we ourselves have found in him. Since we know that he can be of great help in the development of mathematics and of other arts, in historical research, and in the growth of learning in general, it is our intention to employ him, so that sciences and arts may flourish more and more in our realm. In consideration of the said rank of our privy councillor in the judicature it pleases us to appoint his yearly salary at one thousand Albertus-talers, which are to be paid out to him punctually every year on our behalf; for this we shall issue the necessary orders; his service begins from the date indicated below.

In confirmation whereof we issue these letters under our own signature and with our seal of state affixed.

Given at Karlsbad, November 1, 1712.

(Signed) Peter

(Countersigned) Count Golovkin

A Source Book for Russian History from Early Times to 1917, ed. George Vernadsky (New Haven: Yale University Press, 1972), 2:367. Copyright © 1972 Yale University. Reprinted by permission of Yale University Press; Anthony Anemone, "The Monsters of Peter the Great: The Culture of the St. Petersburg Kunstkamera in the Eighteenth Century," *Slavic and East European Journal*, 44:4 (Winter 2000): 592. From T. V. Staniukovich, *Kunstkamera Peterburgskoi Akademii Nauk* (Moscow/Leningrad, 1953).

Draft of Leibniz's Memorandum on the Improvement of Arts and Sciences in Russia, 1716

The improvement of arts and sciences in a great empire involves:

1. Procurement of necessary equipment.
2. Training of men in sciences already established.
3. Discovery of new knowledge.

Equipment consists of books, museums ["curiosity collections"], instruments, and exhibits of works of nature and of human contrivance. . . .

Next to the library comes the museum ["collection of curiosities"], where one should find old and new medals, serving as a source and confirmation of history; remains of Roman, Greek, Hebrew, Chinese, and other antiquity; all kinds of rare objects from the three realms of nature, namely all sorts of mineral stones, ores, plants, insects, and strange animals; also all kinds of works of art—paintings and sculptures; as well as optical, astronomical, architectural, military, nautical, mechanical, and other inventions.

Excerpt from a Decree on "Monsters," 1718

Ignoramuses think that such monsters are born from the action of the devil which is, however, impossible for there is only one creator of all creation, and that is God. And the Evil One has no power over any living creatures. For monsters are the result of internal damage, of fear and the thoughts of the mother during her pregnancy, of which fact there are many examples. For example, when the mother is frightened, hurt or injured in any way the child will be influenced.

READING AND DISCUSSION QUESTIONS

1. What are Leibniz's specific recommendations to Peter? What do they imply about the nature of knowledge, how it should be transmitted, and its value to society?

2. Given Peter's interest in modernizing Russia and bringing it into the European community of great powers, what do you imagine was the value of hiring a German scientist?

3. What does Peter's explanation of "monsters" suggest about the status of women in eighteenth-century Russia?

VIEWPOINTS COMPARATIVE QUESTIONS

1. What did Peter the Great hope to accomplish by hiring Leibniz? What did Leibniz believe was necessary to achieve Peter's goals? What might Bacon have suggested if he had been in a position to advise Peter?

2. Compare the visions of science articulated in these documents with the understanding of science that prevails today. What similarities and differences do you note? Would you describe either Bacon or Leibniz as "scientists"? Why or why not?

19-3 | Science Outside the West

Takyuddin and Other Astronomers at the Galata Observatory (ca. 1581)

The fact that the Scientific Revolution was centered in western Europe does not mean that societies outside of Europe were not interested in science or that they did not help make the Scientific Revolution possible. After all, it was Muslim scholars who preserved Greco-Roman literature and philosophy during the early Middle Ages, providing the West with a critical intellectual foundation for later accomplishments. Moreover, Middle Eastern, Indian, and Chinese rulers all showed considerable interest in the study of nature, offering their patronage to natural philosophers and astronomers. Finally, these same societies all made crucial contributions to the development of scientific and navigational instruments. All of these elements can be seen in this image of Ottoman astronomers at the Galata Observatory, a center of astronomical inquiry built by the Ottoman sultan Suleiman the Magnificent (r. 1520–1566). As you examine the image, think about what it tells you about Ottoman science in the sixteenth century. What clues do the details in the image offer about the scope and focus of Ottoman scientific inquiry?

DOST YAYINEVI/Istanbul University Library, Istanbul, Turkey/Bridgeman Images.

READING AND DISCUSSION QUESTIONS

1. What does the image reveal about the tools of Ottoman science? What books, instruments, and maps were available to Ottoman scientists?

2. What does the image suggest about the social organization of Ottoman science? How might a facility like the Galata Observatory facilitate the exchange of information between scientists?

19-4 | Faith Without Dogma

VOLTAIRE, From *Dictionnaire Philosophique: "Theist"* (1764)

A major figure of the Enlightenment, Voltaire, or François-Marie Arouet (1694–1778), was a literary genius with a keen sense of social responsibility. His writings were immensely popular during his lifetime, although his satirical voice often earned him enemies among France's religious and political elite. The *Dictionnaire Philosophique* (*Philosophical Dictionary*) of 1764 is less an encyclopedic reference than a compilation of Voltaire's critical musings on the nature of religion and intolerance in modern society. Here, his entry for "Theist" outlines the principles of theism (or deism, as it is more commonly known) and indicates his strong approval for the Enlightenment emphasis on secular humanism over sectarian doctrine.

The theist is a man firmly persuaded of the existence of a Supreme Being equally good and powerful, who has formed all extended, vegetating, sentient, and reflecting existences; who perpetuates their species, who punishes crimes without cruelty, and rewards virtuous actions with kindness.

The theist does not know how God punishes, how he rewards, how he pardons; for he is not presumptuous enough to flatter himself that he understands how God acts; but he knows that God does act and that he is just. The difficulties opposed to a Providence do not stagger him in his faith, because they are only great difficulties, not proofs: he submits himself to that Providence, although he only perceives some of its effects and some appearances; and judging of the things he does not see from those he does see, he thinks that this Providence pervades all places and all ages.

United in this principle with the rest of the universe, he does not join any of the sects, who all contradict themselves; his religion is the most ancient and the most extended: for the simple adoration of a God has preceded all the systems in the world. He speaks a language which all nations understand, while they are unable to understand each other's. He has brethren from Pekin to Cayenne,[4] and he reckons all the wise his brothers. He believes that religion consists neither in the opinions of incomprehensible metaphysics, nor in vain decorations, but in

---

M. de Voltaire, *A Philosophical Dictionary* (London: John and Henry L. Hunt, 1824), 6:258–259.

[4] **Pekin to Cayenne:** The cities of Peking (Beijing) and Cayenne, French Guiana.

adoration and justice. To do good—that is his worship: to submit oneself to God—that is his doctrine. The Mahometan [Muslim] cries out to him—"Take care of yourself, if you do not make the pilgrimage to Mecca."—"Woe be to thee," says a Franciscan, "if thou dost not make a journey to our Lady of Loretto."[5] He laughs at Loretto and Mecca; but he succors the indigent and defends the oppressed.

READING AND DISCUSSION QUESTIONS

1. What does Voltaire's treatment of the "theist" reveal about his general attitude toward religion?

2. Is Voltaire concerned more with the theist's beliefs about the divine or with his actions in the world? Explain.

3. Based on this excerpt, what might Voltaire say about atheism? Explain.

19-5 | Kant Challenges His Society to Embrace Reason
IMMANUEL KANT, *What Is Enlightenment?* (1784)

The Prussian professor Immanuel Kant (1724–1804) was perhaps the most influential philosopher of the Enlightenment. In *Critique of Pure Reason* (1781), his best-known work, Kant sought to define what we can know and how we know it, thereby reconciling the previous schools of rationalist and empiricist thought and inspiring philosophical trends to this day. The following excerpt is taken from his "Answer to the Question: What Is Enlightenment?" published in 1784 in a monthly periodical. The short work, more accessible than his 800-page *Critique*, marked his renewed status as a public thinker and spoke to his beliefs about intellectual freedom.

Enlightenment is man's emergence from his self-imposed nonage. Nonage is the inability to use one's understanding without another's guidance. This nonage is self-imposed if its cause lies not in lack of understanding but in indecision and lack of courage to use one's own mind without another's guidance. *Dare to know!* (*Sapere aude.*) "Have the courage to use your own understanding," is therefore the motto of the enlightenment.

Laziness and cowardice are the reasons why such a large part of mankind gladly remain minors all their lives, long after nature has freed them from external guidance. They are the reasons why it is so easy for others to set themselves up as guardians. It is so comfortable to be a minor. If I have a book that thinks for

---

Immanuel Kant, "What Is Enlightenment?" trans. Peter Gay, in *Introduction to Contemporary Civilization in the West* (New York: Columbia University Press, 1954), 1071–1076. Copyright © 1954 Columbia University Press. Reprinted with permission of the publisher.

[5] **Loretto:** Probably Loreto, a Catholic shrine in Italy and a popular destination for pilgrimages.

me, a pastor who acts as my conscience, a physician who prescribes my diet, and so on—then I have no need to exert myself. I have no need to think, if only I can pay; others will take care of that disagreeable business for me. The guardians who have kindly taken supervision upon themselves see to it that the overwhelming majority of mankind—among them the entire fair sex—should consider the step to maturity not only as hard, but as extremely dangerous. First, these guardians make their domestic cattle stupid and carefully prevent the docile creatures from taking a single step without the leading-strings to which they have fastened them. Then they show them the danger that would threaten them if they should try to walk by themselves. Now, this danger is really not very great; after stumbling a few times they would, at last, learn to walk. However, examples of such failures intimidate and generally discourage all further attempts.

Thus it is very difficult for the individual to work himself out of the nonage which has become almost second nature to him. He has even grown to like it and is at first really incapable of using his own understanding, because he has never been permitted to try it. Dogmas and formulas, these mechanical tools designed for reasonable use—or rather abuse—of his natural gifts, are the fetters of an everlasting nonage. The man who casts them off would make an uncertain leap over the narrowest ditch, because he is not used to such free movement. That is why there are only a few men who walk firmly, and who have emerged from nonage by cultivating their own minds.

It is more nearly possible, however, for the public to enlighten itself; indeed, if it is only given freedom, enlightenment is almost inevitable. There will always be a few independent thinkers, even among the self-appointed guardians of the multitude. Once such men have thrown off the yoke of nonage, they will spread about them the spirit of a reasonable appreciation of man's value and of his duty to think for himself. It is especially to be noted that the public which was earlier brought under the yoke by these men afterward forces these very guardians to remain in submission, if it is so incited by some of its guardians who are themselves incapable of any enlightenment. That shows how pernicious it is to implant prejudices: they will eventually revenge themselves upon their authors or their authors' descendants. Therefore, a public can achieve enlightenment only slowly. A revolution may bring about the end of a personal despotism or of avaricious and tyrannical oppression, but never a true reform of modes of thought. New prejudices will serve, in place of the old, as guidelines for the unthinking multitude.

This enlightenment requires nothing but *freedom*—and the most innocent of all that may be called "freedom": freedom to make public use of one's reason in all matters. Now I hear the cry from all sides: "Do not argue!" The officer says: "Do not argue—drill!" The tax collector: "Do not argue—pay!" The pastor: "Do not argue—believe!" Only one ruler in the world says: "Argue as much as you please, and about what you please, but obey!" We find restrictions on freedom everywhere. But which restriction is harmful to enlightenment? Which restriction is innocent, and which advances enlightenment? I reply: the public use of one's reason must be free at all times, and this alone can bring enlightenment to mankind.

On the other hand, the private use of reason may frequently be narrowly restricted without especially hindering the progress of enlightenment. By "public use of one's reason" I mean that use which a man, as *scholar*, makes of it before the reading public. I call "private use" that use which a man makes of his reason in a civic post that has been entrusted to him. In some affairs affecting the interest of the community a certain [governmental] mechanism is necessary in which some members of the community remain passive. This creates an artificial unanimity which will serve the fulfillment of public objectives, or at least keep these objectives from being destroyed. Here arguing is not permitted: one must obey. Insofar as a part of this machine considers himself at the same time a member of a universal community—a world society of citizens—(let us say that he thinks of himself as a scholar rationally addressing his public through his writings) he may indeed argue, and the affairs with which he is associated in part as a passive member will not suffer. Thus, it would be very unfortunate if an officer on duty and under orders from his superiors should want to criticize the appropriateness or utility of his orders. He must obey. But as a scholar he could not rightfully be prevented from taking notice of the mistakes in the military service and from submitting his views to his public for its judgment. The citizen cannot refuse to pay the taxes levied upon him; indeed, impertinent censure of such taxes could be punished as a scandal that might cause general disobedience. Nevertheless, this man does not violate the duties of a citizen if, as a scholar, he publicly expresses his objections to the impropriety or possible injustice of such levies. A pastor too is bound to preach to his congregation in accord with the doctrines of the church which he serves, for he was ordained on that condition. But as a scholar he has full freedom, indeed the obligation, to communicate to his public all his carefully examined and constructive thoughts concerning errors in that doctrine and his proposals concerning improvement of religious dogma and church institutions. This is nothing that could burden his conscience. For what he teaches in pursuance of his office as representative of the church, he represents as something which he is not free to teach as he sees it. He speaks as one who is employed to speak in the name and under the orders of another. He will say: "Our church teaches this or that; these are the proofs which it employs." Thus he will benefit his congregation as much as possible by presenting doctrines to which he may not subscribe with full conviction. He can commit himself to teach them because it is not completely impossible that they may contain hidden truth. In any event, he has found nothing in the doctrines that contradicts the heart of religion. For if he believed that such contradictions existed he would not be able to administer his office with a clear conscience. He would have to resign it. Therefore the use which a scholar makes of his reason before the congregation that employs him is only a private use, for, no matter how sizable, this is only a domestic audience. In view of this he, as preacher, is not free and ought not to be free, since he is carrying out the orders of others. On the other hand, as the scholar who speaks to his own public (the world) through his writings, the minister in the public use of his reason enjoys unlimited freedom to use his own reason and to speak for himself. That the spiritual guardians of the people should themselves be treated as minors is an absurdity which would result in perpetuating absurdities.

But should a society of ministers, say a Church Council, . . . have the right to commit itself by oath to a certain unalterable doctrine, in order to secure perpetual guardianship over all its members and through them over the people? I say that this is quite impossible. Such a contract, concluded to keep all further enlightenment from humanity, is simply null and void even if it should be confirmed by the sovereign power, by parliaments, and by the most solemn treaties. An epoch cannot conclude a pact that will commit succeeding ages, prevent them from increasing their significant insights, purging themselves of errors, and generally progressing in enlightenment. That would be a crime against human nature, whose proper destiny lies precisely in such progress. Therefore, succeeding ages are fully entitled to repudiate such decisions as unauthorized and outrageous. The touchstone of all those decisions that may be made into law for a people lies in this question: Could a people impose such a law upon itself? Now, it might be possible to introduce a certain order for a definite short period of time in expectation of a better order. But while this provisional order continues, each citizen (above all, each pastor acting as a scholar) should be left free to publish his criticisms of the faults of existing institutions. This should continue until public understanding of these matters has gone so far that, by uniting the voices of many (although not necessarily all) scholars, reform proposals could be brought before the sovereign to protect those congregations which had decided according to their best lights upon an altered religious order, without, however, hindering those who want to remain true to the old institutions. But to agree to a perpetual religious constitution which is not to be publicly questioned by anyone would be, as it were, to annihilate a period of time in the progress of man's improvement. This must be absolutely forbidden.

A man may postpone his own enlightenment, but only for a limited period of time. And to give up enlightenment altogether, either for oneself or one's descendants, is to violate and to trample upon the sacred rights of man. What a people may not decide for itself may even less be decided for it by a monarch, for his reputation as a ruler consists precisely in the way in which he unites the will of the whole people within his own. If he only sees to it that all true or supposed [religious] improvement remains in step with the civic order, he can for the rest leave his subjects alone to do what they find necessary for the salvation of their souls. Salvation is none of his business; it *is* his business to prevent one man from forcibly keeping another from determining and promoting his salvation to the best of his ability. Indeed, it would be prejudicial to his majesty if he meddled in these matters and supervised the writings in which his subjects seek to bring their [religious] views into the open, even when he does this from his own highest insight, because then he exposes himself to the reproach: *Caesar non est supra grammaticos.*[6] It is worse when he debases his sovereign power so far as to support the spiritual despotism of a few tyrants in his state over the rest of his subjects.

When we ask, Are we now living in an enlightened age? the answer is, No, but we live in an age of enlightenment. As matters now stand it is still far from true that men are already capable of using their own reason in religious matters confidently and correctly without external guidance. Still, we have some obvious indications that the field of working toward the goal [of religious truth] is now being opened. What is more, the hindrances against general enlightenment or the emergence from self-imposed nonage are gradually diminishing. In this respect this is the age of the enlightenment and the century of Frederick.[7]

A prince ought not to deem it beneath his dignity to state that he considers it his duty not to dictate anything to his subjects in religious matters, but to leave them complete freedom. If he repudiates the arrogant word *tolerant*, he is himself enlightened; he deserves to be praised by a grateful world and posterity as the man who was the first to liberate mankind from dependence, at least on the government, and let everybody use his own reason in matters of conscience. Under his reign, honorable pastors, acting as scholars and regardless of the duties of their office, can freely and openly publish their ideas to the world for inspection, although they deviate here and there from accepted doctrine. This is even more true of every other person not restrained by any oath of office. This spirit of freedom is spreading beyond the boundaries [of Prussia], even where it has to struggle against the external hindrances established by a government that fails to grasp its true interest. [Frederick's Prussia] is a shining example that freedom need not cause the least worry concerning public order or the unity of the community. When one does not deliberately attempt to keep men in barbarism, they will gradually work out of that condition by themselves.

I have emphasized the main point of the enlightenment—man's emergence from his self-imposed nonage—primarily in religious matters, because our rulers have no interest in playing the guardian to their subjects in the arts and sciences. Above all, nonage in religion is not only the most harmful but the most dishonorable. But the disposition of a sovereign ruler who favors freedom in the arts and sciences goes even further: he knows that there is no danger in permitting his subjects to make public use of their reason and to publish their ideas concerning a better constitution, as well as candid criticism of existing basic laws. We already have a striking example [of such freedom], and no monarch can match the one whom we venerate.

But only the man who is himself enlightened, who is not afraid of shadows, and who commands at the same time a well-disciplined and numerous army as guarantor of public peace—only he can say what [the sovereign of] a free state

---

[6] *Caesar non est supra grammaticos:* Latin for "Caesar is not above the grammarians."

[7] **the century of Frederick:** In the eighteenth century, Prussia was ruled by three Fredericks: Frederick I (r. 1701–1713), Frederick William I (r. 1713–1740), and Frederick II (r. 1740–1786).

cannot dare to say: "Argue as much as you like, and about what you like, but obey!" Thus we observe here as elsewhere in human affairs, in which almost everything is paradoxical, a surprising and unexpected course of events: a large degree of civic freedom appears to be of advantage to the intellectual freedom of the people, yet at the same time it establishes insurmountable barriers. A lesser degree of civic freedom, however, creates room to let that free spirit expand to the limits of its capacity. Nature, then, has carefully cultivated the seed within the hard core—namely, the urge for and the vocation of free thought. And this free thought gradually reacts back on the modes of thought of the people, and men become more and more capable of acting in freedom. At last free thought acts even on the fundamentals of government, and the state finds it agreeable to treat man, who is now more than a machine, in accord with his dignity.

READING AND DISCUSSION QUESTIONS

1. Briefly summarize Kant's definition of *enlightenment*. Why is it so difficult for people to achieve enlightenment?

2. According to Kant, who is responsible for enlightening the populace?

3. What is the difference between "public" and "private" freedoms? What examples does Kant give of each?

▪ COMPARATIVE QUESTIONS ▪

1. Religion and spirituality are important components of several excerpts in this chapter. How does each author present religion, and to what end? What might the relative absence of religion in some of the texts signify?

2. Why did the Scientific Revolution emerge in western Europe and not in the Middle East or China? What light do the documents included in this chapter shed on this question?

3. How would you define *science*? How might each of the authors included in this chapter answer this question?

20

Africa and the World

1400–1800

The fifteenth-century voyages of Portuguese mariners eager to identify and exploit new trade opportunities ushered in an era of violence, exploitation, and slavery on the African continent. However, Africa's story during these four centuries was not simply one of involuntary participation in a European-dominated system of colonization and enslavement. For centuries, diverse African states had played an important role in global trade, and foreign and indigenous influences combined to produce powerful and enduring cultures. Neither was slavery new to African culture. However, the traditional African idea of slavery was transformed by the dehumanizing profit motive of European capitalism and plantation economies. Many coastal societies facilitated the massive transatlantic slave trade by capturing people from the African interior and delivering them to European slave ships. The documents in this chapter depict both continuity and transformation in African society during this period of European incursion.

20-1 | A Dutch View of an African King

OLFERT DAPPER, *King Alvaro I of Kongo Receiving the Dutch Ambassadors* (1668)

The history of the powerful central West African state of Kongo was profoundly shaped by European expansion and the emergence of the transatlantic slave trade. Portuguese explorers first arrived in Kongo in 1491. They succeeded in making an alliance with the ruling Kongo Empire, converting the royal family to Catholicism. The alliance gave the Kongo Empire a short-term advantage over their local and regional rivals, but it proved a disaster in the long run. As the slave trade intensified, Kongo became increasingly unstable, descending into endemic warfare and political disorder. Keep this in mind as you examine this image taken from a late-seventeenth-century Dutch book on Africa. What parts of the story of the interaction between Kongo's leaders and Europeans does it highlight? What parts does it leave out?

Private Collection/Bridgeman Images.

READING AND DISCUSSION QUESTIONS

1. How would you characterize the interaction between King Alvaro I and the Dutch ambassadors? What response might the artist have been hoping to evoke in viewers?

2. What importance should we attach to the large chandelier that hangs over the king? What other evidence does the image provide of the importation of European goods into Africa?

3. In the upper left corner of the image, we see a church in the distance. Why might the artist have chosen to include this detail?

20-2 | West African Dependence on the Slave Trade

OSEI BONSU, *An Asante King Questions British Motives in Ending the Slave Trade* (1820)

Osei Bonsu was king of the Asante (also written *Ashanti* or *Ashantee*) state in West Africa from about 1801 to 1824. Under his rule, the Asante state expanded and solidified the sophisticated

David Robinson and Douglas Smith, *Sources of the African Past: Case Studies of Five Nineteenth-Century African Societies* (New York: Africana, 1979), 189–190. Copyright © 1979 by Holmes and Meier Publishers, Inc. Used with permission of Lynne Rienner Publishers, Inc.

bureaucratic structure inaugurated by his predecessors in the late 1700s. The Asante export economy—based historically on the sale of gold, ivory, and slaves—flourished after initial contact with Europeans. His comments, presented here, were recorded by a British trader named Joseph shortly after the British abolition of the slave trade. They indicate both the profound dependence of many African states on the European slave trade and the complex relationships fostered through that system.

"Now," said the king, after a pause, "I have another palaver [topic of discussion], and you must help me to talk it. A long time ago the great king [the king of England] liked plenty of trade, more than now; then many ships came, and they bought ivory, gold, and slaves; but now he will not let the ships come as before, and the people buy gold and ivory only. This is what I have in my head, so now tell me truly, like a friend, why does the king do so?" "His majesty's question," I replied, "was connected with a great palaver, which my instructions did not authorize me to discuss. I had nothing to say regarding the slave trade." "I know that too," retorted the king; "because, if my master liked that trade, you would have told me so before. I only want to hear what you think as a friend: this is not like the other palavers." I was confessedly at a loss for an argument that might pass as a satisfactory reason, and the sequel proved that my doubts were not groundless. The king did not deem it plausible, that this obnoxious traffic should have been abolished from motives of humanity alone; neither would he admit that it lessened the number either of domestic or foreign wars.

Taking up one of my observations, he remarked, "The white men who go to council with your master, and pray to the great God for him, do not understand my country, or they would not say the slave trade was bad. But if they think it bad now, why did they think it good before? Is not your law an old law, the same as the Crammo [Muslim] law? Do you not both serve the same God, only you have different fashions and customs? Crammos are strong people in fetische,[1] and they say the law is good, because the great God made the book; so they buy slaves, and teach them good things, which they knew not before. This makes everybody love the Crammos, and they go everywhere up and down, and the people give them food when they want it. Then these men come all the way from the great water [the Niger River], and from Manding, and Dagomba, and Killinga; they stop and trade for slaves, and then go home. If the great king would like to restore this trade, it would be good for the white men and for me too, because Ashantee is a country for war, and the people are strong; so if you talk that palaver for me properly, in the white country, if you go there, I will give you plenty of gold, and I will make you richer than all the white men."

READING AND DISCUSSION QUESTIONS

1. How does this document complicate your understanding of the racial politics of transatlantic slavery and of slavery in the United States?

---

[1] **fetische:** Fetish, religious practice and observance.

2. In this document, Osei Bonsu uses Muslims (*Crammos*) as an example of moral behavior toward slaves. How does this illustrate his understanding of international affairs?

3. How does the king's description of how Muslims treat slaves compare with their treatment by European Christians?

4. The narrator notes that Osei Bonsu thought it "implausible" that the slave trade was abolished for purely humanitarian reasons. Do you agree, and why?

Debating the Slave Trade

The British dominated the eighteenth-century transatlantic slave trade, and it was in this period that the trade reached its peak. By the end of the century, however, British public opinion was beginning to turn against the slave trade. Inspired by a complex mix of ideological, religious, and economic motives, antislavery organizations emerged to challenge Britain's involvement in the export of human beings from West Africa to the Americas. The efforts of such groups would culminate in the abolition of the slave trade in the British Empire in 1807 and the abolition of slavery itself in 1833. The two documents included in this feature provide an opportunity to gain a better understanding of the public debate that preceded those historic antislavery acts. The first, written by the wife of an English naval surgeon, defends the slave trade on moral and religious grounds. The second, written by a victim of the trade and an antislavery activist, presents the horror, disorientation, and despair of enslavement in vivid detail. As you read these selections, ask yourself how two people could witness similar events and produce such vastly different accounts.

20-3 | An Englishwoman Defends the Slave Trade

ANNA MARIA FALCONBRIDGE, From *Narrative of Two Voyages to the River Sierra Leone* (1794)

Anna Maria Falconbridge (born 1769) was the first modern European woman to write about travels to Africa. She married surgeon and abolitionist Alexander Falconbridge in 1788, whose testimony before the British government became the basis for his 1788 abolitionist

Anna Maria Falconbridge, *Narrative of Two Voyages to the River Sierra Leone*, ed. Christopher Fyfe (Liverpool: Liverpool University Press, 2000), 89–94. Reproduced with permission of Liverpool University Press in the format Republish in a book via Copyright Clearance Center.

work, *An Account of the Slave Trade on the Coast of Africa.* Anna Maria Falconbridge sailed with her husband to Sierra Leone, where a British company had established a settlement of "black poor," or African Americans who had fled the United States after the American Revolution. Her letters from these voyages were published as the *Narrative* upon her return to England in 1794. The excerpt here shows how her initial abolitionist views changed with her firsthand experience.

We embarked and sailed on the ninth of June; nothing could have reconciled me to the idea of taking my passage in a slave ship . . . for I always entertained most horrid notions of being exposed to indelicacies, too offensive for the eyes of an English woman, on board these ships; however, I never was more agreeably disappointed in my life. In the center of the ship a barricade was run across, to prevent any communication between the men and women; the men and boys occupied the forward part, and the women and girls, the after, so I was only liable to see the latter, who were full as well habited as they would have been in Africa. . . . Having heard such a vast deal of the ill treatment to slaves during the middle passage, I did not omit to make the nicest [closest] observations in my power. . . . I would declare I had not the slightest reason to suspect any inhumanity or mal-practice was shewn towards [the slaves], through the whole voyage; on the contrary, I believe they experienced the utmost kindness and care, and after a few days, when they had recovered from sea sickness, I never saw more signs of content and satisfaction, among any set of people, in their or any other country. . . . Regularly every day their rooms were washed out, sprinkled with vinegar, and well dried with chafing dishes of coal; during this operation the slaves were kept on deck, where they were allowed to stay the whole day (when the weather would permit) if they liked it. . . . Their provisions were excellent, consisting of boiled rice and English beans . . . and relished with a piece of beef, salt fish, or palm oil. . . . Great attention was paid the sick, of which, however, there were few. . . .

Whether slaves are equally well treated in common, I cannot pretend to say, but when one recollects how much the masters are interested in their well doing, it is natural to suppose such is the case, for self-interest so unalterably governs the human heart, that it alone must temper the barbarity of any man, and prevent him from committing violence on, or misusing his own property. . . .

For a length of time I viewed the Slave Trade with abhorrence—considering it a blemish on every civilized nation that countenanced or supported it, and that this, our happy enlightened country was more especially stigmatized for carrying it on, than any other; but I am not ashamed to confess, those sentiments were the effect of ignorance, and the prejudice of opinion, imbibed by associating with a circle of acquaintances, *bigoted for the abolition.* . . . So widely opposite are my ideas of the trade from what they were, that I now think it in no shape objectionable either to morality or religion, but on the contrary consistent with both, while neither are to be found in unhappy Africa; and while three-fourths of that populous country come into the world, like hogs or sheep, subject, at any moment, to be rob'd of their lives by the other fourth, I say, while this is the case,

I cannot think the Slave Trade inconsistent with any moral, or religious law—in place of invading the happiness of Africa, tends to promote it; by pacifying the murdering, despotic Chieftains of that country, who only spare the lives of their vassals from a desire of acquiring the manufactures of this and other nations, and by saving millions from perdition, whose future existence is rendered comfortable, by the cherishing hands of Christian masters, who are not only restrained from exercising any improper or unjust cruelties over their slaves, by the fear of reciprocal injury, but by the laws of the land, and their religious tenets. . . .

Pray do not misinterpret my arguments, and suppose me a friend to slavery, or wholly an enemy to abolishing the Slave Trade; lest you should, I must explain myself—by declaring from my heart I wish freedom to every creature formed by God, who knows its value—which cannot be the case with those who have not tasted its sweets; therefore, most assuredly, I must think favorably of the Slave Trade, while those innate prejudices, ignorance, superstition, and savageness, overspread Africa; and while the Africans feel no conviction by continuing it, but remove those errors of nature, teach them the purposes for which they were created, the ignominy of trafficking in their own flesh, and learn them to hold the lives of their fellow mortals in higher estimation, or even let me see a foundation laid, whereupon hopes itself may be built of their becoming proselytes to the doctrine of Abolition; then, no person on earth will rejoice more earnestly to see that trade suppressed in every shape.

READING AND DISCUSSION QUESTIONS

1. How does Falconbridge's letter depict the condition of slaves aboard the slave ship?

2. What is Falconbridge's rationale for her changed attitude toward the slave trade and abolition? Under what conditions would she support abolition?

3. How might an abolitionist respond to Falconbridge's assessment of the slave trade?

20-4 | The Terror of Capture and Enslavement

OLAUDAH EQUIANO, From *The Interesting Narrative of Olaudah Equiano* (1789)

One of the few enslaved Africans able to purchase their freedom, Olaudah Equiano (ca. 1745–1797) drew on his remarkable education and experiences to write an autobiographical account of kidnapping and slavery in Africa and the Americas. It was published with the help of British

Olaudah Equiano, *The Interesting Narrative of Olaudah Equiano* (London, 1789) in *The Atlantic Slave Trade*, ed. David Northrup (Lexington, Mass.: D. C. Heath, 1994), 78–79.

abolitionists, and he promoted his work in Britain with the equivalent of a modern book tour. Some evidence suggests that Equiano may have been born in South Carolina and therefore would not have experienced life in Africa and the Middle Passage. However, his popular narrative is generally consistent with other accounts of the kidnapping and enslavement of Africans, and its power to inspire the abolitionist movement is unquestioned.

One day, when all our people were gone out to their works as usual, and only I and my dear sister were left to mind the house, two men and a woman got over our walls, and in a moment seized us both, and, without giving us time to cry out, or make resistance, they stopped our mouths, and ran off with us into the nearest wood. Here they tied our hands, and continued to carry us as far as they could, till night came on, when we reached a small house, where the robbers halted for refreshment, and spent the night. We were then unbound, but were unable to take any food; and, being quite overpowered by fatigue and grief, our only relief was some sleep, which allayed our misfortune for a short time. The next morning we left the house, and continued traveling all the day. For a long time we had kept [to] the woods, but at last we came to a road which I believed I knew. I now had some hopes of being delivered; for we had advanced but a little way before I discovered some people at a distance, on which I began to cry out for their assistance; but my cries had no other effect than to make them tie me faster and stop my mouth, and then they put me in a large sack. They also stopped my sister's mouth, and tied her hands; and in this manner we proceeded till we were out of sight of these people. When we went to rest the following night, they offered us some victuals, but we refused it; and the only comfort we had was in being in one another's arms all that night, and bathing each other with our tears. But alas! we were soon deprived of even the small comfort of weeping together.

The next day proved a day of greater sorrow than I had yet experienced; for my sister and I were then separated, while we lay clasped in each other's arms. It was in vain that we besought them not to part us; she was torn from me, and immediately carried away, while I was left in a state of distraction not to be described. I cried and grieved continually; and for several days did not eat anything but what they forced into my mouth. At length, after many days' traveling, during which I had often changed masters, I got into the hands of a chieftain, in a very pleasant country. This man had two wives and some children, and they all used me extremely well, and did all they could to comfort me; particularly the first wife, who was something like my mother. Although I was a great many days' journey from my father's house, yet these people spoke exactly the same language with us. . . .

From the time I left my own nation, I always found somebody that understood me till I came to the sea coast. The languages of different nations did not totally differ, nor were they so copious as those of the Europeans,[2] particularly

---

[2] **nor were they so copious . . . Europeans:** Equiano is saying that African languages had less extensive vocabularies than European languages.

the English. They were therefore easily learned; and, while I was journeying thus through Africa, I acquired two or three different tongues. In this manner I had been traveling for a considerable time, when, one evening, to my great surprise, whom should I see brought to the house where I was but my dear sister! As soon as she saw me, she gave a loud shriek, and ran into my arms—I was quite over-powered; neither of us could speak, but, for a considerable time, clung to each other in mutual embraces, unable to do anything but weep. Our meeting affected all who saw us; and, indeed, I must acknowledge, in honor of those sable destroy-ers of human rights, that I never met with any ill treatment, or saw any offered to their slaves, except tying them, when necessary, to keep them from running away.

When these people knew we were brother and sister, they indulged us to be together; and the man, to whom I suppose we belonged, lay with us, he in the middle, while she and I held one another by the hands across his breast all night; and thus for a while we forgot our misfortunes, in the joy of being together; but even this small comfort was soon to have an end; for scarcely had the fatal morn-ing appeared when she was again torn from me forever! I was now more miser-able, if possible, than before. The small relief which her presence gave me from pain, was gone, and the wretchedness of my situation was redoubled by my anx-iety after her fate, and my apprehensions lest her sufferings should be greater than mine, when I could not be with her to alleviate them. . . .

I continued to travel, sometimes by land, sometimes by water, through dif-ferent countries and various nations, till, at the end of six or seven months after I had been kidnapped, I arrived at the sea coast. . . .

The first object which saluted my eyes when I arrived on the coast, was the sea, and a slave ship, which was then riding at anchor, and waiting for its cargo. These filled me with astonishment, which was soon converted into ter-ror, when I was carried on board. I was immediately handled, tossed up to see if I were sound, by some of the crew, and I was now persuaded that I had got-ten into a world of bad spirits, and that they were going to kill me. Their com-plexions, too, differing so much from ours, their long hair, and the language they spoke (which was very different from any I had ever heard), united to confirm me in this belief. Indeed, such were the horrors of my views and fears at the moment, that, if ten thousand worlds had been my own, I would have freely parted with them all to have exchanged my condition with that of the meanest slave in my own country. When I looked round the ship too, and saw a large furnace of copper boiling, and a multitude of black people of every description chained together, every one of their countenances expressing dejection and sorrow. I no longer doubted of my fate, and, quite overpowered with horror and anguish, I fell motionless on the deck and fainted. When I recovered a little, I found some black people about me, who I believed were some of those who had brought me on board, and had been receiving their pay; they talked to me in order to cheer me, but all in vain. I asked them if we were not to be eaten by these white men with horrible looks, red faces, and long hair. They told me I was not, and one of the crew brought me a small portion of spirituous liquor in a wine glass; but being afraid of him, I would not take it out of his hand. One of the blacks therefore took it from him and gave it to me, and I took a little down my palate, which, instead of reviving me, as they thought it would, threw me into the greatest consternation at the strange feeling it produced, having never tasted any such liquor before. Soon after this, the blacks who brought me on board went off, and left me abandoned to despair. . . .

At last, when the ship we were in, had got in all her cargo, they made ready with many fearful noises, and we were all put under deck, so that we could not see how they managed the vessel. But this disappointment was the least of my sorrow. The stench of the hold while we were on the coast was so intolerably loathsome, that it was dangerous to remain there for any time, and some of us had been permitted to stay on the deck for the fresh air; but now that the whole ship's cargo was confined together, it became absolutely pestilential. The closeness of the place, and the heat of the climate, added to the number in the ship, which was so crowded that each had scarcely room to turn himself, almost suffocated us. This produced copious perspirations, so that the air soon became unfit for respiration, from a variety of loathsome smells, and brought on a sickness among the slaves, of which many died — thus falling victims to the improvident avarice, as I may call it, of their purchasers. This wretched situation was again aggravated by the galling of the chains, now became insupportable, and the filth of the necessary tubs [latrines], into which the children often fell, and were almost suffocated. The shrieks of the women, and the groans of the dying, rendered the whole a scene of horror almost inconceivable. Happily, perhaps, for myself, I was soon reduced so low here that it was thought necessary to keep me almost always on deck, and from my extreme youth I was not put in fetters. In this situation I expected every hour to share the fate of my companions, some of whom were almost daily brought upon deck at the point of death, which I began to hope would soon put an end to my miseries. Often did I think of the many inhabitants of the deep much more happy than myself. I envied them [for] the freedom they enjoyed, and as often wished I could change my condition for theirs. Every circumstance I met with, served only to render my state more painful, and heightened my apprehensions, and my opinion of the cruelty of the whites.

One day they had taken a number of fishes; and when they had killed and satisfied themselves with as many as they thought fit, to our astonishment who were on deck, rather than give any of them to us to eat, as we expected, they tossed the remaining fish into the sea again, although we begged and prayed for some as well we could, but in vain. . . .

One day, when we had a smooth sea and a moderate wind, two of my wearied countrymen who were chained together (I was near them at the time), preferring death to such a life of misery, somehow made through the nettings and jumped into the sea; immediately, another quite dejected fellow, who, on account of his illness, was suffered to be out of irons, also followed their example; and I believe many more would have soon done the same, if they had not been prevented by the ship's crew, who were instantly alarmed. . . .

At last we came in sight of the island of Barbadoes, at which the whites on board gave a great shout, and made many signs of joy to us. We did not know what to think of this; but as the vessel grew nearer, we plainly saw the harbor, and other ships of different kinds and sizes, and we soon anchored among them, off Bridgetown. Many merchants and planters now came on board, though it was in the evening. They put us in separate parcels, and examined us attentively. They also made us jump, and pointed to the land, signifying we were to go there. We thought by this, we should be eaten by these ugly men, as they appeared to us; and, when soon after we were all put down under deck again, there was much dread and trembling among us, and nothing but bitter cries to be heard all the night from these apprehensions, insomuch, that at last the white people got some old slaves from the land to pacify us. They told us we were not to be eaten, but to work, and were soon to go on land, where we would see many of our country people. This report eased us much. And sure enough, soon after we were landed, there came to us Africans of all languages.

We were immediately conducted to the merchant's yard, where we were all pent up together, like so many sheep in a fold, without regard to sex or age. As every object was new to me, everything I saw filled me with surprise. What struck me first, was, that the houses were built with bricks and stones, and every other respect different from those I had seen in Africa; but I was still more astonished on seeing people on horseback.[3] I did not know what this could mean; and, indeed, I thought these people were full of nothing but magical arts. While I was in this astonishment, one of my fellow prisoners spoke to a countryman of his, about the horses, who said they were the same kind they had in their country. I understood them, though they were from a distant part of Africa; and I thought it odd I had not seen any horses there; but afterwards, when I came to converse with different Africans, I found they had many horses amongst them, and much larger than those I then saw.

We were not many days in the merchant's custody, before we were sold in the usual manner, which is this: On a signal given (as the beat of a drum), the buyers rush at once into the yard where the slaves are confined, and make a choice of that parcel they like best. The noise and clamor with which this is attended, and the eagerness visible in the countenances of the buyers, serve not a little to increase the apprehension of terrified Africans, who may well be supposed to consider them as the ministers of that destruction to which they think themselves devoted. In this manner, without scruple, are relations and friends separated, most of them never to see each other again.

---

[3] **people on horseback:** Equiano would have been unfamiliar with horses in West Africa, where they were susceptible to sleeping sickness, a lethal disease transmitted by the tsetse fly.

I remember, in the vessel in which I was brought over, in the men's apartment, there were several brothers, who, in the sale, were sold in different lots; and it was very moving on this occasion, to see and hear their cries at parting. O, ye nominal Christians! might not an African ask you—Learned you this from your God, who says unto you, Do unto all men as you would men should do unto you? Is it not enough that we are torn from our country and friends, to toil for your luxury and lust of gain? Must every tender feeling be likewise sacrificed to your avarice? Are the dearest friends and relations, now rendered more dear by their separation from their kindred, still to be parted from each other, and thus prevented from cheering the gloom of slavery, with the small comfort of being together, and mingling their sufferings and sorrows? Why are parents to lose their children, brothers their sisters, or husbands their wives? Surely, this is a new refinement in cruelty, which, while it has no advantage to atone for it, thus aggravates distress, and adds fresh horrors even to the wretchedness of slavery.

READING AND DISCUSSION QUESTIONS

1. How does Equiano contrast his experiences as a slave in Africa with his experiences aboard the slave ship?

2. To whom does Equiano appeal at the end of his narrative, and on what grounds?

3. At times, Equiano describes people as "white" or "black." At others, he distinguishes between people of his own nation and other "blacks," and elsewhere he refers to "Africans." What is the significance of these different categorizations?

VIEWPOINTS COMPARATIVE QUESTIONS

1. Compare and contrast Falconbridge's and Equiano's accounts of life aboard a slave ship. How do you explain the differences you note? In your opinion, did both authors believe their accounts to be truthful? Why or why not?

2. How did each author use Christianity to support his or her position?

3. How might Equiano have responded to Falconbridge's harsh characterization of Africa? Is there any aspect of her account with which he might have agreed?

20-5 | Enslaved Africans March to the Sea

Transportation of Slaves in Africa (ca. 1800–1900)

This nineteenth-century painting depicts the dynamics of the African slave trade and particularly the internal conditions of that trade through the eighteenth and nineteenth centuries. The painting highlights not only the brutal conditions under which Africans were enslaved and transported to the coast, but also the multiple and diverse roles played by Africans in the slave trade. The slavers (the figures holding rifles, a hatchet, or a pistol) are guarding or visibly threatening the enslaved Africans, some of whom are yoked together with a forked wooden device. Victims of violence or deprivation are left alongside the trail, and women and children are clearly visible among the slave ranks.

© RMN–Grand Palais/Art Resource, NY.

READING AND DISCUSSION QUESTIONS

1. What differences and similarities are discernible between the traders and the captured slaves? What do their garments, postures, and expressions reveal?

2. What might the artist have intended to communicate with this illustration? To whom?

3. Note that at least two of the figures in the image are holding firearms. What, if anything, does the presence of firearms indicate about the nature of African slavery?

4. The line of enslaved Africans stretches into the far distance and blurs as it recedes. What impression is created by this visual effect, and what does it communicate about the nature of African slavery?

■ COMPARATIVE QUESTIONS ■

1. What differences between African and European views of African slavery do the documents in this chapter reveal?

2. How might Falconbridge have reacted to the painting of enslaved Africans marching to the sea? What about Equiano? Osei Bonsu?

3. Falconbridge writes of the "ignorance, superstition, and savageness" of Africa based on her observations of Sierra Leone. In what ways does her assessment seem to support or refute the impression of West Africa presented by other sources?

4. What key differences, if any, exist between the two proslavery documents here?

5. Several of the authors in this chapter invoke morality to talk about the slave trade. What, specifically, are the moral standards cited in the various documents?

21

Continuity and Change in East Asia

1400–1800

From 1400 to 1800, East Asian countries experienced important changes at all levels of society. Despite the growing presence of Europeans in East Asia, both China and Japan remained relatively free from the influence of European commercial expansion. Chinese thinkers in the Ming and early Qing periods were primarily concerned with internal development and regional conflicts involving other Asian states. In Japan, the work of the three great unifiers—Oda Nobunaga, Toyotomi Hideyoshi, and Tokugawa Ieyasu—ended the chaotic Warring States Period and led to the relative peace of the Tokugawa regime (1603–1867). In both countries, transitions from older to newer political orders were mirrored by changes in society and culture. In China, the fall of the Ming Dynasty and the founding of the Qing Dynasty (1644–1911) by Jurchen invaders from Manchuria (known as the Manchu) occasioned new unrest and social critique. In Japan, the stability of the Tokugawa family's rule fostered domestic economic and cultural advances, and—despite careful control of international contact—afforded Dutch merchants limited but important access to Japanese society. The documents here illustrate not only the political shifts in East Asia, but also new ways that the Chinese and Japanese tried to define gender and its role in their lives.

21-1 | The Growing British Presence in East Asia

The Viceroy of Canton Giving an Audience to Commodore Anson (1748)

In the mid-eighteenth century, important changes were under way in the East Asian maritime world. The Portuguese had lost considerable ground to the Dutch, and more important in the long run, the British presence in the region was growing. British ambitions were centered on

India, but the British were also determined to expand their trade with China. In the 1830s, this determination would lead to war and a humiliating defeat for the Chinese. In the 1740s and 1750s, however, the Chinese could still treat the British as just another group of foreigners who hoped to grow rich buying and selling Chinese goods. In this illustration from *Anson's Voyage Round the World*, we see the British naval commander and adventurer George Anson in the presence of the viceroy of Canton. As you examine the image, pay particular attention to the relationship between the British visitors and their Chinese host. How did the artist want viewers to see Anson and his party? How did he want them to see the viceroy and his subordinates?

Private Collection/Bridgeman Images.

READING AND DISCUSSION QUESTIONS

1. How are Anson and his party dressed? What impression might they have hoped their attire would make on the viceroy?

2. What does the illustration suggest about Chinese attitudes toward the British? What about British attitudes toward the Chinese?

21-2 | A German Doctor Describes Eighteenth-Century Japan

ENGELBERT KAEMPFER, From *History of Japan* (1727)

Engelbert Kaempfer (1651–1716) was a German physician who traveled extensively in Russia and Asia in the late 1600s. His writings on Japan were published posthumously in 1727 to great public interest, and his exhaustive descriptions of Japanese society, language, environment, culture, and history were so accurate—in many cases—that he earned the suspicion of a later Japanese scholar, who warned in the early 1800s that Kaempfer's careful observations were proof that foreigners should be expelled to prevent espionage. The excerpts here outline his notes on commoners, his understanding of Confucianism, and his description of the Dutch in Japan and their commercial position there.

Judō, the Teaching or the Ways of the Moralists and Philosophers

Judō literally means the way or method of wise men. *Judōsha*, or *judōshū* in the plural, are their philosophers. They do not actually practice a religion but seek perfection and the greatest good in the contentment of the mind resulting from a virtuous and unblemished life and conduct. They believe in only secular punishment and reward, the consequence of virtue and vice. Thus one ought by necessity practice virtue as nature has given birth to us to lead the just life of people, as opposed to dumb animals.

Their founder, the first whose teaching was made public, was the famous Kōshi, born in China 2,238 years ago counting from this fifth year of Genroku, or the 1,692nd year after Christ. He used moral teachings to instruct his disciples in the greatest good and was the first to describe the *Shōgaku*, or book of living ethically, inflicting great damage on the opposing sect of Rōshi, flourishing at the time. After him this sect was continued by the much-praised teacher Mōshi, who established his philosophical Shisho, or Four Books, in this country. Up to this day they have their adherents in all countries where the characters of their writing system are understood.

Their moral philosophy consists of five articles, which they call *jin, gi, rei, chi, shin*. *Jin* teaches ethical living (consequently *jinsha*, virtuous person); *gi*, law and concern for justice; *rei*, politeness and civil behavior; *chi*, practical philosophy, politics, political judgment; *shin* concerns man's conscience and sincerity of heart.

They do not believe in the transmigration of souls but in a universal soul, or a force common to the entire world, which absorbs the souls of the dead, like the ocean takes back all water, and in the generation of matter permits them to depart again without differentiation. They associate this world soul, or universal nature, with the godhead and endow it with the attributes of the prime being. They use the word *ten*, heaven, or nature, in the actions and fortunes of life, thanking

Engelbert Kaempfer, *Kaempfer's Japan: Tokugawa Culture Observed*, ed. and trans. Beatrice M. Bodart-Bailey (Honolulu: University of Hawaii Press, 1999), 132–133, 145, 187–188. Reprinted by permission of the publisher.

heaven or nature for their food. I have spoken to others who conceded an intellect or perfect incorporeal being as the governing agent, but not as the originator of nature. As the highest creation of nature it is produced by *in* and *yō*, that is, from the action of heaven and receptivity of the earth, the principles of generation and corruption. In this fashion they also accept other forces as spiritual and believe that the world is eternal and that men and animals were produced from the *in yō* of heaven and the five elements.

They have neither temple nor gods, but follow the traditions of their forefathers in observing the memory of and commemorating their dead friends. They venerate their dead friends' *byōsho*, or memorial tablet, according to the customs of their forefathers and in the fashion of other believers by placing meat in front of it, lighting candles, and bowing to the ground (as if they were alive). They celebrate their memory monthly and annually and prepare themselves three days in advance by abstaining from sexual intercourse and all sinful matter, cleaning their body, and putting on new clothes. All this they do as a human gesture, prompted by their grateful and virtuous heart. The body of the dead is kept for three days above ground and placed into a European-style coffin, flat on the back, but the head is raised a little. Presumably to prevent decomposition they sometimes also cover the body with spices and scented herbs. Then they accompany it to the place of burial, where they bury the body in the soil without prior cremation.

Suicide is not only permitted in this sect but is considered an extraordinary act of bravery when committed to preempt the enemy or a shameful death.

These atheistic philosophers will only perform heathen celebrations or special duties for the gods out of common politeness. Instead they strive for virtue, a clean conscience, and honorable behavior in accordance with the teaching of [Roman philosopher] Seneca or our Ten Commandments. Thus they are also capable of looking favorably at the Christian teaching and as a result have come under great suspicion. According to the new laws, which came into effect with the banishment of the Christians, they must, against their will, keep in their houses the image of a god or mount, or paste up, the characters of the name of a god with a pot of flowers and an incense burner placed in front of it. Generally they chose Kannon or Amida, whom, according to the custom of the country, they assign a place behind the hearth. Of their own free will they may have a picture of Kōshi in public places of learning or, in their own homes, the *byōsho* of their parents with the posthumous name of, or characters for, a learned man. In the past this now-suspicious sect comprised the greater part of the population and practically held a monopoly on the sciences and liberal arts. But after the martyrdom of the Christians, their numbers decreased yearly and their books were brought into disrepute, even though those books had been valued by all other believers no less than we [Europeans] do the instructive works of Seneca, Plato, and other heathens.

Some thirty years ago it came to pass that the Lord of Bizen, Inaba, an excellent *judōshi* and patron of the liberal arts, attempted to popularize once again in his fief this sect and its stoic manner of living. He founded an academy, appointed learned men and teachers from all parts of the country, and paid them handsomely. Gaining greater understanding and prompted by example of their superiors, the people no longer wanted to believe in the incomprehensible revelation and fantastic tales or to continue supporting the ignorant rabble of priests, who mostly depended for their living on alms. Consequently these gangs (with which the whole country is packed) nearly died of starvation in this fief. But both the emperor and the shogun were so angered about this matter that they were about to deprive this honest patriot of his inherited fief and would have done so had he not taken the precaution of retiring in favor of his son to prevent his family from falling out of favor. His son, who has governed ever since, demonstrates with his stoic conduct that he is still following his father's path. . . .

The Situation of the City of Nagasaki [. . .]

Houses of the Commoners

The houses of common citizens and residents are of poor structure, small and low. They either have no attic at all or one that is low and practically useless. The roof is covered with pine chips, generally secured only by other chips placed across. Like all other houses in this country, they are constructed of wood and clay walls. Inside, the walls are nicely hung with colored paper, and the floors are neatly spread with thickly padded woven rush mats. Further, they are divided into separate rooms by papered sliding windows. They lack chairs or benches and have only as many household items as are essential for daily cooking. At the back there is merely a narrow space for one's private business, which, however poor, does contain some little plants, carefully grown to provide a focus of interest for the eyes. The houses of people of distinction, the rich, and those handling foreign trade rise to two stories, are spacious, and are partly built in Chinese style with a large building with bare floor at the entrance and a garden at the back. . . .

The Situation of the Dutch

At the beginning of the present seventeenth century, very soon after their ships began to travel to Asia and the establishment of their East India Company, the Dutch, enticed by the fertile trade of the Portuguese, began making annual visits to this, the furthest empire of the world. They arrived at the city and island of Hirado and set up their warehouse and living quarters on a spit of land linked to the city by a bridge. Their admission to Japan was all the quicker and easier, the greater their enmity was toward those whom the ruler felt compelled to drive out of the country. Even though the Portuguese still had a lot of influence with the greatest lords of the country, and did much to prevent the entry of the Dutch, they were finally unable to stop the shogun Ieyasu—or Gongen, after his death—from giving the Dutch access to the country in the year of Christ 1611 with a special *goshuin*, which literally means "lofty cinnabar seal" and is a shogunal permit or pass. It is signed by the councilors of the empire and authorized by the red shogunal seal, from the color of which it also takes its name. With this document they were granted in very clear terms, or characters, free trade and access to all provinces and harbors with favorable recommendations to all subjects of the empire. After the death of the shogun they requested to have their privileges renewed and a new pass issued, against the practice of this nation, which considers upholding the laws of its forefathers a sacred duty. This they received, but while outwardly it appeared to be identical in form and shape, it contained much less advantageous conditions. Meanwhile, from the time they settled in Hirado, the Dutch did what they could to profit from the progressive decline of the Portuguese. They did everything possible to please the court, the source of success or failure, as well as the councilors, the lord of Hirado, and any other great men who might proffer help or hindrance. The Dutch spared no cost nor labor to seek out the world's rarest novelties to pay homage to the Japanese annually and to satisfy the ridiculous passion of the Japanese for various strange animals—which nature did not create the way they imagine them—by bringing in as many as possible from the most distant empires of India, Persia, and Europe. The Dutch showed the utmost subservience in everything, even wrongful impositions, to stay in the good books of this nation and conduct profitable trade. Since they valued their lives, they could show no objection when in 1638 the shogun ordered them to tear down as fast as if they were enemy property their own newly built residence and warehouse on the island of Hirado: valuable stone mansions such as Japan had never seen before. The reason was that the buildings were splendid beyond the custom of the country and had the year of the Christian era on the gable [of their roofs]. Soon afterward, in the same year of 1638, this heathen court had no qualms in inflicting upon them a cursed test to find out whether the orders of the shogun or the love for their fellow Christians had greater power over them. It was a matter of us serving the empire by helping to destroy the native Christians, of whom those remaining, some forty thousand people, in desperation over their martyrdom had moved into an old fortress in the province of Shimabara and made preparations to defend themselves. The head of the Dutch, Koekebecker, himself went to the location with the one remaining vessel (for in the face of the impudent demand the remainder had slipped out of the harbor the previous day) and in fourteen days treated the beleaguered Christians to 426 rough cannon salvos, both from land and sea. Although this assistance resulted neither in surrender nor complete defeat, it broke the strength of the besieged. And because the Japanese had the pleasure to order it, he stripped the vessel of a further six cannons (regardless of the fact that she still had to navigate dangerous seas) that the Japanese insisted had to be lent in addition to the first to carry out their cruel designs.

It is true that this show of total obedience was instrumental in keeping a foothold in the country when the court was considering completely closing it to all Christians. At the same time, however, they gained a bad reputation among the more high-minded at court and throughout the country, for they judged that people who so easily permitted themselves to be used in the destruction of those with whom they basically shared the same belief and the path of Christ—as they had been amply told by the padres from Portugal and Manila—could not be true of heart, honest, and loyal towards a foreign ruler. I was told this by the locals in these very same words. Thus far from earning the trust and deep friendship of this exceedingly suspicious nation by their compliance, the reputation of the Dutch was ruined unjustly, regardless of their merits. Shortly afterward, in 1641, the Dutch, having assisted in the confinement of the Portuguese by word and deed, were to undergo the same experience. For they were told to leave the island of Hirado with all their belongings and to exchange subordination to a lenient territorial lord for directions from a new and zealous administration directly responsible to the shogun, while retiring under strict guard and manifold supervision within the limits of the prison built for the Portuguese. Submission to these proud heathens into such servitude and imprisonment, forgoing all celebrations of feast days and Sundays, all devotion with religious song and prayer, the use of the name of Christ, the symbol of the cross, and all outward proof or signs of being a Christian, and, added to that, good-natured acceptance of their despicable impudence, an affront to any high-minded soul, all that for the love of profit and to gain control of the veins of ore in their mountains.

READING AND DISCUSSION QUESTIONS

1. Kaempfer was criticized for his favorable presentation of a "heathen" culture. How does he address religion in these excerpts?

2. Kaempfer's description of Japan fascinated the European public. What might have particularly intrigued European readers in the early 1700s, and why?

3. What light does Kaempfer's account shed on the relative power of the Dutch and the Japanese in the seventeenth century?

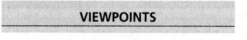

VIEWPOINTS

Gender in East Asia

Over the course of the early modern period, family and marriage systems in China and Japan converged, with Japan moving closer to the Chinese model of strict subordination of women to men. In both societies, women moved into their husband's house upon marriage. Once there, they were expected to show total obedience to both their husbands and their in-laws. Deprived of independent wealth by inheritance practices that favored sons over daughters, women had little leverage with which to resist the demands of their relatives. Thus, women were, in a sense, seen as perpetual children, with no identity separate from their roles as daughters, wives, and mothers. The documents included in this feature highlight this subordination, but they also reveal some of its limits. Most women worked in some capacity outside of the home, taking on roles that required more of them than humble acquiescence and a pretty smile. Moreover, contemporary observers were aware of the gender inequities in their society, and they did not always approve of them. As you explore the documents, think about the limits on the subordination of women in Japanese and Chinese society. Why was it impossible for the reality of gender relations to ever be in complete accord with theory?

21-3 | Teaching Values to Japanese Children

KAIBARA EKIKEN AND KAIBARA TŌKEN, *Common Sense Teachings for Japanese Children* and *Greater Learning for Women* (ca. 1700)

Kaibara Ekiken (1630–1714) was a physician, educator, and author from the samurai class during the enforced peace of the Tokugawa period (1603–1867). His works combined Neo-Confucian principles of self-reliance and humaneness with careful and practical attention to life in early modern Japan. His writings were printed and distributed widely, thanks to the vibrant publishing world of urban Tokugawa Japan. The following selections (the second probably coauthored with his wife, Tōken) show his concern with daily life and "common sense" and his interest in maintaining gender and social roles in the Confucian social order.

Common Sense Teachings for Japanese Children

In January when children reach the age of six, teach them numbers one through ten, and the names given to designate 100, 1,000, 10,000, and 100,000,000. Let them know the four directions, East, West, North, and South. Assess their native intelligence and differentiate between quick and slow learners. Teach them Japanese pronunciation from the age of six or seven, and let them learn how to write. . . . From this time on, teach them to respect their elders, and let them know the distinctions between the upper and lower classes and between the young and old. Let them learn to use the correct expressions.

When the children reach the age of seven, do not let the boys and girls sit together, nor must you allow them to dine together. . . .

For the eighth year. This is the age when the ancients began studying the book *Little Learning*.[1] Beginning at this time, teach the youngsters etiquette befitting their age, and caution them not to commit an act of impoliteness. Among those which must be taught are: daily deportment, the manners set for appearing

David J. Lu, *Japan: A Documentary History* (Armonk, N.Y.: M. E. Sharpe, 1997), 258–261. Translation copyright © 1997 by David J. Lu. Reprinted with permission of M. E. Sharpe, Inc. All rights reserved. Not for Reproduction.

[1] **Little Learning:** An instruction book for young children that contained rules of behavior.

before one's senior and withdrawing from his presence, how to speak or respond to one's senior or guest, how to place a serving tray or replace it for one's senior, how to present a wine cup and pour rice wine and to serve side dishes to accompany it, and how to serve tea. Children must also learn how to behave while taking their meals.

Children must be taught by those who are close to them the virtues of filial piety and obedience. To serve the parents well is called filial piety, and to serve one's seniors well is called obedience. The one who lives close to the children and who is able to teach must instruct the children in the early years of their life that the first obligation of a human being is to revere the parents and serve them well. Then comes the next lesson which includes respect for one's seniors, listening to their commands and not holding them in contempt. One's seniors include elder brothers, elder sisters, uncles, aunts, and cousins who are older and worthy of respect. . . . As the children grow older, teach them to love their younger brothers and to be compassionate to the employees and servants. Teach them also the respect due the teachers and the behavior codes governing friends. The etiquette governing each movement toward important guests—such as standing, sitting, advancing forward, and retiring from their presence—and the language to be employed must be taught. Teach them how to pay respect to others according to the social positions held by them. Gradually the ways of filial piety and obedience, loyalty and trustworthiness, right deportment and decorum, and sense of shame must be inculcated in the children's minds and they must know how to implement them. Caution them not to desire the possessions of others, or to stoop below one's dignity in consuming excessive amounts of food and drink. . . .

Once reaching the age of eight, children must follow and never lead their elders when entering a gate, sitting, or eating and drinking. From this time on they must be taught how to become humble and yield to others. Do not permit the children to behave as they please. It is important to caution them against "doing their own things."

At the age of ten, let the children be placed under the guidance of a teacher, and tell them about the general meaning of the five constant virtues and let them understand the way of the five human relationships.[2] Let them read books by the Sage [Confucius] and the wise men of old and cultivate the desire for learning. . . . When not engaged in reading, teach them the literary and military arts. . . .

Fifteen is the age when the ancients began the study of the *Great Learning*.[3] From this time on, concentrate on the learning of a sense of justice and duty. The students must also learn to cultivate their personalities and investigate the way of governing people. . . .

---

[2] **five constant virtues . . . human relationships:** The *five virtues* are human heartedness, righteousness, propriety, wisdom, and good faith. The *five relationships* are ruler-subject, father-son, husband-wife, older brother–younger brother, and friend-friend.

[3] **Great Learning:** A chapter in the *Record of Rituals*, one of the four works that came to be known within the Confucian classics as the Four Books.

Those who are born in the high-ranking families have the heavy obligations of becoming leaders of the people, of having people entrusted to their care, and of governing them. Therefore, without fail, a teacher must be selected for them when they are still young. They must be taught how to read and be informed of the ways of old, of cultivating their personalities, and of the way of governing people. If they do not learn the way of governing people, they may injure the many people who are entrusted to their care by the Way of Heaven. That will be a serious disaster. . . .

Greater Learning for Women

Seeing that it is a girl's destiny, on reaching womanhood, to go to a new home, and live in submission to her father-in-law, it is even more incumbent upon her than it is on a boy to receive with all reverence her parents' instructions. Should her parents, through their tenderness, allow her to grow up self-willed, she will infallibly show herself capricious in her husband's house, and thus alienate his affection; while, if her father-in-law be a man of correct principles, the girl will find the yoke of these principles intolerable. She will hate and decry her father-in-law, and the end of those domestic dissensions will be her dismissal from her husband's house and the covering of herself with ignominy. Her parents, forgetting the faulty education they gave her, may indeed lay all the blame on the father-in-law. But they will be in error; for the whole disaster should rightly be attributed to the faulty education the girl received from her parents.

* * *

More precious in a woman is a virtuous heart than a face of beauty. The vicious woman's heart is ever excited; she glares wildly around her, she vents her anger on others, her words are harsh and her accent vulgar. When she speaks, it is to set herself above others, to upbraid others, to envy others, to be puffed up with individual pride, to jeer at others, to outdo others—all things at variance with the way in which a woman should walk. The only qualities that befit a woman are gentle obedience, chastity, mercy, and quietness.

From her earliest youth a girl should observe the line of demarcation separating women from men. The customs of antiquity did not allow men and women to sit in the same apartment, to keep their wearing apparel in the same place, to bathe in the same place, or to transmit to each other anything directly from hand to hand. A woman . . . must observe a certain distance in her relations even with her husband and with her brothers. In our days the women of lower classes, ignoring all rules of this nature, behave disorderly; they contaminate their reputations, bring down reproach upon the head of their parents and brothers, and spend their whole lives in an unprofitable manner. Is not this truly lamentable?

* * *

It is the chief duty of a girl living in the parental house to practice filial piety towards her father and mother. But after marriage her duty is to honor her father-in-law and mother-in-law, to honor them beyond her father and mother, to love and reverence them with all ardor, and to tend them with practice of every filial piety. . . . Even if your father-in-law and mother-in-law are inclined to hate and vilify you, do not be angry with them, and murmur not. If you carry piety towards them to its utmost limits, and minister to them in all sincerity, it cannot be but that they will end by becoming friendly to you.

* * *

The great lifelong duty of a woman is obedience. . . . When the husband issues his instructions, the wife must never disobey them. In a doubtful case, she should inquire of her husband and obediently follow his commands. . . .

Should her husband be roused at any time to anger, she must obey him with fear and trembling, and not set herself up against him in anger and forwardness. A woman should look upon her husband as if he were Heaven itself, and never weary of thinking how she may yield to her husband and thus escape celestial castigation.

Her treatment of her servant girls will require circumspection. Those low-born girls have had no proper education; they are stupid, obstinate, and vulgar in their speech. . . . Again, in her dealings with those lowly people, a woman will find many things to disapprove of. But if she be always reproving and scolding, and spend her time in hustle and anger, her household will be in a continual state of disturbance. When there is real wrongdoing, she should occasionally notice it, and point out the path of amendment, while lesser faults should be quietly endured without anger.

READING AND DISCUSSION QUESTIONS

1. What values does Ekiken emphasize for children's education? How are they to be instilled?

2. How is concern for social hierarchy and propriety evident in Ekiken's work on children? In his work on women?

3. Based on these excerpts, what role were women supposed to play in Tokugawa society?

4. What assumptions, if any, does Ekiken make about his likely audience? What gives you that impression?

21-4 | Pleasure and Gender in Tokugawa Edo

TORII KIYONAGA, *Women of the Gay Quarters* (Late Eighteenth Century)

For Japanese daimyo, Tokugawa-era Edo was a gilded prison. On the one hand, the city boasted an astonishing variety of establishments devoted to providing urban elites with every possible pleasure, luxury, and form of diversion. Providing he had the money to pay for his desires, a daimyo living in Edo could indulge his every whim. On the other hand, the alternate residence system required all daimyo to live in Edo every other year and to leave their families there. Thus, the decision to maintain a residence in Edo, with all the costs that entailed, was not a choice for daimyo, but a legal requirement that resulted in the eventual bankruptcy of many once-powerful daimyo families. Think about these issues as you examine this eighteenth-century woodblock print of a wealthy Japanese man surrounded by "women of the gay quarters" of Edo. In what ways might this image comment on the effects of city life on elite Japanese men?

Pushkin Museum, Moscow, Russia/Bridgeman Images.

READING AND DISCUSSION QUESTIONS

1. How would you characterize the lone male figure in the print? What is his relationship to the women who surround him?

2. In your opinion, should we see this image as a reflection of male dominance in Japanese society? Why or why not? What alternative interpretations of the image are possible?

21-5 | Chinese Gender Norms Turned Upside Down

LI RUZHEN (LI JU-CHEN), From *Flowers in the Mirror* (1827)

Li Ruzhen (1763–1830) was a Chinese scholar and novelist in the Qing Dynasty. Objecting to the constraints of the Confucian examination system, he achieved only the lowest official rank of scholarship, but his work in linguistics earned him a reputation as an intellectual. His novel *Flowers in the Mirror* (*Jing Hua Yuan*) is a fantastic and satirical take on Chinese society during the Tang Dynasty (618–907). In this excerpt, the main characters Tang Ao and Merchant Lin have traveled from the Kingdom on Earth to the Country of Women. Their experiences there call attention to gender dynamics during the Qing Dynasty, and especially the practice of foot binding, a popular but controversial procedure in which women's feet were crushed into a shape thought to be appealing to men.

When Tang Ao heard that they had arrived at the Country of Women, he thought that the country was populated entirely by women, and was afraid to go ashore. But Old Tuo said, "Not at all! There are men as well as women, only they call men women, and women men. The men wear the skirts and take care of the home, while the women wear hats and trousers and manage affairs outside." . . .

"If the men dress like women, do they use cosmetics and bind their feet?" asked Tang Ao.

"Of course they do!" cried Lin, and took from his pocket a list of the merchandise he was going to sell, which consisted of huge quantities of rouge, face powder, combs and other women's notions. "Lucky I wasn't born in this country," he said. "Catch me mincing around on bound feet!" . . .

Merchant Lin had been told by one of his customers that the "King's uncle" wanted to buy some of his goods. Following instructions, he went to the "Royal Uncle's" Residence in the Palace, and handed his list of merchandise to the gatekeeper. Soon, the gatekeeper came back and said that it was just what the "King" was looking for for his "concubines" and "maids," and asked Lin to be shown into the inner apartments. . . .

Li Ju-chen, *Flowers in the Mirror*, trans. and ed. Lin Tai-yi (Berkeley: University of California Press, 1965), 107–113. Reprinted with permission of Peter Owen Publishers.

Merchant Lin followed the guard inside, and was soon in the presence of the "King." After making a deep bow, he saw that she was a woman of about thirty years old, with a beautiful face, fair skin and cherry-red lips. Around her there stood many palace "maids."

The "King" spoke to Lin in a light voice[,] . . . looking at him with interest as he answered her questions.

"I wonder what she is staring at me like this for," Merchant Lin thought to himself. "Hasn't she ever seen a man from the Kingdom on Earth before?" . . .

In a little time, Merchant Lin was ushered to a room upstairs, where victuals of many kinds awaited him. . . . Several palace "maids" ran upstairs soon, and calling him "Your Highness" kowtowed to him and congratulated him. Before he knew what was happening, Merchant Lin was being stripped completely bare by the maids and led to a perfumed bath. Against the powerful arms of these maids, he could scarcely struggle. Soon he found himself being anointed, perfumed, powdered and rouged, and dressed in a skirt. His big feet were bound up in strips of cloth and socks, and his hair was combed into an elaborate braid over his head and decorated with pins. . . .

Merchant Lin thought he must be drunk, or dreaming, and began to tremble. He asked the maids what was happening, and was told that he had been chosen by the "King" to be the Imperial Consort, and that a propitious day would be chosen for him to enter the "King's" chambers.

Before he could utter a word, another group of maids, all tall and strong and wearing beards, came in. One was holding a threaded needle. "We are ordered to pierce your ears," he said, as the other four "maids" grabbed Lin by the arms and legs. The white-bearded one seized Lin's right ear, and after rubbing the lobe a little, drove the needle through it.

"Ooh!" Merchant Lin screamed. . . .

Having finished what they came to do, the maids retreated, and a black-bearded fellow came in with a bolt of white silk. Kneeling down before him, the fellow said, "I am ordered to bind Your Highness's feet."

Two other maids seized Lin's feet as the black-bearded one sat down on a low stool, and began to rip the silk into ribbons. Seizing Lin's right foot, he set it upon his knee, and sprinkled white alum powder between the toes and the grooves of the foot. He squeezed the toes tightly together, bent them down so that the whole foot was shaped like an arch, and took a length of white silk and bound it tightly around it twice. One of the others sewed the ribbon together in small stitches. Again the silk went around the foot, and again, it was sewn up.

Merchant Lin felt as though his feet were burning, and wave after wave of pain rose to his heart. When he could stand it no longer, he let out his voice and began to cry. . . .

Before two weeks were over, Lin's feet had begun to assume a permanently arched form, and his toes begun to rot. Daily medical ablutions were given to them, and the pain persisted. . . .

In due course, his feet lost much of their original shape. Blood and flesh were squeezed into a pulp and then little remained of his feet but dry bones and skin, shrunk, indeed, to a dainty size. Responding to daily anointing, his hair became shiny and smooth, and his body, after repeated ablutions of perfumed water, began to look very attractive indeed. His eyebrows were plucked to resemble a new moon. With blood-red lipstick and powder adorning his face, and jade and pearl adorning his coiffure and ears, Merchant Lin assumed, at last, a not unappealing appearance.

READING AND DISCUSSION QUESTIONS

1. What does Li's novel tell us about gender norms in his society? What role were women supposed to play? What about men?

2. How should we see Li's work—as a comedy in which the absurdity of the situation serves to reinforce traditional gender roles, or as a work of social satire and criticism in which the oppression of women is revealed by placing male characters in traditional female roles?

VIEWPOINTS COMPARATIVE QUESTIONS

1. How might Li have responded to Kaibara Ekiken and Kaibara Tōken's advice book? How might they have responded to his work?

2. What might Kaibara Ekiken and Kaibara Tōken have made of the Japanese use of "antipollution passes"?

3. How do the works included in this feature demonstrate the power of traditional gender norms in Chinese and Japanese society? How do they reveal the limits of that power?

■ COMPARATIVE QUESTIONS ■

1. Several of the documents in this chapter address, directly or indirectly, the construction of gender in East Asian societies. Based on these documents, what conclusions can you draw about how men and women related to one another in early modern China and Japan? How did these relations change, and why?

2. Compare and contrast the illustration from *Anson's Voyage Round the World* and Kaempfer's account of the Dutch presence in Japan. What common themes are present in both documents?

3. Both Kaempfer and Li write about the experience of being in a foreign culture. In Li's case, the fictional account is designed as a commentary on his own time and place. How might Kaempfer's writing say as much about his own culture as it does about early modern Japan? In what ways does his writing reflect a European perspective? How might it have been different if written by a Japanese observer?

22

Revolutions in the Atlantic World
1775–1825

Beginning with the American Revolution in 1775, the intellectual projects of the Enlightenment in Europe intersected with the economic logic of overseas colonial empires to generate optimism and upheaval in the Atlantic world. Colonists in British North America, members of the third estate in France, and slaves in the French colony of Saint-Domingue (Haiti) all used Enlightenment values to justify rebellion. The bloody expression of notions of freedom, equality, and national integrity in the American, French, and Haitian Revolutions, along with the Napoleonic wars of conquest in Europe, challenged many aspects of traditional European society at home and in the colonies. However, the endurance of sexual, class-based, and ethnic discrimination and the recurrence of violence and war complicate the era's story of egalitarianism and democracy.

VIEWPOINTS

Defining the Citizen

At the heart of the revolutionary movement that swept France in 1789 was the replacement of the term *subject* with the term *citizen*. Subjects were given their rights by a divinely appointed ruler. Since rights were assigned to subjects at the discretion of the monarch, it followed that not all subjects would necessarily enjoy the same rights and that those rights could be withdrawn at any time. In sharp contrast, the rights of the citizen were the product of natural law and hence universal, immutable, and irrevocable.

Government did not exist in order to dispense rights and privileges; it existed to protect them. Likewise, the purpose of the law was not to enforce inequality, but to create conditions in which all citizens could enjoy the full expression of their national rights. However, almost as quickly as this vision was articulated in the Declaration of the Rights of Man and of the Citizen (see Document 22-1), critics noted an important omission in this foundational document of the Revolution. While the authors had taken great care to define the rights of citizens, they had been less precise in identifying which groups were to be included as citizens. Were women to have the same rights as men? Was slavery compatible with the new political order? Think about these questions as you read the selections included in this feature. What traditional social and political structures did the National Assembly challenge? Which were left in place?

22-1 | The National Assembly Presents a New Vision of Government

The Declaration of the Rights of Man and of the Citizen (1789)

On June 17, 1789, during a meeting of the Estates General, the traditional advisory body under the absolutist French monarchy, delegates of the third estate voted to form a new National Assembly of France. They were joined by clergy and noblemen from the first and second estates, one of whom, the Marquis de Lafayette (1757–1834), outlined the assembly's aims in the Declaration of the Rights of Man. The assembly approved the document in August, after the Revolution had begun, and trumpeted it throughout Europe and the world. The Declaration is an important codification of Enlightenment ideas that embodies the National Assembly's vision of the relationship between the individual and government.

The representatives of the French people, organized as a National Assembly, believing that the ignorance, neglect, or contempt of the rights of man are the sole cause of public calamities and of the corruption of governments, have determined to set forth in a solemn declaration the natural, inalienable, and sacred rights of man, in order that this declaration, being constantly before all the members of the social body, shall remind them continually of their rights and duties; in order that the acts of the legislative power, as well as those of the executive power, may be compared at any moment with the objects and purposes of all political institutions and may thus be more respected; and, lastly, in order that the grievances of the citizens, based hereafter upon simple and incontestable principles, shall tend to the maintenance of the constitution and redound to the happiness of all. Therefore the National Assembly recognizes and proclaims, in

James Harvey Robinson, ed., *Readings in European History* (Boston: Ginn, 1904), 2:409–411.

the presence and under the auspices of the Supreme Being, the following rights of man and of the citizen:

ARTICLE 1. Men are born and remain free and equal in rights. Social distinctions may be founded only upon the general good.

2. The aim of all political association is the preservation of the natural and imprescriptible rights of man. These rights are liberty, property, security, and resistance to oppression.

3. The principle of all sovereignty resides essentially in the nation. No body nor individual may exercise any authority which does not proceed directly from the nation.

4. Liberty consists in the freedom to do everything which injures no one else; hence the exercise of the natural rights of each man has no limits except those which assure to the other members of the society the enjoyment of the same rights. These limits can only be determined by law.

5. Law can only prohibit such actions as are hurtful to society. Nothing may be prevented which is not forbidden by law, and no one may be forced to do anything not provided for by law.

6. Law is the expression of the general will. Every citizen has a right to participate personally, or through his representative, in its formation. It must be the same for all, whether it protects or punishes. All citizens, being equal in the eyes of the law, are equally eligible to all dignities and to all public positions and occupations, according to their abilities, and without distinction except that of their virtues and talents.

7. No person shall be accused, arrested, or imprisoned except in the cases and according to the forms prescribed by law. Any one soliciting, transmitting, executing, or causing to be executed, any arbitrary order, shall be punished. But any citizen summoned or arrested in virtue of the law shall submit without delay, as resistance constitutes an offense.

8. The law shall provide for such punishments only as are strictly and obviously necessary, and no one shall suffer punishment except it be legally inflicted in virtue of a law passed and promulgated before the commission of the offense.

9. As all persons are held innocent until they shall have been declared guilty, if arrest shall be deemed indispensable, all harshness not essential to the securing of the prisoner's person shall be severely repressed by law.

10. No one shall be disquieted on account of his opinions, including his religious views, provided their manifestation does not disturb the public order established by law.

11. The free communication of ideas and opinions is one of the most precious of the rights of man. Every citizen may, accordingly, speak, write, and print with freedom, but shall be responsible for such abuses of this freedom as shall be defined by law.

12. The security of the rights of man and of the citizen requires public military forces. These forces are, therefore, established for the good of all and not for the personal advantage of those to whom they shall be intrusted.

13. A common contribution is essential for the maintenance of the public forces and for the cost of administration. This should be equitably distributed among all the citizens in proportion to their means.

14. All the citizens have a right to decide, either personally or by their representatives, as to the necessity of the public contribution; to grant this freely; to know to what uses it is put; and to fix the proportion, the mode of assessment and of collection and the duration of the taxes.

15. Society has the right to require of every public agent an account of his administration.

16. A society in which the observance of the law is not assured, nor the separation of powers defined, has no constitution at all.

17. Since property is an inviolable and sacred right, no one shall be deprived thereof except where public necessity, legally determined, shall clearly demand it, and then only on condition that the owner shall have been previously and equitably indemnified.

READING AND DISCUSSION QUESTIONS

1. According to the Declaration, what is the source of individual rights? What traditional ideas about such rights does the Declaration implicitly challenge?

2. Which rights did the authors see as most important? Why? What did they see as the essential elements of a just and prosperous society?

3. What importance should we attach to the fact that the authors failed to include any discussion of race, gender, or social status in the Declaration? Should we assume that men and women of all races and all social backgrounds were intended to be included in the category "citizen"? Why or why not?

22-2 | A Female Author Revises the Declaration of the Rights of Man

OLYMPE DE GOUGES, From the *Declaration of the Rights of Woman* (1791)

Olympe de Gouges (1748–1793) was a French playwright who turned to political activism in the late 1780s. In plays and other writings, she advocated for the rights of enslaved people in France's colonies. After her initial enthusiasm with the Revolution, she became increasingly outspoken on gender equality. She continued to speak out against injustice, opposing the execution of Louis XVI and offering her opinion on factional revolutionary politics. She was arrested for the latter, and—thanks in part to her own refusal to plead ignorance—was

Darline G. Levy, Harriet B. Applewhite, and Mary D. Johnson, eds., *Women in Revolutionary Paris, 1789–1795* (Champaign: University of Illinois Press, 1979), 89–92. Copyright 1979 by the Board of Trustees of the University of Illinois. Used with permission of the University of Illinois Press.

executed in November 1793. The pamphlet excerpted here is her best-known work. In it, she skillfully reproduces the form of the Declaration of the Rights of Man and of the Citizen (see Document 22-1) to direct attention to women's rights.

For the National Assembly to decree in its last sessions, or in those of the next legislature:

Preamble

Mothers, daughters, sisters [and] representatives of the nation demand to be constituted into a national assembly. Believing that ignorance, omission, or scorn for the rights of woman are the only causes of public misfortunes and of the corruption of governments, [the women] have resolved to set forth in a solemn declaration the natural, inalienable, and sacred rights of woman in order that this declaration, constantly exposed before all the members of the society, will ceaselessly remind them of their rights and duties; in order that the authoritative acts of women and the authoritative acts of men may be at any moment compared with and respectful of the purpose of all political institutions; and in order that citizens' demands, henceforth based on simple and incontestable principles, will always support the constitution, good morals, and the happiness of all.

Consequently, the sex that is as superior in beauty as it is in courage during the sufferings of maternity recognizes and declares in the presence and under the auspices of the Supreme Being, the following Rights of Woman and of Female Citizens.

Article I

Woman is born free and lives equal to man in her rights. Social distinctions can be based only on the common utility.

Article II

The purpose of any political association is the conservation of the natural and imprescriptible rights of woman and man; these rights are liberty, property, security, and especially resistance to oppression.

Article III

The principle of all sovereignty rests essentially with the nation, which is nothing but the union of woman and man; no body and no individual can exercise any authority which does not come expressly from it [the nation].

Article IV

Liberty and justice consist of restoring all that belongs to others; thus, the only limits on the exercise of the natural rights of woman are perpetual male tyranny; these limits are to be reformed by the laws of nature and reason.

Article V

Laws of nature and reason proscribe all acts harmful to society; everything which is not prohibited by these wise and divine laws cannot be prevented, and no one can be constrained to do what they do not command.

Article VI

The law must be the expression of the general will; all female and male citizens must contribute either personally or through their representatives to its formation; it must be the same for all: male and female citizens, being equal in the eyes of the law, must be equally admitted to all honors, positions, and public employment according to their capacity and without other distinctions besides those of their virtues and talents.

Article VII

No woman is an exception; she is accused, arrested, and detained in cases determined by law. Women, like men, obey this rigorous law.

Article VIII

The law must establish only those penalties that are strictly and obviously necessary, and no one can be punished except by virtue of a law established and promulgated prior to the crime and legally applicable to women.

Article IX

Once any woman is declared guilty, complete rigor is [to be] exercised by the law.

Article X

No one is to be disquieted for his very basic opinions; woman has the right to mount the scaffold; she must equally have the right to mount the rostrum [podium], provided that her demonstrations do not disturb the legally established public order.

Article XI

The free communication of thoughts and opinions is one of the most precious rights of woman, since that liberty assures the recognition of children by their fathers. Any female citizen thus may say freely, I am the mother of a child which belongs to you, without being forced by a barbarous prejudice to hide the truth; [an exception may be made] to respond to the abuse of this liberty in cases determined by the law.

Article XII

The guarantee of the rights of woman and the female citizen implies a major benefit; this guarantee must be instituted for the advantage of all, and not for the particular benefit of those to whom it is entrusted.

Article XIII

For the support of the public force and the expenses of administration, the contributions of woman and man are equal; she shares all the duties and all the painful tasks; therefore, she must have the same share in the distribution of positions, employment, offices, honors, and jobs.

Article XIV

Female and male citizens have the right to verify, either by themselves or through their representatives, the necessity of the public contribution. This can only apply to women if they are granted an equal share, not only of wealth, but also of public administration, and in the determination of the proportion, the base, the collection, and the duration of the tax.

Article XV

The collectivity of women, joined for tax purposes to the aggregate of men, has the right to demand an accounting of his administration from any public agent.

Article XVI

No society has a constitution without the guarantee of rights and the separation of powers; the constitution is null if the majority of individuals comprising the nation have not cooperated in drafting it.

Article XVII

Property belongs to both sexes whether united or separate; for each it is an inviolable and sacred right; no one can be deprived of it, since it is the true patrimony of nature, unless the legally determined public need obviously dictates it, and then only with a just and prior indemnity.

READING AND DISCUSSION QUESTIONS

1. How does de Gouges define "the nation"? What does her definition tell you about her view of the ideal polity?

2. What distinctions, if any, does de Gouges make between the rights of men and the rights of women?

3. Why did de Gouges believe that the full participation of women was necessary in all aspects of the life of the nation?

VIEWPOINTS COMPARATIVE QUESTIONS

1. What ideals are championed both in the Declaration of the Rights of Man and in the Declaration of the Rights of Woman?

2. How might the authors of the Declaration of the Rights of Man have responded to de Gouges's critique? How might they explain their failure to address gender inequality?

22-3 | Robespierre Justifies Terror as a Tool of Revolutionary Change

MAXIMILIEN ROBESPIERRE, *Revolutionary Speech* (February 5, 1794)

Maximilien Robespierre (1758–1794) was one of the most important figures during the French Revolution. His skills as an orator and his control of the influential Committee of Public Safety helped lead to the period known as the Reign of Terror, during which Robespierre and his political allies not only executed political rivals, but also encouraged the population through laws and example to practice their own persecution of fellow citizens deemed to be "counter-revolutionary." Thousands were executed by government tribunals without evidence, while many others were killed by mobs. Robespierre himself was executed by members of the National Convention on July 27, 1794. This excerpt from a speech he had delivered to the Convention several months earlier demonstrates Robespierre's extreme commitment to revolutionary values, even to the point of violence.

After having marched for a long time at hazard, and, as it were, carried away by the movement of contrary factions, the representatives of the people have at last formed a government. A sudden change in the nation's fortune announced to Europe the regeneration which had been operated in the national representation; but up to this moment, we must admit that *we have been rather guided in these stormy circumstances by the love of good, and by a sense of the country's wants, than by any exact theory, or precise rules of conduct.*

It is time to distinguish clearly the aim of the revolution, and the term to which we would arrive. It is time for us to render account to ourselves, both of the obstacles which still keep us from that aim, and of the means which we ought to take to attain it.

What is the aim to which we tend?

The peaceful enjoyment of liberty and equality; the reign of that eternal justice, of which the laws have been engraved, not upon marble, but upon the hearts of all mankind; even in the hearts of the slaves who forget them, or of the

G. H. Lewes, ed., *The Life of Maximilien Robespierre: With Extracts of His Unpublished Correspondence* (Philadelphia: Carey and Hart, 1849), 270–273.

tyrants who have denied them! We desire a state of things wherein all base and cruel passions shall be enchained; all generous and beneficent passions awakened by the laws; wherein ambition should be the desire of glory, and glory the desire of serving the country; wherein distinctions should arise but from equality itself; wherein the citizen should submit to the magistrate, the magistrate to the people, and the people to justice; wherein the country assures the welfare of every individual; wherein every individual enjoys with pride the prosperity and the glory of his country; wherein all minds are enlarged by the continual communication of republican sentiments, and by the desire of meriting the esteem of a great people; wherein arts should be the decorations of that liberty which they ennoble, and commerce the source of public wealth, and not the monstrous opulence of some few houses. We desire to substitute morality for egotism, probity for honor, principles for usages, duties for functions, the empire of reason for the tyranny of fashion, the scorn of vice for the scorn of misfortune, pride for insolence, greatness of soul for vanity, the love of glory for the love of money, good citizens for good society, merit for intrigue, genius for cleverness, truth for splendor, the charm of happiness for the *ennui* of voluptuousness, the grandeur of man for the pettiness of the great, a magnanimous people, powerful, happy, for a people amiable, frivolous, and miserable; that is to say, all the virtues and all the miracles of a republic, for all the vices and all the follies of a monarchy.

What is the nature of the government which can realize these prodigies? The democratic or republican government.

Democracy is that state in which the people, guided by laws which are its own work, executes for itself all that it can well do, and, by its delegates, all that it cannot do itself. But to found and consolidate democracy, we must first end the war of liberty against tyranny, and traverse the storm of the revolution. Such is the aim of the revolutionary system which you have organized; you ought, therefore, to regulate your conduct by the circumstances in which the republic finds itself; and the plan of your administration ought to be the result of the spirit of revolutionary government, combined with the general principles of democracy.

The great purity of the French revolution, the sublimity even of its object, is precisely that which makes our force and our weakness. Our force, because it gives us the ascendency of truth over imposture, and the rights of public interest over private interest. Our weakness, because it rallies against us all the vicious; all those who in their heart meditate the robbery of the people; all those who, having robbed them, seek impunity; and all those who have rejected liberty as a personal calamity, and those who have embraced the revolution as a trade, and the republic as a prey. Hence the defection of so many ambitious men, who have abandoned us on our route, because they did not commence the journey to arrive at the same object as we did. We must crush both the interior and exterior enemies of the republic, or perish with her. And in this situation, the first maxim of your policy should be to conduct the people by reason, and the enemies of the people by terror. If the spring of popular government during peace is virtue, the spring of popular government in rebellion is at once both virtue and terror; virtue, without which terror is fatal! terror, without which virtue is powerless! Terror is nothing else than justice, prompt, secure, and inflexible! It is, therefore, an emanation of virtue; it is less a particular principle, than a consequence of the general principles of democracy, applied to the most urgent wants of the country.

It has been said that terror is the instrument of a despotic government. Does yours then resemble despotism? Yes, as the sword which glitters in the hand of a hero of liberty, resembles that with which the satellites of tyranny are armed! The *government of a revolution is the despotism of liberty against tyranny.* Is force then only made to protect crime? Is it not also made to strike those haughty heads which the lightning has doomed? Nature has imposed upon every being the law of self-preservation. Crime massacres innocence to reign, and innocence struggles with all its force in the hands of crime. Let tyranny but reign one day, and on the morrow there would not remain a single patriot. Until when will the fury of tyranny continue to be called justice, and the justice of the people barbarity and rebellion? How tender they are to oppressors: how inexorable to the oppressed! Nevertheless, it is necessary that one or the other should succumb. Indulgence for the Royalist! exclaimed certain people. Pardon for wretches! No! Pardon for innocence, pardon for the weak, pardon for the unhappy, pardon for humanity!

READING AND DISCUSSION QUESTIONS

1. What are the aims of the French Revolution as Robespierre describes them? Are they achievable goals or unreasonable goals for society? Cite evidence to support your position.

2. How does Robespierre justify his vision of terror? Against whom should terror be directed?

3. Robespierre advocates for democracy. How might he define democracy? How does he imagine terror will help to achieve democracy?

22-4 | A Former Slave Calls on France to Support the Cause of Freedom

FRANÇOIS DOMINIQUE TOUSSAINT L'OUVERTURE, *Letter to the French National Assembly* (1797)

The impact of the French Revolution and the Napoleonic Wars was not limited to Europe. Societies across the Americas were shaken by events in France. In the United States, support

François Dominique Toussaint L'Ouverture, Letter, in C. L. R. James, ed., *The Black Jacobins,* 2d ed. (New York: Vintage Books, 1963), 195–197. Reprinted with permission of the Estate of C. L. R. James c/o The Curtis Brown Group.

READING AND DISCUSSION QUESTIONS

1. Who is the intended audience of this document? What is Toussaint L'Ouverture trying to convince them to do?

2. What reasons might persuade the French to reimpose slavery in Haiti, and what reasons might they have for defending its abolition?

3. How does Toussaint L'Ouverture use the ideas and rhetoric of the French Revolution to argue for the rights of Haitian slaves?

22-5 | Slaves into Citizens
The Haitian Declaration of Independence (1804)

The Haitian Revolution represents one of modern history's most thorough political and social transformations. Beginning in 1791, slaves of African descent on the sugar and coffee plantations in the French colony of Saint-Domingue staged a series of uprisings against white plantation owners, ultimately forcing France to abolish slavery in its colonies. After Napoleonic forces sought to regain control of the colony and imprisoned Saint-Domingue's charismatic leader, Toussaint L'Ouverture, his lieutenant Jean-Jacques Dessalines (1758–1806) took command and expelled the French in 1803. His declaration of independence in 1804 invoked Enlightenment values and rhetoric to address racial inequality.

The Commander in Chief to the People of Haiti

Citizens:

It is not enough to have expelled the barbarians who have bloodied our land for two centuries; it is not enough to have restrained those ever-evolving factions that one after another mocked the specter of liberty that France dangled before you. We must, with one last act of national authority, forever ensure liberty's reign in the country of our birth; we must take any hope of re-enslaving us away from the inhuman government that for so long kept us in the most humiliating stagnation. In the end we must live independent or die.

Independence or death . . . let these sacred words unite us and be the signal of battle and of our reunion.

Citizens, my countrymen, on this solemn day I have brought together those courageous soldiers who, as liberty lay dying, spilled their blood to save it; these generals who have guided your efforts against tyranny have not yet done enough for your happiness; the French name still haunts our land.

Everything revives the memories of the cruelties of this barbarous people: our laws, our habits, our towns, everything still carries the stamp of the French. Indeed! There are still French in our island, and you believe yourself free and

Thomas Madiou, *Histoire d'Haïti* (Port-au-Prince, 1847–1848), 3:146–150. Excerpted in *Slave Revolution in the Caribbean, 1789–1804: A Brief History with Documents*, Laurent Dubois and John D. Garrigus, eds. (Boston: Bedford/St. Martin's, 2006), 188–191. Reprinted by permission of the publisher.

independent of that republic, which, it is true, has fought all the nations, but which has never defeated those who wanted to be free.

What! Victims of our [own] credulity and indulgence for fourteen years; defeated not by French armies, but by the pathetic eloquence of their agents' proclamations; when will we tire of breathing the air that they breathe? What do we have in common with this nation of executioners? The difference between its cruelty and our patient moderation, its color and ours, the great seas that separate us, our avenging climate, all tell us plainly that they are not our brothers, that they never will be, and that if they find refuge among us, they will plot again to trouble and divide us.

Native citizens, men, women, girls, and children, let your gaze extend on all parts of this island: look there for your spouses, your husbands, your brothers, your sisters. Indeed! Look there for your children, your suckling infants, what have they become? . . . I shudder to say it . . . the prey of these vultures.

Instead of these dear victims, your alarmed gaze will see only their assassins, these tigers still dripping with their blood, whose terrible presence indicts your lack of feeling and your guilty slowness in avenging them. What are you waiting for before appeasing their spirits? Remember that you had wanted your remains to rest next to those of your fathers after you defeated tyranny; will you descend into their tombs without having avenged them? No! Their bones would reject yours.

And you, precious men, intrepid generals, who, without concern for your own pain, have revived liberty by shedding all your blood, know that you have done nothing if you do not give the nations a terrible, but just example of the vengeance that must be wrought by a people proud to have recovered its liberty and jealous to maintain it. Let us frighten all those who would dare try to take it from us again; let us begin with the French. Let them tremble when they approach our coast, if not from the memory of those cruelties they perpetrated here, then from the terrible resolution that we will have made to put to death anyone born French whose profane foot soils the land of liberty.

We have dared to be free, let us be thus by ourselves and for ourselves. Let us imitate the grown child: his own weight breaks the boundary that has become an obstacle to him. What people fought for us? What people wanted to gather the fruits of our labor? And what dishonorable absurdity to conquer in order to be enslaved. Enslaved? . . . Let us leave this description for the French; they have conquered but are no longer free.

Let us walk down another path; let us imitate those people who, extending their concern into the future and dreading to leave an example of cowardice for posterity, preferred to be exterminated rather than lose their place as one of the world's free peoples.

Let us ensure, however, that a missionary spirit does not destroy our work; let us allow our neighbors to breathe in peace; may they live quietly under the laws that they have made for themselves, and let us not, as revolutionary firebrands, declare ourselves the lawgivers of the Caribbean, nor let our glory consist in troubling the peace of the neighboring islands. Unlike that which we inhabit, theirs has not been drenched in the innocent blood of its inhabitants; they have no vengeance to claim from the authority that protects them.

Fortunate to have never known the ideals that have destroyed us, they can only have good wishes for our prosperity.

Peace to our neighbors; but let this be our cry: "Anathema to the French name! Eternal hatred of France!"

Natives of Haiti! My happy fate was to be one day the sentinel who would watch over the idol to which you sacrifice; I have watched, sometimes fighting alone, and if I have been so fortunate as to return to your hands the sacred trust you confided to me, know that it is now your task to preserve it. In fighting for your liberty, I was working for my own happiness. Before consolidating it with laws that will guarantee your free individuality, your leaders, who I have assembled here, and I, owe you the final proof of our devotion.

Generals and you, leaders, collected here close to me for the good of our land, the day has come, the day which must make our glory, our independence, eternal.

If there could exist among us a lukewarm heart, let him distance himself and tremble to take the oath which must unite us. Let us vow to ourselves, to posterity, to the entire universe, to forever renounce France, and to die rather than live under its domination; to fight until our last breath for the independence of our country.

And you, a people so long without good fortune, witness to the oath we take, remember that I counted on your constancy and courage when I threw myself into the career of liberty to fight the despotism and tyranny you had struggled against for fourteen years. Remember that I sacrificed everything to rally to your defense; family, children, fortune, and now I am rich only with your liberty; my name has become a horror to all those who want slavery. Despots and tyrants curse the day that I was born. If ever you refused or grumbled while receiving those laws that the spirit guarding your fate dictates to me for your own good, you would deserve the fate of an ungrateful people. But I reject that awful idea; you will sustain the liberty that you cherish and support the leader who commands you. Therefore, vow before me to live free and independent and to prefer death to anything that will try to place you back in chains. Swear, finally, to pursue forever the traitors and enemies of your independence.

Done at the headquarters of Gonaïves, the first day of January 1804, the first year of independence.

READING AND DISCUSSION QUESTIONS

1. How does the Haitian Declaration of Independence inspire nationalist feelings in its audience?

2. How does the document justify the Haitian Revolution?

3. Describe the tone of the declaration. Who is speaking, and to whom?

▪ COMPARATIVE QUESTIONS ▪

1. Compare and contrast the three declarations excerpted in this chapter: the Declaration of the Rights of Man, the Declaration of the Rights of Woman, and the Haitian Declaration of Independence. How does each document describe past problems, and how does each present a vision of a new world? What values do all three embrace, and where do the documents diverge?

2. What is the role of violence in each of this chapter's documents? According to each, when is violence justified in order to bring about positive social change? Which documents do not address the problem of violence?

3. Which is the most radical of these documents? Which is the most conservative? Explain.

4. How might Robespierre have responded to the author of the Haitian Declaration of Independence? Would he have supported him? Why or why not?

23

The Revolution in Energy and Industry

1760–1850

The Industrial Revolution, though less visibly dramatic than the bloody political and social revolutions taking place in Europe and the Americas, did more to transform human societies around the world than any single development since the beginning of agriculture. Changes in farming, manufacturing, and domestic and foreign trade—first in Britain, and then in Europe and beyond—resulted in unprecedented economic growth. At the same time, shifts in social relations revealed obvious and disturbing inequalities between prosperous business owners and their often-abused workers. In the following documents, politicians, workers, and intellectuals address some of the social effects of rapid modernization. Whether seeking protection for women and children in the workplace, demanding universal male suffrage, analyzing the challenges of a rapidly increasing population, or outlining the international effects of industrialization, these texts show ways in which people tried to understand and navigate their changing social and economic worlds.

23-1 | Thomas Malthus Predicts Demographic Collapse

THOMAS ROBERT MALTHUS, From *"An Essay on the Principle of Population"* (1798)

Anglican priest and scholar Thomas Robert Malthus (1766–1834) revised and republished his influential 1798 work on population numerous times to respond to critics and changing circumstances. His views on the relationships between population, resources, and human

---

Thomas Robert Malthus, "An Essay on the Principle of Population," in Walter Arnstein, ed., *The Past Speaks*, 2d ed. (Lexington, Mass.: D. C. Heath, 1993), 2:144–146.

happiness met with considerable opposition, especially from thinkers such as William Godwin (1756–1836), husband of the author Mary Wollstonecraft and author of a book that Malthus attacked directly. Malthus's attempts to fold natural and social sciences together, though frequently misunderstood or misappropriated, continue to inform debates over social policy and natural resources.

I have read some of the speculations on the perfectibility of man and of society with great pleasure. I have been warmed and delighted with the enchanting picture which they hold forth. I ardently wish for such happy improvements. But I see great, and, to my understanding, unconquerable difficulties in the way to them. These difficulties it is my present purpose to state; declaring, at the same time, that so far from exulting in them, as a cause of triumphing over the friends of innovation, nothing would give me greater pleasure than to see them completely removed. . . .

I think I may fairly make two postulata.

First, That food is necessary to the existence of man.

Secondly, That the passion between the sexes is necessary, and will remain nearly in its present state. . . .

Assuming, then, my postulata as granted, I say, that the power of population is indefinitely greater than the power in the earth to produce subsistence for man.

Population, when unchecked, increases in a geometrical ratio. Subsistence only increases in an arithmetical ratio. A slight acquaintance with numbers will show the immensity of the first power in comparison of the second.

By that law of our nature which makes food necessary to the life of man, the effects of these two unequal powers must be kept equal.

This implies a strong and constantly operating check on population from the difficulty of subsistence. This difficulty must fall some where; and must necessarily be severely felt by a large portion of mankind. . . .

The ultimate check to population appears then to be a want of food arising necessarily from the different ratios according to which population and food increase. But this ultimate check is never the immediate check, except in cases of actual famine.

The immediate check may be stated to consist in all those customs, and all those diseases which seem to be generated by a scarcity of the means of subsistence; and all those causes, independent of this scarcity, whether of a moral or physical nature, which tend prematurely to weaken and destroy the human frame.

In every country some of these checks are, with more or less force, in constant operation; yet, notwithstanding their general prevalence, there are few states in which there is not a constant effort in the population to increase beyond the means of subsistence. This constant effort as constantly tends to subject the lower classes of society to distress, and to prevent any great permanent melioration of their condition.

These effects, in the present state of society, seem to be produced in the following manner. We will suppose the means of subsistence in any country just equal to the easy support of its inhabitants. The constant effort toward population, which is found to act even in the most vicious societies, increases the number of people before the means of subsistence are increased. The food, therefore, which before supported eleven millions, must now be divided among eleven millions and a half. The poor consequently must live much worse, and many of them be reduced to severe distress. The number of laborers also being above the proportion of work in the market, the price of labor must tend to fall, while the price of provisions would at the same time tend to rise. The laborer therefore must do more work to earn the same as he did before. During this season of distress, the discouragements to marriage and the difficulty of rearing a family are so great, that the progress of population is retarded. In the meantime, the cheapness of labor, the plenty of laborers, and the necessity of an increased industry among them, encourage cultivators to employ more labor upon their land, to turn up fresh soil, and to manure and improve more completely what is already in tillage, till ultimately the means of subsistence may become in the same proportion to the population as at the period from which we set out. The situation of the laborer being then again tolerably comfortable, the restraints to population are in some degree loosened; and, after a short period, the same retrograde and progressive movements, with respect to happiness, are repeated.

READING AND DISCUSSION QUESTIONS

1. According to Malthus, what features are constant in modern populations?

2. In Malthus's view, who bears the brunt of the cycle of human reproduction and food production? What seems to be Malthus's attitude toward these people?

3. What are possible solutions to the cycle that Malthus describes?

VIEWPOINTS

The Realities of Manufacturing

In the earliest phases of industrialization, entire families often worked together in the same factory, with children working side by side with their parents. Over time, however, changes in factory design and machinery led to new labor patterns that took the supervision and control of child workers out of the hands of parents. As familial connections and control broke down, public concern about the potential for the abuse of child laborers, particularly young girls and women, intensified. The documents included in this feature focus on the impact of industrialization on workers in general and on working-class families in particular. As you read them, ask yourself how industrialization changed the lives of Britain's laboring classes. How and why did the British government seek to exert greater control over factory conditions and the composition of the industrial labor force?

23-2 | A Mill Owner Describes the Human Costs of Industrialization

ROBERT OWEN, From *Observations on the Effect of the Manufacturing System* (1815)

Robert Owen (1771–1858), a British socialist from a coal-rich area of Wales, first gained fame through his management of a cotton mill in New Lanark, Scotland. As part owner, Owen incorporated philanthropy with capitalism, and his concern for working conditions, education, and workers' lives helped establish New Lanark's international reputation as a model industrial community. Beginning in 1815, Owen lobbied the British Parliament for legislation to protect British workers, but the many concessions made to industrialists in the 1819 law left him disappointed. Owen penned his *Observations* in 1815; although he would not develop utopian socialist ideals until later, his interest in public welfare and his distrust of naked capitalism are evident here.

Those who were engaged in the trade, manufactures, and commerce of this country thirty or forty years ago, formed but a very insignificant portion of the knowledge, wealth, influence, or population of the Empire.

Prior to that period, Britain was essentially agricultural. But, from that time to the present, the home and foreign trade have increased in a manner so rapid and extraordinary as to have raised commerce to an importance, which it never previously attained in any country possessing so much political power and influence. This change has been owing chiefly to the mechanical inventions which introduced the cotton trade into this country, and to the cultivation of the cotton-tree in America. The wants, which this trade created for the various materials requisite to forward its multiplied operations, caused an extraordinary demand for almost all the manufactures previously established, and, of course, for human labor. The numerous fanciful and useful fabrics manufactured from cotton soon became objects of desire in Europe and America: and the consequent extension of the British foreign trade was such as to astonish and confound the most enlightened statesmen both at home and abroad.

The immediate effects of this manufacturing phenomenon were a rapid increase of the wealth, industry, population and political influence of the British empire; and by the aid of which it has been enabled to contend for five-and-twenty years against the most formidable military and *immoral* power that the world perhaps ever contained.[1]

These important results, however, great as they really are, have not been obtained without accompanying evils of such a magnitude as to raise a doubt whether the latter do not preponderate over the former.

Robert Owen, *Observations on the Effect of the Manufacturing System: With Hints for the Improvement of Those Parts of It Which Are Most Injurious to Health and Morals* (London: R. and A. Taylor, 1817), 3–6.

[1] **the most formidable . . . contained:** Owen is referring to Revolutionary and Napoleonic France.

Hitherto, legislators have appeared to regard manufactures only in one point of view, as a source of national wealth. The other mighty consequences, which proceed from extended manufactures, *when left to their natural progress*, have never yet engaged the attention of any legislature. Yet the political and moral effects to which we allude, well deserve to occupy the best faculties of the greatest and the wisest statesmen.

The general diffusion of manufactures throughout a country generates a new character in its inhabitants; and as this character is formed upon a principle quite unfavorable to individual or general happiness, it will produce the most lamentable and permanent evils, unless its tendency be counteracted by legislative interference and direction.

The manufacturing system has already so far extended its influence over the British empire, as to effect an essential change in the general character of the mass of the people. This alteration is still in rapid progress; and ere long, the comparatively happy simplicity of the agricultural peasant will be wholly lost amongst us: It is even now scarcely any where to be found, without a mixture of those habits, which are the offspring of trade, manufactures, and commerce.

The acquisition of wealth, and the desire which it naturally creates for a continued increase, have introduced a fondness for essentially injurious luxuries among a numerous class of individuals, who formerly never thought of them, and they have also generated a disposition which strongly impels its possessors to sacrifice the best feelings of human nature to this love of accumulation. To succeed in this career, the industry of the lower orders from whose labor this wealth is now drawn, has been carried by new competitors striving against those of longer standing, to a point of real oppression, reducing them by successive changes, as the spirit of competition increased, and the ease of acquiring wealth diminished, to a state more wretched than can be imagined by those who have not attentively observed the changes as they have gradually occurred. In consequence, they are at present in a situation infinitely more degraded and miserable than they were before the introduction of these manufactories, upon the success of which their bare subsistence now depends.

READING AND DISCUSSION QUESTIONS

1. What is the principal product that characterizes industry for Owen?

2. How does Owen situate British industry in the larger context of international relations?

3. What, in Owen's view, has been the attitude of government toward industry? What is government's implicit responsibility?

23-3 | Child Labor in Industrial Britain

SADLER COMMITTEE AND ASHLEY COMMISSION, *Testimonies Before Parliamentary Committees on Working Conditions in England* (1832, 1842)

The Industrial Revolution depended on men, women, and children working under harsh and often deadly conditions. Troubled by the social changes wrought by Britain's rapid industrialization, politician Michael Sadler (1780–1835) formed the Committee on the Labour of Children in the Mills and Factories of the United Kingdom. The committee's 1832 report shocked the public and mobilized support for labor reform. In 1840, another labor reform advocate, Lord Ashley (1801–1885), established the Children's Employment Commission. Its 1842 report shed light on the practice of child labor in coal mines, or "collieries." Both of these reports prompted legislation and raised public awareness of the human cost of the Industrial Revolution.

Testimony Before the Sadler Committee, 1832[2]

Elizabeth Bentley, Called in; and Examined

What age are you?—Twenty-three. . . .

What time did you begin to work at a factory?—When I was six years old. . . .

What kind of mill is it?—Flax-mill. . . .

What was your business in that mill?—I was a little doffer.[3]

What were your hours of labor in that mill?—From 5 in the morning till 9 at night, when they were thronged [busy].

For how long a time together have you worked that excessive length of time?—For about half a year.

What were your usual hours of labor when you were not so thronged?—From 6 in the morning till 7 at night.

What time was allowed for your meals?—Forty minutes at noon.

Had you any time to get your breakfast or drinking?—No, we got it as we could.

And when your work was bad, you had hardly any time to eat it at all?—No; we were obliged to leave it or take it home, and when we did not take it, the over-looker took it, and gave it to his pigs.

Do you consider doffing a laborious employment?—Yes.

Explain what it is you had to do.—When the frames are full, they have to stop the frames, and take the flyers off, and take the full bobbins off, and carry them to the roller; and then put empty ones on, and set the frames on again.

Does that keep you constantly on your feet?—Yes, there are so many frames and they run so quick.

Your labor is very excessive?—Yes; you have not time for anything.

John Bowditch, ed., *Voices of the Industrial Revolution* (Ann Arbor: University of Michigan Press, 1961), 82–90.

[2] **Testimony . . . 1832:** Michael Sadler first proposed a ten-hour workday in 1831; his bill was rejected by Parliament but prompted the formation of this investigative committee.

[3] **doffer:** A young child whose job was to clean the machinery.

Suppose you flagged a little, or were too late, what would they do?—Strap us.

Are they in the habit of strapping those who are last in doffing?—Yes.

Constantly?—Yes.

Girls as well as boys?—Yes.

Have you ever been strapped?—Yes.

Severely?—Yes.

Could you eat your food well in that factory?—No, indeed, I had not much to eat, and the little I had I could not eat it, my appetite was so poor, and being covered with dust; and it was no use to take it home, I could not eat it, and the overlooker took it, and gave it to the pigs. . . .

Did you live far from the mill?—Yes, two miles.

Had you a clock?—No, we had not.

Supposing you had not been in time enough in the morning at the mills, what would have been the consequence?—We should have been quartered.

What do you mean by that?—If we were a quarter of an hour too late, they would take off half an hour; we only got a penny an hour, and they would take a halfpenny more. . . .

Were you generally there in time?—Yes, my mother has been up at 4 o'clock in the morning, and at 2 o'clock in the morning; the colliers used to go to their work about 3 or 4 o'clock, and when she heard them stirring she has got up out of her warm bed, and gone out and asked them the time, and I have sometimes been at Hunslet Car at 2 o'clock in the morning, when it was streaming down with rain, and we have had to stay till the mill was opened. . . .

Testimony Before the Ashley Commission on the Conditions in Mines, 1842[4]

Edward Potter

I am a coal viewer, and the manager of the South Hetton colliery. We have about 400 bound people (contract laborers), and in addition our bank people (foremen), men and boys about 700. In the pits 427 men and boys; of these, 290 men. . . .

Of the children in the pits we have none under eight, and only three so young. We are constantly beset by parents coming making application to take children under the age, and they are very anxious and very dissatisfied if we do not take the children; and there have been cases in times of brisk trade, when the parents have threatened to leave the colliery, and go elsewhere if we did not comply. At every successive binding, which takes place yearly, constant attempts are made to get the boys engaged to work to which they are not competent from their years. In point of fact, we would rather not have boys until nine years of age complete. If younger than that, they are apt to fall asleep and get hurt; some get killed. It is no interest to the company to take any boys under nine. . . .

---

[4] **Testimony . . . 1842:** This testimony led to the Mines Act of 1842, which prohibited boys under the age of ten and women from working in the mines.

Hannah Richardson

I've one child that works in the pit; he's going on ten. He is down from 6 to 8. . . . He's not much tired with the work, it's only the confinement that tires him. He likes it pretty well, for he'd rather be in the pit than to go to school. There is not much difference in his health since he went into the pit. He was at school before, and can read pretty well, but can't write. He is used pretty well; I never hear him complain. I've another son in the pit, 17 years old. . . . He went into the pit at eight years old. It's not hurt his health nor his appetite, for he's a good size. It would hurt us if children were prevented from working till 11 or 12 years old, because we've not jobs enough to live now as it is. . . .

Mr. George Armitage

I am now a teacher at Hoyland school; I was a collier at Silkstone until I was 22 years old and worked in the pit above 10 years. . . . I hardly know how to reprobate the practice sufficiently of girls working in pits; nothing can be worse. I have no doubt that debauchery is carried on, for which there is every opportunity; for the girls go constantly, when hurrying, to the men, who work often alone in the bank-faces apart from every one. I think it scarcely possible for girls to remain modest who are in pits, regularly mixing with such company and hearing such language as they do—it is next to impossible. I dare venture to say that many of the wives who come from pits know nothing of sewing or any household duty, such as women ought to know—they lose all disposition to learn such things; they are rendered unfit for learning them also by being overworked and not being trained to the habit of it. I have worked in pits for above 10 years, where girls were constantly employed, and I can safely say it is an abominable system; indecent language is quite common. I think, if girls were trained properly, as girls ought to be, that there would be no more difficulty in finding suitable employment for them than in other places. Many a collier spends in drink what he has shut up a young child the whole week to earn in a dark cold corner as a trapper. The education of the children is universally bad. They are generally ignorant of common facts in Christian history and principles, and, indeed, in almost everything else. Little can be learned merely on Sundays, and they are too tired as well as indisposed to go to night schools. . . .

The Rev. Robert Willan, Curate of St. Mary's, Barnsley

I have been resident here as chief minister for 22 years. I think the morals of the working classes here are in an appalling state. . . . The ill manners and conduct of the weavers are daily presented to view in the streets, but the colliers work under ground and are less seen, and we have less means of knowing. . . . The master-sin among the youths is that of gambling; the boys may be seen playing at pitch-and-toss on the Sabbath and on week-days; they are seen doing this in all directions. The next besetting sin is promiscuous sexual intercourse; this may be much induced by the manner in which they sleep—men, women, and children often sleeping in one bed-room. I have known a family of father and mother and 12 children, some of them up-grown, sleeping on a kind of sacking and straw bed, reaching from one side of the room to the other, along the floor; they were an English family. Sexual intercourse begins very young. This and gambling pave the way; then drinking ensues, and this is the vortex which draws in every other sin.

Thomas Wilson, Esq., Owner of Three Collieries

I object on general principles to government interference in the conduct of any trade, and I am satisfied that in the mines it would be productive of the greatest injury and injustice. The art of mining is not so perfectly understood as to admit of the way in which a colliery shall be conducted being dictated by any person, however experienced, with such certainty as would warrant an interference with the management of private business. I should also most decidedly object to placing collieries under the present provisions of the Factory Act[5] with respect to the education of children employed therein. First, because, if it is contended that coal-owners, as employers of children, are bound to attend to their education, this obligation extends equally to all other employers, and therefore it is unjust to single out one class only; secondly, because, if the legislature asserts a right to interfere to secure education, it is bound to make that interference general; and thirdly, because the mining population is in this neighborhood so intermixed with other classes, and is in such small bodies in any one place, that it would be impossible to provide separate schools for them.

READING AND DISCUSSION QUESTIONS

1. How do these testimonies present the realities of child labor? Give specific examples.

2. Both reports make particular note of the gender of workers. What is the effect of calling attention to female labor? Describe the attitudes toward gender differences conveyed in these reports.

3. Summarize the arguments presented in the Ashley Commission report for and against the regulation of female and child labor in mines. How is the issue of education used in each argument?

VIEWPOINTS COMPARATIVE QUESTIONS

1. How might Owen have explained the harsh conditions described by the witnesses before the Sadler Committee and the Ashley Commission? How might the Reverend Robert Willan have explained those conditions?

2. What light do these two documents shed on the social consequences of industrialization? How did industrialization change both work and family life?

---

[5] **Factory Act:** The Factory Act of 1833 restricted the workday to eight hours for children between the ages of nine and fourteen and twelve hours for those between fourteen and eighteen.

23-4 | The British East India Company Battles for Control of the Subcontinent

An Incident During the Sikh Wars (ca. 1850)

When non-Western peoples resisted efforts to reshape long-standing economic relationships or refused to give up control of natural resources, the industrialized nations of the West proved willing to use force to remake the global economic map to their own advantage. The activities of the British East India Company provide a case in point. Although formed as a commercial organization, the British East India Company had its own military forces, which it used to gain direct or indirect control of Indian territories and principalities. The image included here shows a scene from the Sikh Wars (1845–1846, 1848–1849), which pitted the British East India Company against the Sikh Kingdom of Punjab. Although the Sikhs put up a stiff defense, aided by Western artillery and other advanced military technology, their eventual defeat led to the annexation of the Punjab by the British, in effect completing the British conquest of India. As you examine the image, compare and contrast the two sides. What do they have in common? In what important ways do the opposing forces differ?

National Army Museum, London/Bridgeman Images.

READING AND DISCUSSION QUESTIONS

1. What evidence does the image provide of the "modernization" of the Sikh army?

2. Which side appears to be winning? What details support your answer?

3. What advantages do the British forces seem to enjoy that might help explain their eventual victory over the Sikhs?

23-5 | Britain Forces the Ottoman Empire to Make Economic Concessions

The Treaty of Balta-Liman (August 16, 1838)

The British Industrial Revolution led to increased demands for overseas markets. In 1838, the United Kingdom signed a treaty with the Ottoman Empire at Balta-Liman, near Istanbul. The treaty responded to complaints by British merchants that their goods were subject to a high tariff or other taxes when shipped into or across Egypt. Egypt, nominally a territory of the Ottoman Empire but virtually independent under the rule of Muhammad Ali (or Mehmet Ali), had embarked on its own efforts to industrialize, including high tariffs and state monopolies of important industrial sectors. These excerpts from the treaty show how the United Kingdom's demands and the Ottoman Empire's acquiescence helped destroy Egypt's industries by flooding its markets with cheap British goods.

Article I

All rights, privileges, and immunities which have been conferred on the subjects or ships of Great Britain by the existing Capitulations and Treaties, are confirmed now and for ever, except in as far as they may be specifically altered by the present Convention: and it is moreover expressly stipulated, that all rights, privileges, or immunities which the Sublime Porte[6] now grants, or may hereafter grant, to the ships and subjects of any other foreign Power, or which it may suffer the ships and subjects of any other foreign Power to enjoy, shall be equally granted to, and exercised and enjoyed by, the subjects and ships of Great Britain.

Article II

The subjects of Her Britannic Majesty, or their agents, shall be permitted to purchase at all places in the Ottoman Dominions (whether for the purposes of internal trade or exportation) all articles, without any exception whatsoever, the produce, growth, or manufacture of the said Dominions; and the Sublime Porte formally engages to abolish all monopolies of agricultural produce, or of any other articles whatsoever, as well as all *Permits* from the local Governors, either for the purchase of any article, or for its removal from one place to another when purchased; and any attempt to compel the subjects of Her Britannic Majesty to receive such *Permits* from the local Governors, shall be considered as an infraction of Treaties, and the Sublime Porte shall immediately punish with severity any Vizirs [ministers] and other officers who shall have been guilty of such misconduct, and render full justice to British subjects for all injuries or losses which they may duly prove themselves to have suffered. . . .

Convention of Commerce and Navigation Between Her Majesty and the Sultan of the Ottoman Empire (London: J. Harrison and Son, 1839), 3–6.

[6] **Sublime Porte:** Literally, the gate of the sultan's palace; the term refers to the sultan and his sovereignty.

Additional Articles

Certain difficulties having arisen between the Ambassador of Her Britannick Majesty and the Plenipotentiaries of the Sublime Porte, in fixing the new conditions which should regulate the commerce in British goods imported into the Turkish Dominions, or passing through the same in transit, it is agreed between His Excellency the British Ambassador and the Plenipotentiaries of the Sublime Porte, that the present Convention should receive their signatures, without the articles which have reference to the above-mentioned subjects forming part of the body of the said Convention.

But at the same time it is also agreed,—the following Articles having been consented to by the Turkish Government,—that they shall be submitted to the approbation of Her Majesty's Government, and should they be approved and accepted by Her Majesty's Government, they shall then form an integral part of the Treaty now concluded.

The Articles in question are the following:

Article I

All articles being the growth, produce, or manufacture of the United Kingdom of Great Britain and Ireland and its dependencies, and all merchandise, of whatsoever description, embarked in British vessels, and being the property of British subjects, or being brought over land, or by sea, from other countries by the same, shall be admitted, as heretofore, into all parts of the Ottoman Dominions, without exception, on the payment of three per cent. duty, calculated upon the value of such articles.

And in lieu of all other and interior duties, whether levied on the purchaser or seller, to which these articles are at present subject, it is agreed that the importer, after receiving his goods, shall pay, if he sells them at the place of reception, or if he sends them thence to be sold elsewhere in the interior of the Turkish Empire, one fixed duty of two per cent.; after which such goods may be sold and resold in the interior, or exported, without any further duty whatsoever being levied or demanded on them.

But all goods that have paid the three per cent. import duty at one port, shall be sent to another free of any further duty, and it is only, when sold there or transmitted thence into the interior, that the second duty shall be paid.

It is always understood that Her Majesty's Government do not pretend, either by this Article or any other in the present Treaty, to stipulate for more than the plain and fair construction of the terms employed; nor to preclude, in any manner, the Ottoman Government from the exercise of its rights of internal administration, where the exercise of those rights does not evidently infringe upon the privileges accorded by ancient Treaties, or the present Treaty, to British merchandise or British subjects.

Article II

All foreign goods brought into Turkey from other countries, shall be freely purchased and traded in, in any manner, by the subjects of Her Britannic Majesty or the agents of the same, at any place in the Ottoman Dominions; and if such foreign goods have paid no other duty than the duty paid on importation, then the British subject or his agent shall be able to purchase such foreign goods on paying the extra duty of two per cent., which he will have to pay on the sale of his own imported goods, or on their transmission for sale into the interior; and after that such foreign goods shall be resold in the interior, or exported, without further duty; or should such foreign goods have already paid the amount of the two duties (*i.e.* the import duty and the one fixed interior duty), then they shall be purchased by the British subject or his agent, and afterwards resold or exported, without being ever submitted to any further duty.

Article III

No charge whatsoever shall be made upon British goods,—(such being the growth, produce, or manufacture of the United Kingdom or its dependencies, or the growth, produce, or manufacture of any foreign country, and charged in British vessels and belonging to British subjects)—passing through the straits of the Dardanelles, of the Bosphorus, and of the Black Sea, whether such goods shall pass through those straits in the ships that brought them, or are transshipped in those straits, or, destined to be sold elsewhere, are landed with a view to their being transferred to other vessels (and thus to proceed on their voyage) within a reasonable time. All merchandise imported into Turkey for the purpose of being transmitted to other countries, or which, remaining in the hands of the importer, shall be transmitted by him for sale to other countries, shall only pay the duty of three per cent. paid on importation, and no other duty whatsoever.

READING AND DISCUSSION QUESTIONS

1. The first article stipulates that any future concession to any other foreign power will be matched by a concession to Great Britain. This is known as a "most-favored nation clause." What does this clause tell you about this treaty? What does it tell you about international relations between the Ottoman Empire and other powers at this point in history?

2. What is the significance of eliminating Ottoman monopolies on any particular item? What is the significance of establishing lowered tariffs and shipping duties?

3. Does this treaty benefit both parties equally? Explain. If it provides benefit primarily to one party, then why might the other have signed it?

▪ COMPARATIVE QUESTIONS ▪

1. What is the relationship between the British government and British business in each document?

2. The Viewpoints documents in this chapter point to the effect on human society of the modern age and specifically the Industrial Revolution. How do the different documents describe this effect?

3. Which documents portray industry most positively? Cite examples and explain.

4. Do Owen's observations support or refute Malthus's theory of population? Explain.

5. What do the image from the Sikh Wars and the Treaty of Balta-Liman tell you about the willingness of the British to use force, and the threat of force, to advance their global economic agenda?

Ideologies of Change in Europe

1815–1914

Following the defeat of Napoleon and his imperial aspirations, a period of ideological development promised to transform the economic and political foundations of Europe. Born in part out of calls for national mobilization in revolutionary France, nationalism gained strength as cultural groups began to seek their own political identity as nation-states. While nationalist rhetoric in Europe often emphasized language, territory, or ethnicity as unifying principles, other movements coalesced around shared identities of gender or social class. In many cases, nationalism, socialism, and other ideologies led to uprisings, revolutions, and wars. In most cases, nationalist movements strengthened states through standardized culture, language, and history as they created both internal solidarity and external threats. Some nationalist movements fought unsuccessfully for recognition, and socialism threatened new nation-states and their nationalist ideologies with a universal call to recognize and respond to the social divisions wrought by the Industrial Revolution. The documents in this chapter present these ideologies as they were proposed and understood by European men and women.

24-1 | Marx and Engels Predict the Coming of a New Social Order

KARL MARX AND FRIEDRICH ENGELS, From *The Communist Manifesto* (1848)

Published in 1848, *The Communist Manifesto* was commissioned by the Communist League, an early socialist organization that advocated for workers' rights and societal reforms. Party

Karl Marx and Friedrich Engels, "The Communist Manifesto," in Arthur P. Mendel, *The Essential Works of Marxism* (New York: Bantam, 1961), 13–17, 19, 23, 40–44.

members Karl Marx (1818–1883) and Friedrich Engels (1820–1895) set forth the group's analysis of social conditions under capitalism, their historical basis, and the roles of the bourgeoisie (middle-class property holders) and the proletariat (urban workers) in social change. Written in German, the document was translated into English in 1850 but received little attention. In later years, however, Marx's writings spurred great debate in England and around the world.

A specter is haunting Europe—the specter of communism. All the powers of old Europe have entered into a holy alliance to exorcise this specter: Pope and Czar, Metternich and Guizot,[1] French Radicals and German police-spies. . . .

Communism is already acknowledged by all European powers to be itself a power.

It is high time that Communists should openly, in the face of the whole world, publish their views, their aims, their tendencies, and meet this nursery tale of the specter of communism with a Manifesto of the party itself. . . .

The history of all hitherto existing society is the history of class struggles. . . .

Modern industry has established the world market, for which the discovery of America paved the way. This market has given an immense development to commerce, to navigation, to communication by land. This development has, in its turn, reacted on the extension of industry; and in proportion as industry, commerce, navigation, railways extended, in the same proportion the bourgeoisie developed, increased its capital, and pushed into the background every class handed down from the Middle Ages. . . .

The bourgeoisie, historically, has played a most revolutionary part.

The bourgeoisie, wherever it has got the upper hand, has put an end to all feudal, patriarchal, idyllic relations. It has pitilessly torn asunder the motley feudal ties that bound man to his "natural superiors," and has left remaining no other nexus between man and man than naked self-interest, than callous "cash payment." It has drowned the most heavenly ecstasies of religious fervor, of chivalrous enthusiasm, of philistine sentimentalism, in the icy water of egotistical calculation. It has resolved personal worth into exchange value, and in place of the numberless indefeasible chartered freedoms, has set up that single, unconscionable freedom—Free Trade. In a word, for exploitation, veiled by religious and political illusions, it has substituted naked, shameless, direct, brutal exploitation.

The bourgeoisie has stripped of its halo every occupation hitherto honored and looked up to with reverent awe. It has converted the physician, the lawyer, the priest, the poet, and the man of science into its paid wage-laborers.

The bourgeoisie has torn away from the family its sentimental veil and has reduced the family relation to a mere money relation. . . .

The bourgeoisie has subjected the country to the rule of the towns. It has created enormous cities, greatly increased the urban population as compared with

---

[1] **Metternich and Guizot:** Prince Klemens von Metternich (1773–1859) was foreign minister and chancellor of the Austrian Empire (1809–1848); François Guizot (1787–1874) was a French politician who served as prime minister from 1847 to 1848.

the rural, and thus rescued a considerable part of the population from the idiocy of rural life. . . .

The bourgeoisie, during its rule of scarcely one hundred years, has created more massive and more colossal productive forces than have all preceding generations together. . . .

But not only has the bourgeoisie forged the weapons that bring death to itself; it has also called into existence the men who are to wield those weapons—the modern working class—the proletariat.

In proportion as the bourgeoisie, i.e., capital, develops, in the same proportion the proletariat, the modern working class, develops—a class of laborers, who live only so long as they find work, and who find work only so long as their labor increases capital. These laborers, who must sell themselves piece-meal, are a commodity, like every other article of commerce, and are consequently exposed to all the vicissitudes of competition, to all the fluctuations of the market. . . .

Of all the classes that stand face to face with the bourgeoisie today, the proletariat alone is a really revolutionary class. The other classes decay and finally disappear in the face of modern industry; the proletariat is its special and essential product. . . .

The socialist and communist systems properly so called, those of Saint-Simon, Fourier, Owen[2] and others, spring into existence in the early undeveloped period, described above, of the struggle between proletariat and bourgeoisie. . . .

Such fantastic pictures of future society, painted at a time when the proletariat is still in a very undeveloped state and has but a fantastic conception of its own position, correspond with the first instinctive yearnings of that class for a general reconstruction of society.

But these socialist and communist publications contain also a critical element. They attack every principle of existing society. . . .

The Communists fight for the attainment of the immediate aims, for the enforcement of the momentary interests of the working class; but in the movement of the present, they also represent and take care of the future of that movement. . . .

The Communists turn their attention chiefly to Germany, because that country is on the eve of a bourgeois revolution that is bound to be carried out under more advanced conditions of European civilization, and with a much more developed proletariat, than that of England was in the seventeenth, and of France in the eighteenth century, and because the bourgeois revolution in Germany will be but the prelude to an immediately following proletarian revolution.

---

[2] **Saint-Simon, Fourier, Owen:** French utopian socialists Henri de Saint-Simon (1760–1825) and Charles Fourier (1772–1837) and Welsh utopian socialist Robert Owen (1771–1858) believed that capitalists and workers could overcome their antagonism and work cooperatively for the common good.

In short, the Communists everywhere support every revolutionary movement against the existing social and political order of things.

In all these movements they bring to the fore, as the leading question in each, the property question, no matter what its degree of development at the time.

Finally, they labor everywhere for the union and agreement of the democratic parties of all countries.

The Communists disdain to conceal their views and aims. They openly declare that their ends can be attained only by the forcible overthrow of all existing social conditions. Let the ruling classes tremble at a Communistic revolution. The proletarians have nothing to lose but their chains. They have a world to win.

WORKING MEN OF ALL COUNTRIES, UNITE!

READING AND DISCUSSION QUESTIONS

1. Evaluate the actions of the bourgeoisie described by Marx and Engels. Which actions seem positive, and which seem negative?

2. What do Engels and Marx mean when they say that the bourgeoisie "has played a most revolutionary part" in history?

3. According to Marx and Engels, what is the purpose of their manifesto? How successful is it in achieving that purpose?

<hr>

VIEWPOINTS

Peoples Without Nations

European nationalism came in many forms and drew on a variety of intellectual and cultural traditions. Nonetheless, all nationalists agreed on one thing: to achieve its historical potential, a people needed a nation, a defined geographic space in which to live and develop. For French and British nationalists, this imperative created no real obstacle to the fulfillment of the nationalist dream since the people they identified as "French" or "British" were already concentrated within the boundaries of autonomous states. For other European nationalists, however, the situation was not as straightforward. In the early nineteenth century, Johann Gottlieb Fichte (Document 24-2) dreamed of a Germany "of Germans" and "for Germans"; however, not only were ethnic German populations scattered across central and eastern Europe, but there was no unified German nation at that time in which they could gather. At the end of the nineteenth century, Zionists like Max Nordau (Document 24-3) faced an even more difficult challenge. Convinced that Jews would never be accepted as full citizens of

European nations, and at the same time committed to the notion that the full development of the Jewish people could only take place within a nation, Zionists had to look further back in history and outside of Europe for a potential solution to their dilemma. As you read these excerpts from the writings of Fichte and Nordau, look for areas of agreement between the two authors. What assumptions do both men make about the importance of a nation to the development of a people?

24-2 | Fichte Imagines a Future Germany

JOHANN GOTTLIEB FICHTE, *Address to the German Nation* (1808)

Johann Gottlieb Fichte (1762–1814) was a German philosopher who wrote and studied widely but is perhaps best known for his contributions to political theory. During the Napoleonic Wars in the early nineteenth century, Fichte fled Berlin and the French forces attacking Prussia. Returning in 1807, he was disheartened to find French troops and a dispirited greater German public in the city. The anti-imperial (anti-French) sentiment of the day found form in Fichte's celebration of German identity, which fostered German pride through an exaggerated litany of German accomplishments and virtues. His speeches (1807–1808) were published in 1808, inspiring citizens of German states to help fight and defeat Napoleon and laying the foundation for German nationalism.

Time is taking giant strides with us more than with any other age since the history of the world began. . . . At some point self-seeking has destroyed itself, because by its own complete development it has lost its self and the independence of that self; and since it would not voluntarily set itself any other aim but self, an external power has forced upon it another and a foreign purpose. He who has once undertaken to interpret his own age must make his interpretation keep pace with the progress of that age, if progress there be. It is, therefore, my duty to acknowledge as past what has ceased to be the present, before the same audience to whom I characterized it as the present.

   . . . Whatever has lost its independence has at the same time lost its power to influence the course of events and to determine these events by its own will. If it remain in this state its age, and itself with the age, are conditioned in their development by that alien power which governs its fate. From now onwards it has no longer any time of its own, but counts its years by the events and epochs of alien nations and kingdoms. From this state, in which all its past world is removed from its independent influence and in its present world only the merit of obedience remains to it, it could raise itself only on condition that a new world should arise for it, the creation of which would begin, and its development fill, a new

Johann Gottlieb Fichte, *Addresses to the German Nation*, trans. R. F. Jones and G. H. Turnbull (Chicago: Open Court Publishing, 1922), 2–4.

epoch of its own in history. . . . Now if, for a race which has lost its former self, its former age and world, such a world should be created as the means of producing a new self and a new age, a thorough interpretation of such a possible age would have to give an account of the world thus created.

Now for my part I maintain that there is such a world, and it is the aim of these addresses to show you its existence and its true owner, to bring before your eyes a living picture of it, and to indicate the means of creating it. . . .

I speak for Germans simply, of Germans simply, not recognizing, but setting aside completely and rejecting, all the dissociating distinctions which for centuries unhappy events have caused in this single nation. You, gentlemen, are indeed to my outward eye the first and immediate representatives who bring before my mind the beloved national characteristics, and are the visible spark at which the flame of my address is kindled. But my spirit gathers round it the educated part of the whole German nation, from all the lands in which they are scattered. It thinks of and considers our common position and relations; it longs that part of the living force, with which these addresses may chance to grip you, may also remain in and breathe from the dumb printed page which alone will come to the eyes of the absent, and may in all places kindle German hearts to decision and action. Only of Germans and simply for Germans, I said. In due course we shall show that any other mark of unity or any other national bond either never had truth and meaning or, if it had, that owing to our present position these bonds of union have been destroyed and torn from us and can never recur; it is only by means of the common characteristic of being German that we can avert the downfall of our nation which is threatened by its fusion with foreign peoples, and win back again an individuality that is self-supporting and quite incapable of any dependence upon others. With our perception of the truth of this statement its apparent conflict (feared now, perhaps, by many) with other duties and with matters that are considered sacred will completely vanish.

Therefore, as I speak only of Germans in general, I shall proclaim that many things concern us which do not apply in the first instance to those assembled here, just as I shall pronounce as the concern of all Germans other things which apply in the first place only to us. In the spirit, of which these addresses are the expression, I perceive that organic unity in which no member regards the fate of another as the fate of a stranger. I behold that unity (which shall and must arise if we are not to perish altogether) already achieved, completed, and existing.

READING AND DISCUSSION QUESTIONS

1. In 1808, there were more than two dozen German states, most of which had yielded to Napoleonic control in 1806. What does Fichte mean when he talks about "the whole German nation"?

2. What is the tone of Fichte's address? Who is his intended audience? What is the purpose of his address?

3. What does Fichte mean when he speaks of the "organic unity" that exists between Germans?

24-3 | Nordau Calls on Jews to Forge Their Own Nation

MAX NORDAU, *On Zionism* (1905)

Max Nordau (1849–1923) cofounded, with Theodor Herzl, the World Zionist Organization in 1897. His first work, *Die Conventionellen Lügen der Kulturmenschheit (The Conventional Lies of Civilization)*, published in 1883, critiqued modern society for its failure to relate to humanity's "natural" characteristics. His *Entartung (Degeneration)* of 1893 drew even more directly on his training as a physician by lamenting the effects of civilization on the healthy physiques of modern humans. Nordau saw Zionism as a means to combat the "degeneration" he identified in modern society. Excerpted here is his 1905 definition of Zionism.

The generations that were under the influence of the Mendelssohnian rhetoric and enlightenment—of reform and assimilation—were followed in the last twenty years of the 19th century by a new generation which strove to secure for the Zionist question a different position from the traditional one. These new Jews shrug their shoulders at the talk of Rabbis and writers about a "Mission of Judaism" that has been in vogue these hundred years.

The Mission is said to consist in this, that the Jews must always live in dispersion among the nations in order to be unto them teachers and models of morality and to educate them gradually to a pure rationalism, to a universal brotherhood of man, and to an ideal cosmopolitanism. They declare this Mission to be a piece of presumption or folly. More modern and practical in their attitude, they demand for the Jewish people only the right to live and to develop in accordance with its own powers to the natural limits of its type. They have found, however, that this is impossible in a state of dispersion, as under such circumstances prejudice, hatred, contempt ever pursue and oppress them, and either inhibit their development or else tend to reduce them to an ethnic mimicry. Thus, instead of their being originals worthy of their existence, this striving at imitation will mold them into mediocre or wretched copies of foreign models. They are therefore working systematically to make the Jewish people once again a normal people, which shall live on its own soil and discharge all the economic, spiritual, moral and political functions of a civilized people. . . .

This goal is not to be attained immediately. It lies in a near or a more distant future. It is an ideal, a wish, a hope, just as Messianic Zionism was and is. But the new Zionism, which is called political, is distinguished from the old religious Messianic Zionism in this, that it repudiates all mysticism, and does not rely upon the return to Palestine to be accomplished by a miracle, but is resolved to bring it about through its own efforts. . . .

The new Zionism has partly arisen out of the inner impulses of Jewry, out of the enthusiasm of modern educated Jews for their history and martyrology, out of the awakened consciousness of their racial fitness, out of their ambition to preserve the ancient stock to as distant a future as possible and to follow up the worthy deeds of ancestors with worthy deeds of descendants. . . .

Max Nordau, "Zionism," from the English Zionist Federation, *Zionism, Its History and Its Aims*, trans. Israel Cohen (London: English Zionist Federation, 1905), 3–20.

But it is also partly the effect of two influences that have come from without: first, the national idea that has dominated European thought and feeling for half a century and determined international politics; secondly, Anti-Semitism, under which the Jews of all countries have to suffer more or less. . . .

The national idea has educated all nations to self-consciousness; it has taught them to feel that their peculiarities are so many valuable factors, and it has inspired them with the passionate wish for independence. It could not fail to exert a deep influence upon educated Jews. It stimulated them to reflect about themselves, to feel once again what they had unlearned, and to demand for themselves the normal destinies of a people. This task of re-discovering their national individuality, although not free from pain, was lightened for them by the attitude of the nations who isolated them as a foreign element and did not hesitate to emphasize the real and imagined contrasts, or rather differences, existing between them and the Jews. . . .

The national idea has, in its extravagances, deteriorated in different directions. It has been distorted into Chauvinism, transformed into an imbecile hatred of foreigners, besotted into grotesque self-deification. Jewish nationalism is quite secure from these self-caricatures. The Jewish nationalist does not suffer from vanity; on the contrary, he feels that he must put forth unremitting effort to render the name of Jew a name of honor. He discreetly recognizes the good qualities of other nations, and eagerly strives to acquire them so far as they harmonize with his natural powers. He knows what terrible injuries have been wrought upon his originally proud and upright character by centuries of slavery and denial of rights, and he endeavors to heal them by strenuous self-education. But while Jewish nationalism is secure from distortion, it, moreover, is a natural phase of the process of development from barbarian self-seeking individualism to the status of noble manhood and altruism, a phase the justification and necessity of which can be denied only by him who knows nothing of the laws of organic evolution and is utterly void of historical sense. . . .

Anti-Semitism has likewise taught many educated Jews how to find the way back to their people. It has had the effect of a severe ordeal, which the weak cannot withstand, but from which the strong step forth stronger, or rather with a keener self-consciousness. It is not correct to say that Zionism is merely a gesture of defiance or an act of despair in the face of Anti-Semitism. Doubtless many an educated Jew has been constrained only through Anti-Semitism to attach himself again to Judaism, and he would again fall away if his Christian compatriots would welcome him as a friend. But in the case of most Zionists, Anti-Semitism was only a stimulus causing them to reflect upon their relation to the nations, and their reflection has led them to results that must remain for them a permanent intellectual and spiritual possession, even if Anti-Semitism were to vanish completely from the world. . . .

Let it be clearly understood. The Zionism that has hitherto been analyzed is that of the free and educated Jews, the Jewish élite. The uneducated multitude that cling to old traditions are Zionistic without much reflection, out of sentiment, out of instinct, out of affliction and longing. They suffer too grievously from the misery of life, from the hatred of the nations, from legal restrictions and social proscriptions. They feel that they cannot hope for any permanent improvement of their position so long as they must live as a helpless minority in the midst of evil-disposed majorities. They want to be a people, to renew their youth in intimate touch with Mother Earth, and to become master of their own fate. A certain proportion of this Zionistic multitude are not altogether free from mystical tendencies. They allow Messianic reminiscences to flit through their Zionism, which they transfuse with religious emotions. They are quite clear about the goal, the national re-union, but not about the ways to attain it. Yet upon them, too, has been borne the necessity of putting forth their own efforts, and a vast difference exists between their organized activity with its voluntary labors and the prayerful passivity of the purely religious Messianist.

READING AND DISCUSSION QUESTIONS

1. How does Nordau differentiate between ancient and contemporary Zionism? For whom does he seem to be defining Zionism?

2. According to Nordau, what role does evolution play in Zionism?

3. Does Nordau's Zionism seem like nationalism to you? Why or why not?

VIEWPOINTS COMPARATIVE QUESTIONS

1. Why did Fichte think it was so important for each people to have its own nation? Did Nordau agree? Why?

2. How did the success of Fichte's nationalist vision help bring about the conditions that gave rise to Nordau's Zionism?

24-4 | Embodying the French Nation
EUGÈNE DELACROIX, *Liberty Leading the People* (1830)

Marianne, a female figure representing liberty and reason, became a central element in French political iconography during the French Revolution. From that point forward, French artists have used Marianne to connect the political events of their day to France's revolutionary legacy, drawing on this powerful symbol of the promise of the Revolution to give meaning to their own struggles. The work of French artist Eugène Delacroix (1798–1863) provides an example of this phenomenon. In 1830, with France once again convulsed by revolutionary upheaval, Delacroix placed Marianne in the thick of the Parisian street fighting, leading a crowd of revolutionaries forward over their fallen comrades, pointing the way toward the realization of France's national destiny.

Liberty Leading the People, 28 July 1830, ca. 1830–31 (oil on canvas)/ Ferdinand Victor Eugène Delacroix (1798–1863)/Louvre-Lens, France/ Bridgman Images.

READING AND DISCUSSION QUESTIONS

1. How might we interpret the fact that liberty is portrayed as a young woman? What significance might we attach to the fact that her dress is torn, revealing her breasts?

2. What does Delacroix's painting suggest about the place of the French Revolution in French national identity in the early nineteenth century?

24-5 | A Socialist Describes Her Own Political Journey

BEATRICE WEBB, From *My Apprenticeship: Why I Became a Socialist* (1926)

Beatrice Webb (1858–1943) was a cofounder of the London School of Economics. In the course of research into the urban poor of London, she met her future husband, Sidney, with whom she would engage in a range of social reform efforts. From 1905 to 1909, she worked

Beatrice Webb, *My Apprenticeship* (London: Cambridge University Press, 1979), 346–349. Copyright © 1980 Cambridge University Press. Reprinted with the permission of Cambridge University Press.

on the Royal Commission into the Operation of the Poor Laws and recommended the social safety net of a welfare state. Webb and her husband also wrote several works on socialism, trade unions, and other topics, and she is credited with inventing the term *collective bargaining*. Webb's meditations on becoming a Socialist highlight not only a sense of social crisis, but her firm belief that socialism would provide an important remedy to many of the problems plaguing nineteenth-century Britain.

The industrial revolution in Britain, which had its most intense phase in the latter end of the eighteenth and the beginning of the nineteenth century, cast out of our rural and urban life the yeoman cultivator and the copyholder, the domestic manufacturer and the independent handicraftsman, all of whom owned the instruments by which they earned their livelihood; and gradually substituted for them a relatively small body of capitalist entrepreneurs employing at wages an always multiplying mass of propertyless men, women and children, struggling, like rats in a bag, for the right to live. This bold venture in economic reconstruction had now been proved to have been, so it seemed to me, at one and the same time, a stupendous success and a tragic failure. The accepted purpose of the pioneers of the new power-driven machine industry was the making of pecuniary profit; a purpose which had been fulfilled, as Dr. Johnson observed about his friend Thrale's brewery, "beyond the dreams of avarice." Commodities of all sorts and kinds rolled out from the new factories at an always accelerating speed with ever falling costs of production, thereby promoting what Adam Smith had idealized as *The Wealth of Nations*. The outstanding success of this new system of industry was enabling Great Britain, through becoming the workshop of the world, to survive the twenty years' ordeal of the Napoleonic Wars intact, and not even invaded, whilst her ruling oligarchy emerged in 1815 as the richest and most powerful government of the time.

On the other hand, that same revolution had deprived the manual workers—that is, four-fifths of the people of England—of their opportunity for spontaneity and freedom of initiative in production. It had transformed such of them as had been independent producers into hirelings and servants of another social class; and, as the East End of London in my time only too vividly demonstrated, it had thrust hundreds of thousands of families into the physical horrors and moral debasement of chronic destitution in crowded tenements in the midst of mean streets. There were, however, for the manual working class as a whole, certain compensations. The new organization of industry had the merit of training the wage-earners in the art of team-work in manufacture, transport and trading. Even the oppressions and frauds of the capitalist profit-maker had their uses in that they drove the proletariat of hired men, which capitalism had made ubiquitous, to combine in Trade Unions and co-operative societies; and thus to develop their instinct of fellowship, and their capacity for representative institutions, alike in politics and in industry. Moreover, the contrast between the sweated workers of East London and the

Lancashire textile operatives made me realize how the very concentration of wage-earners in the factory, the ironworks and the mine had made possible, in their cases, what the sweater's workshop, the independent craftsman's forge and the out-worker's home had evaded, namely, a collective regulation of the conditions of employment, which, in the Factory Acts and Mines Regulation Acts[3] on the one hand, and in the standard rates of wage and the normal working day of the Trade Unions on the other, had, during the latter part of the nineteenth century, wrought so great an improvement in the status of this regulated section of the World of Labor. It was, in fact, exactly this collective regulation of the conditions of employment, whether by legislative enactment or by collective bargaining, that had raised the cotton operatives, the coal-miners and the workers of the iron trades into an effective democracy; or, at least, into one which, in comparison with the entirely unorganized workers of East London, was eager for political enfranchisement and education; and which, as the chapels, the co-operative societies and the Trade Unions had demonstrated, was capable of self-government. I wished to probe further this contrast between the wage-earners who had enjoyed the advantages of collective regulation and voluntary combinations, and those who had been abandoned to the rigors of unrestrained individual competition. But I wanted also to discover whether there was any practicable alternative to the dictatorship of the capitalist in industry, and his reduction of all the other participants in production to the position of subordinate "hands." For it was persistently asserted that there was such an alternative. In this quest I did not turn to the socialists. *Fabian Essays*[4] were still unwritten and unpublished; and such socialists as I had happened to meet at the East End of London belonged to the Social Democratic Federation, and were at that time preaching what seemed to me nothing but a catastrophic overturning of the existing order, by forces of whose existence I saw no sign, in order to substitute what appeared to me the vaguest of incomprehensible utopias.

There was, however, another alternative lauded by idealists of all classes: by leading Trade Unionists and the more benevolent employers, by revolutionary socialists and by Liberal and Conservative philanthropists: an experiment in industrial organization actually, so it was reported, being brought into operation on a small scale by enthusiastic working men themselves. This was the ideal of "self-employment," and the peaceful elimination from industry of the capitalist *entrepreneur*; to be secured by the manual workers themselves acquiring the ownership, or at any rate the use, of the capital, and managing the industry by which they gained their livelihood. It was this ideal, so I was told, that animated the Co-operative Movement in the North of England and the Lowlands of Scotland—a movement barely represented in the London that I knew.

---

[3] **Factory Acts and Mines Regulation Acts:** Various laws passed by the British Parliament limiting hours worked by women and children in industrial jobs and by coal miners.

[4] *Fabian Essays: Fabian Essays in Socialism* by George Bernard Shaw et al., published in 1889, was an important collection of essays arguing for socialism through gradual reform.

READING AND DISCUSSION QUESTIONS

1. How does Webb link the Industrial Revolution to her own political beliefs? What is her argument?

2. What are the positive effects of industry, according to Webb?

3. How does Webb contrast herself to other Socialists? What form of socialism does she embrace, and why?

■ COMPARATIVE QUESTIONS ■

1. National identity was a major theme of the nineteenth century. How does each document in this chapter either encourage or discourage national identity?

2. Fichte and Nordau speak about the unity of the German and Jewish nations, respectively. Compare and contrast the way that each author defines national unity and presents it as a motivating factor.

3. How does the communism presented by Marx and Engels relate to Webb's socialism? How are they similar, and how are they different?

4. What is the role of gender in each document? How is a person's gender a part of national or class identity? Juxtapose Webb's perspective with that of the male authors and subjects of this chapter. What should we make of Delacroix's *Liberty Leading the People* in this context?

5. What social or political problem is defined in each document? What are the different ways in which each document presents a crisis, and what kind of language or imagery is used to motivate the intended audience?

25

Africa, the Ottoman Empire, and the New Imperialism
1800–1914

The rise of industrial economies in Europe drove European nations to expand their empires in Africa and Asia. In search of markets, resources, and occasionally adventure, Europeans gained control of an increasingly large part of the globe through commerce and colonization. At the same time, states like the Ottoman Empire mixed western European notions of civilization with their own cultures to develop alternative visions of a "modern society." The documents in this chapter present different perspectives on the global progress of modernization and westernization: from the Ottoman Empire's government as it sought to draw on modern Western ideas to reform and strengthen its state, from a leading voice of British imperialism, from an African who fought and then submitted to British colonial rule, and from Africans who endured terrible abuses in the Belgian Congo. All of the documents offer insight on how non-Western peoples adapted and endured as nationalism, progress, and empire changed their worlds.

25-1 | Ottoman Reform from the Top Down
SULTAN ABDUL MEJID, *Imperial Rescript* (1856)

Building on the work of previous rulers to enact military and administrative reforms, many of which were inspired by modern Western institutions, Sultan Abdul Mejid or Abdülmecid (r. 1839–1861) instituted a period of "reorganization," or *Tanzimat*, in the aging Ottoman Empire. Various non-Turkish groups had been pulling away from Ottoman rule since the early 1800s, and large-scale violence against non-Muslim subjects was not uncommon. In this imperial rescript, or official proclamation, the sultan affirms his policy of "Ottomanism," or

E. A. Van Dyck, *Report upon the Capitulations of the Ottoman Empire Since the Year 1150*, pt. 1 (Washington, D.C.: U.S. Government Printing Office, 1881, 1882), 106–108.

equal treatment of all citizens without regard to race, language, or religion. Ottomanism may be seen as a doomed and even hypocritical attempt to reassert central authority; however, the rescript represented real reform in Ottoman society.

Let it be done as herein set forth. . . . It being now my desire to renew and enlarge still more the new Institutions ordained with the view of establishing a state of things conformable with the dignity of my Empire and . . . by the kind and friendly assistance of the Great Powers, my noble Allies.[1] . . . The guarantees promised on our part by the Hatti-Humaïoun of Gülhané,[2] and in conformity with the Tanzimat, . . . are today confirmed and consolidated, and efficacious measures shall be taken in order that they may have their full and entire effect.

All the privileges and spiritual immunities granted by my ancestors from time immemorial, and at subsequent dates, to all Christian communities or other non-Muslim persuasions established in my empire, under my protection, shall be confirmed and maintained.

Every Christian or other non-Muslim community shall be bound within a fixed period, and with the concurrence of a commission composed . . . of members of its own body, to proceed with my high approbation and under the inspection of my Sublime Porte,[3] to examine into its actual immunities and privileges, and to discuss and submit to my Sublime Porte the reforms required by the progress of civilization and of the age. The powers conceded to the Christian Patriarchs and Bishops[4] by the Sultan Mehmed II[5] and his successors, shall be made to harmonize with the new position which my generous and beneficent intentions ensure to these communities. . . . The ecclesiastical dues, of whatever sort of nature they be, shall be abolished and replaced by fixed revenues of the Patriarchs and heads of communities. . . . In the towns, small boroughs, and villages, where the whole population is of the same religion, no obstacle shall be offered to the repair, according to their original plan, of buildings set apart for religious worship, for schools, for hospitals, and for cemeteries. . . .

Every distinction or designation tending to make any class whatever of the subjects of my Empire inferior to another class, on account of their religion, language, or race, shall be forever effaced from Administrative Protocol. The laws shall be put in force against the use of any injurious or offensive term, either among private individuals or on the part of the authorities. . . .

---

[1] **the Great Powers, my noble allies:** During the Crimean War (1853–1856), the Ottoman Empire fought with Great Britain and France against Russia.

[2] **The guarantees . . . Gülhané:** The Noble Rescript of 1839, also written by Sultan Abdul Mejid, guaranteed personal security, a fair tax system, controlled military conscriptions, and full rights to citizens regardless of faith.

[3] **Sublime Porte:** The term refers to the sultan and his sovereignty.

[4] **Christian Patriarchs and Bishops:** Ruling officials of the Greek and Armenian churches in the Ottoman Empire.

[5] **Sultan Mehmed II:** Ottoman ruler from 1451 to 1481.

As all forms of religion are and shall be freely professed in my dominions, no subject of my Empire shall be hindered in the exercise of the religion that he professes. . . . No one shall be compelled to change their religion . . . and . . . all the subjects of my Empire, without distinction of nationality, shall be admissible to public employments. . . . All the subjects of my Empire, without distinction, shall be received into the civil and military schools of the government. . . . Moreover, every community is authorized to establish public schools of science, art, and industry. . . .

All commercial, correctional, and criminal suits between Muslims and Christian or other non-Muslim subjects, or between Christian or other non-Muslims of different sects, shall be referred to Mixed Tribunals. The proceedings of these Tribunals shall be public; the parties shall be confronted, and shall produce their witnesses, whose testimony shall be received, without distinction, upon an oath taken according to the religious law of each sect. . . .

Penal, correctional, and commercial laws, and rules of procedure for the Mixed Tribunals, shall be drawn up as soon as possible, and formed into a code. . . . Proceedings shall be taken, for the reform of the penitentiary system. . . .

The organization of the police . . . shall be revised in such a manner as to give to all the peaceable subjects of my Empire the strongest guarantees for the safety both of their persons and property. . . . Christian subjects, and those of other non-Muslim sects, . . . shall, as well as Muslims, be subject to the obligations of the Law of Recruitment [for military service]. The principle of obtaining substitutes, or of purchasing exemption, shall be admitted.

Proceedings shall be taken for a reform in the constitution of the Provincial and Communal Councils, in order to ensure fairness in the choice of the deputies of the Muslim, Christian, and other communities, and freedom of voting in the Councils. . . .

As the laws regulating the purchase, sale, and disposal of real property are common to all the subjects of my Empire, it shall be lawful for foreigners to possess landed property in my dominions. . . .

The taxes are to be levied under the same denomination from all the subjects of my Empire, without distinction of class or of religion. The most prompt and energetic means for remedying the abuses in collecting the taxes, and especially the tithes, shall be considered. The system of direct collection shall gradually, and as soon as possible, be substituted for the plan of farming,[6] in all the branches of the revenues of the state.

A special law having been already passed, which declares that the budget of the revenue and the expenditure of the state shall be drawn up and made known every year, the said law shall be most scrupulously observed. . . .

The heads of each community and a delegate, designated by my Sublime Porte, shall be summoned to take part in the deliberations of the Supreme

---

[6] **farming:** Tax farming, in which the government contracted with private financiers who collected taxes for a profit.

Council of Justice on all occasions which might interest the generality of the subjects of my Empire. . . .

Steps shall be taken for the formation of banks and other similar institutions,
so as to effect a reform in the monetary and financial system, as well as to create
funds to be employed in augmenting the sources of the material wealth of my
Empire.

Everything that can impede commerce or agriculture shall be abolished. To
accomplish these objects means shall be sought to profit by science, the art, and
the funds of Europe, and thus gradually to execute them.

READING AND DISCUSSION QUESTIONS

1. What specific measures does the sultan take to ensure religious and ethnic equality? What do these measures imply about life in the Ottoman Empire before the
   rescript was issued?

2. The sultan is careful to extend military service to people of all religious and ethnic backgrounds. How does this right compare to rights regarding public
   employment, education, taxation, and real estate?

3. The rescript mentions communities of Christian and non-Muslim people and
   villages or small areas where all people share a common religion. What does
   this imply about the integration of different religious groups in Ottoman society?

4. In explaining the purpose of his rescript, the sultan refers to the "dignity" of his
   empire and mentions the Ottoman Empire's relationship with European "Great
   Powers." How do you think the ideas of religious equality, social reform, and
   international relations and the dignity of the empire work together?

VIEWPOINTS

The Colonial Encounter in Africa

The scramble for Africa brought almost all of the continent under European colonial rule in only a few short decades. Against industrialized
European adversaries with overwhelming technological advantages, African forces could offer little sustained military resistance. This does not
mean, however, that conquest and colonization brought African resistance
to an end. Instead, resistance took on new forms as the European powers
settled into the difficult task of governing their new colonies. British busi-
nessman and financier Cecil Rhodes (Document 25-2) may have imagined
that African peoples would simply disappear, washed away by a tidal
wave of racially superior "Anglo-Saxon" settlers, but they did not. The
European presence had a profound impact on African society and culture,
but it was a complex one, forged out of cross-cultural interactions and the

ongoing efforts of Africans to regain control of their lives and destinies. As you read the documents included in this feature, think about the African reaction to colonization. Why did African peoples never fully accept the legitimacy and permanence of colonial rule?

25-2 | Cecil Rhodes Dreams of Global Domination
CECIL RHODES, From *Confession of Faith* (ca. 1877)

Perhaps no single man exemplified European colonial exploitation of the African continent more than Cecil Rhodes (1853–1902). He was sent as a child from England to South Africa—then the British Cape Colony—for his health, and there he amassed a fortune by controlling diamond production. He entered politics in the Cape Colony and quickly parlayed his wealth and political influence into expanded colonial control of South African territories, one of which (comprising present-day Zambia and Zimbabwe) was named Rhodesia in his honor. Rhodes sent the following text to British journalist William Thomas Stead as representative of his thoughts on empire and race; it has survived as a marker of European pride and global ambitions in the late nineteenth century.

It often strikes a man to inquire what is the chief good in life; to one the thought comes that it is a happy marriage, to another great wealth, and as each seizes on his idea, for that he more or less works for the rest of his existence. To myself thinking over the same question the wish came to render myself useful to my country. I then asked myself how could I and after reviewing the various methods I have felt that at the present day we are actually limiting our children and perhaps bringing into the world half the human beings we might owing to the lack of country for them to inhabit that if we had retained America there would at this moment be millions more of English living. I contend that we are the finest race in the world and that the more of the world we inhabit the better it is for the human race, just fancy those parts that are at present inhabited by the most despicable specimens of human beings what an alteration there would be if they were brought under Anglo-Saxon influence, look again at the extra employment a new country added to our dominions gives. I contend that every acre added to our territory means in the future birth to some more of the English race who otherwise would not be brought into existence. Added to this the absorption of the greater portion of the world under our rule simply means the end of all wars, at this moment had we not lost America I believe we could have stopped the Russian-Turkish war[7] by merely refusing money and supplies. Having these ideas what scheme could we think of to forward this object. I look into history

John Flint, *Cecil Rhodes* (New York: Hachette, 1974), appendix.

[7] **Russian-Turkish war:** This 1870s conflict between the Ottoman Empire and Russia was spurred in part by various ethnic or religious nationalisms in Ottoman territories.

and I read the story of the Jesuits[8] I see what they were able to do in a bad cause and I might say under bad leaders.

In the present day I become a member in the Masonic order[9] I see the wealth and power they possess the influence they hold and I think over their ceremonies and I wonder that a large body of men can devote themselves to what at times appear the most ridiculous and absurd rites without an object and without an end.

The idea gleaming and dancing before one's eyes like a will-of-the-wisp at last frames itself into a plan. Why should we not form a secret society with but one object the furtherance of the British Empire and the bringing of the whole uncivilized world under British rule for the recovery of the United States for the making the Anglo-Saxon race but one Empire. What a dream, but yet it is probable, it is possible. I once heard it argued by a fellow in my own college, I am sorry to own it by an Englishman, that it was a good thing for us that we have lost the United States. There are some subjects on which there can be no arguments, and to an Englishman this is one of them, but even from an American's point of view just picture what they have lost, look at their government, are not the frauds that yearly come before the public view a disgrace to any country and especially theirs which is the finest in the world. Would they have occurred had they remained under English rule great as they have become how infinitely greater they would have been with the softening and elevating influences of English rule, think of those countless 000's of Englishmen that during the last 100 years would have crossed the Atlantic and settled and populated the United States. Would they have not made without any prejudice a finer country of it than the low class Irish and German emigrants? All this we have lost and that country loses owing to whom? Owing to two or three ignorant pig-headed statesmen of the last century, at their door lies the blame. Do you ever feel mad? Do you ever feel murderous? I think I do with those men. I bring facts to prove my assertion. Does an English father when his sons wish to emigrate ever think of suggesting emigration to a country under another flag, never—it would seem a disgrace to suggest such a thing I think that we all think that poverty is better under our own flag than wealth under a foreign one.

Put your mind into another train of thought. Fancy Australia discovered and colonized under the French flag, what would it mean merely several millions of English unborn that at present exist we learn from the past and to form our future. We learn from having lost to cling to what we possess. We know the size of the world we know the total extent. Africa is still lying ready for us it is our duty to take it. It is our duty to seize every opportunity of acquiring more territory and

---

[8] **the Jesuits:** The Society of Jesus, or the Jesuits, was founded in 1534 as a missionary arm of the Roman Catholic Church and in partial response to the Protestant Reformation. Rhodes seems to be voicing anti-Catholic sentiments in his assessment of the "bad cause" and "bad leaders" of the Jesuits.

[9] **Masonic order:** A male fraternal organization largely centered in Great Britain, northwest Europe, and the United States.

we should keep this one idea steadily before our eyes that more territory simply means more of the Anglo-Saxon race more of the best the most human, most honorable race the world possesses.

READING AND DISCUSSION QUESTIONS

1. How is race a part of Rhodes's justification for empire? What does British society possess that he most admires?

2. What are the different races that Rhodes mentions? How do they relate to one another?

3. What is the purpose of the secret society that Rhodes proposes?

25-3 | A Firsthand Account of Imperial Conquest

NDANSI KUMALO, *On the British Incursion in Zimbabwe* (1932)

Ndansi Kumalo was a member of the Ndebele people who lived in what is now Zimbabwe, where the Ndebele had settled after years of struggle with Zulu and Dutch forces. The Ndebele sovereign, Lobengula, negotiated with the new wave of British colonizers intent on access to the region's mineral resources, but tensions mounted and conflict broke out in the 1890s. Kumalo, a witness to the British incursion, was hired to play the role of Lobengula in a 1932 British film about the life of colonizer Cecil Rhodes (see Document 25-2). While filming in England, Kumalo met the African scholar Margery Perham, who recorded the following firsthand account of British colonization.

We were terribly upset and very angry at the coming of the white men, for Lobengula . . . was under her . . . [the Queen's] protection and it was quite unjustified that white men should come with force into our country.[10] . . . Lobengula had no war in his heart: he had always protected the white men and been good to them. If he had meant war, would he have sent our regiments far away to the north at this moment? As far as I know the trouble began in this way. Gandani, a chief who was sent out, reported that some of the Mashona[11] had taken the king's cattle; some regiments were detailed to follow and recover them. They followed the Mashona to Ziminto's people. Gandani had strict instructions not to molest

---

Margery Perham, ed., *Ten Africans* (London: Faber and Faber, 1936). Originally published by Faber and Faber Ltd. in 1936. Used by permission of the Trustees of the Will of the Late Dame Margery Perham.

[10] **under her . . . our country:** In an 1888 agreement Lobengula made with Cecil Rhodes, the British government guaranteed that there would be no incursion of English settlers on Ndebele land and that Lobengula's authority would continue. Unhappy with Lobengula's concessions, many Ndebele warriors began to press for war against the Europeans.

[11] **the Mashona:** A people who raised livestock and were ruled by the Ndebele.

the white people established in certain parts and to confine himself to the people who had taken the cattle. The commander was given a letter which he had to produce to the Europeans and tell them what the object of the party was. But the members of the party were restless and went without reporting to the white people and killed a lot of Mashonas. The pioneers were very angry and said, "You have trespassed into our part." They went with the letter, but only after they had killed some people, and the white men said, "You have done wrong, you should have brought the letter first and then we should have given you permission to follow the cattle." The commander received orders from the white people to get out, and up to a certain point which he could not possibly reach in the time allowed. A force followed them up and they defended themselves. When the pioneers turned out there was a fight at Shangani and at Bembezi. . . .

The next news was that the white people had entered Bulawayo; the King's kraal [stockade] had been burnt down and the King had fled. Of the cattle very few were recovered; most fell into the hands of the white people. Only a very small portion were found and brought to Shangani where the King was, and we went there to give him any assistance we could. . . . Three of our leaders mounted their horses and followed up the King and he wanted to know where his cattle were; they said they had fallen into the hands of the whites, only a few were left. He said, "Go back and bring them along." But they did not go back again; the white forces had occupied Bulawayo and they went into the Matoppos [hills]. Then the white people came to where we were living and sent word round that all chiefs and warriors should go into Bulawayo and discuss peace, for the King had gone and they wanted to make peace. . . . The white people said, "Now that your King has deserted you, we occupy your country. Do you submit to us?" What could we do? "If you are sincere, come back and bring in all your arms, guns, and spears." We did so. . . .

So we surrendered to the white people and were told to go back to our homes and live our usual lives and attend to our crops. But the white men sent native police who did abominable things; they were cruel and assaulted a lot of our people and helped themselves to our cattle and goats. These policemen were not our own people; anybody was made a policeman. We were treated like slaves. They came and were overbearing and we were ordered to carry their clothes and bundles. They interfered with our wives and our daughters and molested them. In fact, the treatment we received was intolerable. We thought it best to fight and die rather than bear it. How the rebellion started I do not know; there was no organization, it was like a fire that suddenly flames up. We had been flogged by native police and then they rubbed salt water in the wounds. There was much bitterness because so many of our cattle were branded and taken away from us; we had no property, nothing we could call our own. We said, "It is no good living under such conditions; death would be better — let us fight." Our King gone, we had submitted to the white people and they ill-treated us until we became desperate and tried to make an end of it all. We knew that we had very little chance because their weapons were so much superior to ours. But we meant to fight to the last, feeling that even if we could not beat them we might at least kill a few of them and so have some sort of revenge.

I fought in the rebellion. We used to look out for valleys where the white men were likely to approach. We took cover behind rocks and trees and tried to ambush them. We were forced by the nature of our weapons not to expose ourselves. I had a gun, a breech-loader [rear-loading gun]. They—the white men—fought us with big guns and Maxims [early machine guns] and rifles.

I remember a fight in the Matoppos when we charged the white men. There were some hundreds of us; the white men also were as many. We charged them at close quarters: we thought we had a good chance to kill them but the Maxims were too much for us. We drove them off at the first charge, but they returned and formed up again. We made a second charge, but they were too strong for us. I cannot say how many white people were killed, but we think it was quite a lot. . . . Many of our people were killed in this fight: I saw four of my cousins shot. One was shot in the jaw and the whole of his face was blown away—like this—and he died. One was hit between the eyes; another here, in the shoulder; another had part of his ear shot off. We made many charges but each time we were beaten off, until at last the white men packed up and retreated. But for the Maxims, it would have been different. . . .

So peace was made. Many of our people had been killed, and now we began to die of starvation; and then came the rinderpest [an infectious cow disease] and the cattle that were still left to us perished. We could not help thinking that all these dreadful things were brought by the white people. We struggled, and the Government helped us with grain; and by degrees we managed to get crops and pulled through. Our cattle were practically wiped out, but a few were left and from them we slowly bred up our herds again. We were offered work in the mines and farms to earn money and so were able to buy back some cattle. At first, of course, we were not used to going out to work, but advice was given that the chief should advise the young people to go out to work, and gradually they went. At first we received a good price for our cattle and sheep and goats. Then the tax came. It was 10s.[12] a year. Soon the Government said, "That is too little, you must contribute more; you must pay £1." We did so. Then those who took more than one wife were taxed; 10s. for each additional wife. The tax is heavy, but that is not all. We are also taxed for our dogs; 5s. for a dog. Then we were told we were living on private land; the owners wanted rent in addition to the Government tax; some 10s. some £1, some £2 a year. . . .

Would I like to have the old days back? Well, the white men have brought some good things. For a start, they brought us European implements—plows; we can buy European clothes, which are an advance. The Government has arranged for education and through that, when our children grow up, they may rise in status. We want them to be educated and civilized and make better citizens. Even in our own time there were troubles, there was much fighting and many innocent people were killed. It is infinitely better to have peace instead of war, and our treatment generally by the officials is better than it was at first. But,

---

[12] **10s.:** Ten shillings.

under the white people, we still have our troubles. Economic conditions are telling on us very severely. We are on land where the rainfall is scanty, and things will not grow well. In our own time we could pick our own country, but now all the best land has been taken by the white people. We get hardly any price for our cattle; we find it hard to meet our money obligations. If we have crops to spare we get very little for them; we find it difficult to make ends meet and wages are very low. When I view the position, I see that our rainfall has diminished, we have suffered drought and have poor crops and we do not see any hope of improvement, but all the same our taxes do not diminish. We see no prosperous days ahead of us. There is one thing we think an injustice. When we have plenty of grain the prices are very low, but the moment we are short of grain and we have to buy from Europeans at once the price is high. If when we have hard times and find it difficult to meet our obligations some of these burdens were taken off us it would gladden our hearts. As it is, if we do raise anything, it is never our own: all, or most of it, goes back in taxation. We can never save any money. If we could, we could help ourselves: we could build ourselves better houses; we could buy modern means of traveling about, a cart, or donkeys or mules.

As to my own life, I have had twelve wives altogether, five died and seven are alive. I have twenty-six children alive, five have died. Of my sons five are married and are all at work farming; three young children go to school. I hope the younger children will all go to school. I think it is a good thing to go to school.

There are five schools in our district. Quite a number of people are Christians, but I am too old to change my ways. In our religion we believe that when anybody dies the spirit remains and we often make offerings to the spirits to keep them good-tempered. But now the making of offerings is dying out rapidly, for every member of the family should be present, but the children are Christians and refuse to come, so the spirit-worship is dying out. A good many of our children go to the mines in the Union, for the wages are better there. Unfortunately a large number do not come back at all. And some send money to their people — others do not. Some men have even deserted their families, their wives, and children. If they cannot go by train they walk long distances.

READING AND DISCUSSION QUESTIONS

1. What reasons does Kumalo give for rebelling against British colonial forces? What caused the initial violence, and what was the outcome?

2. If the Ndebele leader Gandani had delivered the letter to the British and not acted in haste, do you think the British pioneers would have responded as violently as they did? What gives you that impression?

3. What is Kumalo's opinion of British colonial influence in Africa? Cite examples to support your answer.

25-4 | The Law as a Form of Resistance

JOHN MENSAH SARBAH, *Fanti Customary Law* (1897)

John Mensah Sarbah (1864–1910) was born in the Gold Coast, a British colony in West Africa that would become the nation Ghana upon gaining independence in 1957. As one of the Gold Coast's African elite, Sarbah studied law in England and passed the bar in 1887. He dedicated his life to using his legal training to protect the rights of his people and to resist British domination. It was in this context that he wrote *Fanti Customary Law*, an introduction to the laws and customs of one of the Gold Coast's most important ethnic groups. Sarbah believed that for laws to be effective they had to reflect local conditions, social norms, and experiences. Thus, if the British wanted to administer genuine justice in the Gold Coast, they had to be familiar with local customs and traditions. As you read this excerpt, think about the implications of Sarbah's argument. How might it have been used to support calls for the Gold Coast's independence?

Words which cause or produce any injury to the reputation of another are called defamatory, and, if false, are actionable. False defamatory words, when spoken, constitute slander. Where a person has been found guilty for using slanderous words, he is bound to retract his words publicly, in addition to paying a small fine by way of compensation to the aggrieved party. Words imputing witchcraft, adultery, immoral conduct, crime, and all words which sound to the disreputation of a person of whom they are spoken are actionable. The native custom is more in accordance with natural justice, equity, and good conscience than the English law, which has been denounced by many a learned judge. Says Lord Chancellor Campbell, in *Lynch* v. *Knight and Wife*, "I may lament the unsatisfactory state of our law, according to which the imputation by words, however gross, on an occasion however public, upon the chastity of a modest matron or a pure virgin is not actionable, without proof that it has actually produced special temporal damage to her." Instead of the word "unsatisfactory" I should substitute the word "barbarous," said Lord Brougham on the same occasion.

An effective way of punishing a person guilty of slander of serious consequences, is to make him walk through the town or village carrying a heavy stone in front of an officer of the Court, who, at convenient halting-places, beats a gong; the guilty slanderer is compelled to recant his base falsehoods, and to confess his disgraceful behavior, amid the sneers and jeers of the multitude. The heavy stone so carried is called *oturbiba*.

READING AND DISCUSSION QUESTIONS

1. Why did Sarbah believe that the Fanti approach to slander was superior to the British approach?

2. What does the punishment that Sarbah described suggest about the nature of Fanti society?

3. In what ways was Sarbah's publication of Fanti customs, traditions, and laws an anti-imperialist act?

John Mensah Sarbah, *Fanti Customary Law* (London: William Clowes and Sons, 1897), 93–94.

VIEWPOINTS COMPARATIVE QUESTIONS

1. How might Kumalo and Sarbah have responded to Rhodes's claim that the world would be a better place if it were inhabited solely by the "Anglo-Saxon race"?

2. What aspects of British culture did Kumalo and Sarbah value? Why did both believe that their people would be better off if the British left?

25-5 | The Brutality of Colonial Rule

ROGER CASEMENT AND DAVID ENGOHAHE, *Victims of Belgian Congo Atrocities* (ca. 1904–1905)

In 1903, the British consul Roger Casement investigated abuses in the Congo Free State for the British government. The Congo Free State was the private holding of King Leopold II of Belgium from 1885 to 1908, and under Leopold's control the extraction of rubber led to gross human rights abuses. Casement's report led to a public outcry in Europe. The report, upheld by an independent commission in 1905 and verified through later research, detailed the mutilation and murder practiced by Leopold's representatives to ensure rubber production. Here, an excerpt from Casement's report shows the testimony of eyewitness David Engohahe—a member of the Bolia ethnicity—detailing the violence employed to ensure the continued profits from rubber cultivation. The photographs of three residents of the Congo show the human cost of the atrocities Engohahe describes.

At the time the district headquarters of the Basengele[13] was at Mbongo.[14] When the rubber was prepared you took it to Mbongo. . . . The State man[15] would stretch [the lengths of rubber] . . . out, and if they split he would reject them and throw them to one side. At the end of the count, if the rubber was bad, out of a village complement of 25 men he might shoot 5, out of 30, perhaps 10; and perhaps 20 out of 50. It was dreadful persecution. He then sent the rest of the men back to the forest to collect more rubber to make up the quota. . . . He forbad us to harvest the things in our own gardens so much so that our immediate forefathers did not eat manioc.[16] He forbad us the palm nuts in our own trees, and the plantains and all the garden produce, and sugar cane. It was all kept for his soldiers and his followers. . . . Many fled and some were mutilated. I myself saw a

---

Roger Anstey, "The Congo Rubber Atrocities: A Case Study," *African Historical Studies*, 4:1 (1971): 72.

[13] **Basengele:** A Bantu-language ethnic group.
[14] **Mbongo:** Near present-day Isoko, Democratic Republic of the Congo.
[15] **State man:** A representative of Leopold.
[16] **manioc:** A popular West African root crop, also called cassava.

man at Likange who had had both his hands cut off. Sometimes they cut them at the wrist, sometimes farther up . . . with a machete. Also there is a Muboma[17] . . . who has a long scar across the back of his neck. There is another man called Botei at Ihanga with the same sort of scar, where they wounded him maliciously, expecting him to die. They didn't cut his head off, they didn't get to the bone, but expected him to bleed to death. It was sheer cruelty; the State treated us abominably.

© Everett Collections Inc./Alamy Stock Photo.

READING AND DISCUSSION QUESTIONS

1. How does Engohahe connect the production of rubber to the presence or absence of subsistence agriculture?

2. How does the system of labor described here compare or contrast with your impression of slavery in the Americas?

3. Engohahe describes Leopold's representative as "the State man," but Leopold operated the territory as his own private holding rather than as a colony of Belgium. How might Leopold's relationship to the territory change your impression of the abuses described here?

4. What is the effect of the photographs? Do they look posed or natural? What might have been the purpose of these photographs?

---

[17] **Muboma:** An ethnic group.

▪ COMPARATIVE QUESTIONS ▪

1. Most of the documents in this chapter are written from a non-Western point of view; two, however, present a European view of non-Europeans. How do the photographs and Rhodes's "Confession" each present Africans? What is the role of Africans in each document?

2. Each of these documents deals in some way with the intersection of non-Western cultures and modern (if not Western) ideas and influences. How does each present the idea of modernization? What is the influence of the modern world in each case?

3. Consider the 1856 Ottoman rescript on equality and Rhodes's 1877 "Confession." How does each present the idea of managing diverse populations?

4. Taken together, what do the documents in this chapter tell you about the nature of colonial rule in the late nineteenth and early twentieth centuries? What do they reveal about the motives behind the New Imperialism?

26

Asia and the Pacific in the Era of Imperialism
1800–1914

Though not colonized as directly or thoroughly as Africa, Asia was heavily influenced by the imperial aspirations of Western industrial societies. British colonial rule directly reshaped the Indian economy and Indian culture, forcibly incorporating many Indians into the British-dominated world economy. In East Asia, treaties gave multiple Western powers—and Japan—economic, political, and military control over key areas of China. Spared the full brunt of Western attention, Japan incorporated Western ideas as it pushed to become an industrial power in its own right. But in every case, Asian nations wrestled with the presence of Westerners and Western ideas as well as their own domestic transformations. The documents in this chapter reflect the broad range of strategies that Asians used to appropriate or contest what they understood to be a new framework of international power.

VIEWPOINTS

Reactions to Imperialism and Modernity

Most Western proponents of imperialism had little doubt that the conquest and colonization of Africa and Asia were a moral undertaking. Starting with the assumption that their own societies represented the pinnacle of human achievement, that they were citizens of the most "civilized" nations the world had ever seen, they argued that the West had a right, even a duty, to rule. The "backwards" peoples of the world could only benefit from Western guidance. Westerners were likened to firm but fair teachers, patiently pointing unruly and unpromising students in the direction of progress and morality. Not surprisingly, many non-Western critics of imperialism rejected such analogies, pointing out both the defects in Western societies and the value of their own traditions and accomplishments. As you read the documents included in this feature, focus on the counter-arguments they offer to Western justifications of imperialism. How do these authors characterize the West? What claims do they make about their own societies?

26-1 | A Chinese Official Denounces the British Opium Trade

LIN ZEXU, *From a Letter to Queen Victoria* (1839)

Lin Zexu (1785–1850) was a Confucian scholar-bureaucrat of the highest rank, who was tapped by the Daoguang Emperor in 1838 to stop the illegal importation of opium by Great Britain and other foreign powers. In 1839, he arrived in Guangzhou and, after increasingly hostile negotiations, seized and destroyed more than two million pounds of raw opium from British warehouses. This action, viewed as heroic by Chinese and Britons alike, ignited the first Opium War (1839–1842). Lin wrote to Queen Victoria, pleading with her to stop the British opium trade. Although his letter was never sent to the queen, it was published in Guangdong and later in Britain, where it aroused both outrage and sympathy.

It is only our high and mighty emperor, who alike supports and cherishes those of the Inner Land [China], and those from beyond the seas—who looks upon all mankind with equal benevolence—who, if a source of profit exists anywhere, diffuses it over the whole world—who, if the tree of evil takes root anywhere, plucks it up for the benefit of all nations:—who, in a word, hath implanted in his breast that heart (by which beneficent nature herself) governs the heavens and the earth! You, the queen of your honorable nation, sit upon a throne occupied through successive generations by predecessors, all of whom have been styled respectful and obedient. Looking over the public documents accompanying the tribute sent (by your predecessors) on various occasions, we find the following:—"All the people of my (i.e. the king of England's) country, arriving at the Central Land for purposes of trade, have to feel grateful to the great emperor for the most perfect justice, for the kindest treatment," and other words to that effect. Delighted did we feel that the kings of your honorable nation so clearly understood the great principles of propriety, and were so deeply grateful for the heavenly goodness (of our emperor):—therefore, it was that we of the heavenly dynasty nourished and cherished your people from afar, and bestowed upon them redoubled proofs of our urbanity and kindness. It is merely from these circumstances, that your country—deriving immense advantage from its commercial intercourse with us, which has endured now two hundred years—has become the rich and flourishing kingdom that it is said to be!

The Chinese Repository, 20 vols. (Japan: Canton Press, 1840), 8:497–593.

But, during the commercial intercourse which has existed so long, among the numerous foreign merchants resorting hither, are wheat and tares, good and bad; and of these latter are some, who, by means of introducing opium by stealth, have seduced our Chinese people, and caused every province of the land to overflow with that poison. These then know merely to advantage themselves, they care not about injuring others! This is a principle which heaven's Providence repugnates; and which mankind conjointly look upon with abhorrence! Moreover, the great emperor hearing of it, actually quivered with indignation, and especially dispatched me, the commissioner, to Canton, that in conjunction with the viceroy and lieut.-governor of the province, means might be taken for its suppression! . . .

We find that your country is distant from us about sixty or seventy thousand [Chinese] miles, that your foreign ships come hither striving the one with the other for our trade, and for the simple reason of their strong desire to reap a profit. Now, out of the wealth of our Inner Land, if we take a part to bestow upon foreigners from afar, it follows, that the immense wealth which the said foreigners amass, ought properly speaking to be portion of our own native Chinese people. By what principle of reason then, should these foreigners send in return a poisonous drug, which involves in destruction those very natives of China? Without meaning to say that the foreigners harbor such destructive intentions in their hearts, we yet positively assert that from their inordinate thirst after gain, they are perfectly careless about the injuries they inflict upon us! And such being the case, we should like to ask what has become of that conscience which heaven has implanted in the breasts of all men?

We have heard that in your own country opium is prohibited with the utmost strictness and severity:—this is a strong proof that you know full well how hurtful it is to mankind. Since then you do not permit it to injure your own country, you ought not to have the injurious drug transferred to another country, and above all others, how much less to the Inner Land! Of the products which China exports to your foreign countries, there is not one which is not beneficial to mankind in some shape or other. There are those which serve for food, those which are useful, and those which are calculated for re-sale;—but all are beneficial. Has China (we should like to ask) ever yet sent forth a noxious article from its soil? Not to speak of our tea and rhubarb, things which your foreign countries could not exist a single day without, if we of the Central Land were to grudge you what is beneficial, and not to compassionate [pity] your wants, then wherewithal could you foreigners manage to exist? And further, as regards your woolens, camlets, and longells [all woolen, woven fabrics], were it not that you get supplied with our native raw silk, you could not get these manufactured! If China were to grudge you those things which yield a profit, how could you foreigners scheme after any profit at all? Our other articles of food, such as sugar, ginger, cinnamon, &c., and our other articles for use, such as silk piece-goods, chinaware, &c., are all so many necessaries of life to you; how can we reckon up their number! On the other hand, the things that come from your foreign countries are only calculated to make presents of, or serve for mere amusement. It is quite the same to us if we have them, or if we have them not. If then these are of no material consequence to us of the Inner Land, what difficulty would there be in prohibiting and shutting our market against them? It is only that our heavenly dynasty most freely permits you to take off her tea, silk, and other commodities, and convey them for consumption everywhere, without the slightest stint or grudge, for no other reason, but that where a profit exists, we wish that it be diffused abroad for the benefit of all the earth!

. . . Now we have always heard that your highness possesses a most kind and benevolent heart, surely then you are incapable of doing or causing to be done unto another, that which you should not wish another to do unto you! We have at the same time heard that your ships which come to Canton do each and every of them carry a document granted by your highness' self, on which are written these words "you shall not be permitted to carry contraband goods"; this shows that the laws of your highness are in their origin both distinct and severe, and we can only suppose that because the ships coming here have been very numerous, due attention has not been given to search and examine; and for this reason it is that we now address you this public document, that you may clearly know how stern and severe are the laws of the central dynasty, and most certainly you will cause that they be not again rashly violated!

Moreover, we have heard that in London the metropolis where you dwell, as also in Scotland, Ireland, and other such places, no opium whatever is produced. It is only in sundry parts of your colonial kingdom of Hindostan, such as Bengal, Madras, Bombay, Patna, Malwa, Benares, Malacca, and other places where the very hills are covered with the opium plant, where tanks are made for the preparing of the drug; month by month, and year by year, the volume of the poison increases, its unclean stench ascends upwards, until heaven itself grows angry, and the very gods thereat get indignant! You, the queen of the said honorable nation, ought immediately to have the plant in those parts plucked up by the very root! Cause the land there to be hoed up afresh, sow in its stead the five grains, and if any man dare again to plant in these grounds a single poppy, visit his crime with the most severe punishment. By a truly benevolent system of government such as this, will you indeed reap advantage, and do away with a source of evil. Heaven must support you, and the gods will crown you with felicity! This will get for yourself the blessing of long life, and from this will proceed the security and stability of your descendants! . . .

Suppose the subject of another country were to come to England to trade, he would certainly be required to comply with the laws of England, then how much more does this apply to us of the celestial empire! Now it is a fixed statute of this empire, that any native Chinese who sells opium is punishable with death, and even he who merely smokes it, must not less die. Pause and reflect for a moment: if you foreigners did not bring the opium hither, where should our Chinese people get it to re-sell? It is you foreigners who involve our simple natives in the pit of death, and are they alone to be permitted to escape alive? If so much as one of those deprive one of our people of his life, he must forfeit his life in requital for that which he has taken:—how much more does this apply to him who by means of opium destroys his fellow-men? Does the havoc which he commits stop with a single life? Therefore it is that those foreigners who now import opium into the Central Land are condemned to be beheaded and strangled by the new statute, and this explains what we said at the beginning about plucking up the tree of evil, wherever it takes root, for the benefit of all nations.

We further find that during the second month of this present year, the superintendent of your honorable country, Elliot, viewing the law in relation to the prohibiting of opium as excessively severe, duly petitioned us, begging for "an extension of the term already limited, say five months for Hindostan and the different parts of India, and ten for England, after which they would obey and act in conformity with the new statute," and other words to the same effect. Now we, the high commissioner and colleagues, upon making a duly prepared memorial to the great emperor, have to feel grateful for his extraordinary goodness, for his redoubled compassion. Any one who within the next year and a half may by mistake bring opium to this country, if he will but voluntarily come forward, and deliver up the entire quantity, he shall be absolved from all punishment for his crime. If, however, the appointed term shall have expired, and there are still persons who continue to bring it, then such shall be accounted as knowingly violating the laws, and shall most assuredly be put to death! On no account shall we show mercy or clemency! This then may be called truly the extreme of benevolence, and the very perfection of justice!

Our celestial empire rules over ten thousand kingdoms! Most surely do we possess a measure of godlike majesty which ye cannot fathom! Still we cannot bear to slay or exterminate without previous warning, and it is for this reason that we now clearly make known to you the fixed laws of our land. If the foreign merchants of your said honorable nation desire to continue their commercial intercourse, they then must tremblingly obey our recorded statutes, they must cut off for ever the source from which the opium flows, and on no account make an experiment of our laws in their own persons! Let then your highness punish those of your subjects who may be criminal, do not endeavor to screen or conceal them, and thus you will secure peace and quietness to your possessions, thus will you more than ever display a proper sense of respect and obedience, and thus may we unitedly enjoy the common blessings of peace and happiness. What greater joy! What more complete felicity than this!

Let your highness immediately, upon the receipt of this communication, inform us promptly of the state of matters, and of the measures you are pursuing utterly to put a stop to the opium evil. Please let your reply be speedy. Do not on any account make excuses or procrastinate. A most important communication.

P. S. We annex an abstract of the new law, now about to be put in force. "Any foreigner or foreigners bringing opium to the Central Land, with design to sell the same, the principals shall most assuredly be decapitated, and the accessories strangled;—and all property (found on board the same ship) shall be confiscated. The space of a year and a half is granted, within the which, if any one bringing opium by mistake, shall voluntarily step forward and deliver it up, he shall be absolved from all consequences of his crime."

READING AND DISCUSSION QUESTIONS

1. Describe the tone of Lin's letter. What language or phrases establish his under-standing of the relationship between China and Great Britain?

2. According to Lin, what should motivate Queen Victoria to halt the opium trade? How will she be rewarded?

3. What does Lin say about trade between China and the world? In his opinion, whom does this trade benefit? How do you imagine a British trader would respond to Lin's assertions?

26-2 | The Boxers Declare War on the "Foreign Devils"
Two Proclamations of the Boxer Rebellion (1898, 1900)

Following the Guangxu Emperor's optimistic but unsuccessful attempt to modernize China during the Hundred Days' Reform period of 1898, a local martial arts organization in Shandong village, the Society of Righteous and Harmonious Boxers, emerged as a violently antimodern, anti-Western, and anti-Christian force. Encouraged by the Qing government and eschewing modern military techniques, the Boxers killed thousands of foreign and Chinese Christians and in 1900 laid siege to the area in Beijing where foreign officials were quartered. A multinational force, including both Western and Japanese troops, ended the siege within two months, and the resulting Boxer Protocol of 1901 forced the Qing government to pay war reparations. The proclamations here outline the Boxers' beliefs and their exhortations to Chinese citizens.

1898 Proclamation

The Gods assist the Boxers,
The Patriotic Harmonious corps,
It is because the "Foreign Devils" disturb the "Middle Kingdom" [China].
Urging the people to join their religion,
To turn their backs on Heaven,
Venerate not the Gods and forget the ancestors.
Men violate the human obligations,
Women commit adultery,
"Foreign Devils" are not produced by mankind,
If you do not believe,
Look at them carefully.
The eyes of all the "Foreign Devils" are bluish,
No rain falls,
The earth is getting dry,
This is because the churches stop Heaven,

The Society of Righteous and Harmonious Boxers, "The Gods Assist the Boxers" in the Peking and Tientsin *Times*, May 5, 1900; "Attention" in Ssu-ya Teng and John K. Fairbank, eds., *China's Response to the West* (Cambridge, Mass.: Harvard University Press, 1954), 190.

The Gods are angry;
The Genii [minor spirits] are vexed;
Both come down from the mountain to deliver the doctrine.
This is no hearsay,
The practices of boxing[1] will not be in vain;
Reciting incantations and pronouncing magic words,
Burn up yellow written prayers,
Light incense sticks
To invite the Gods and Genii of all the grottoes.
The Gods come out from grottoes,
The Genii come down from mountains,
Support the human bodies to practice the boxing.
When all the military accomplishments or tactics
Are fully learned,
It will not be difficult to exterminate the "Foreign Devils" then.
Push aside the railway tracks,
Pull out the telegraph poles,
Immediately after this destroy the steamers.
The great France
Will grow cold and downhearted.
The English and Russians will certainly disperse.
Let the various "Foreign Devils" all be killed.
May the whole Elegant Empire of the Great Qing Dynasty[2] be ever prosperous!

1900 Proclamation

Attention: all people in markets and villages of all provinces in China—now, owing to the fact that Catholics and Protestants have vilified our gods and sages, have deceived our emperors and ministers above, and oppressed the Chinese people below, both our gods and our people are angry at them, yet we have to keep silent. This forces us to practice the Yike[3] magic boxing so as to protect our country, expel the foreign bandits and kill Christian converts, in order to save our people from miserable suffering. After this notice is issued to instruct you villagers, no matter which village you are living in, if there are Christian converts, you ought to get rid of them quickly. The churches which belong to them should be unreservedly burned down. Everyone who intends to spare someone, or to disobey our order by concealing Christian converts, will be punished according to the regulation when we come to his place, and he will be burned to

---

[1] **practices of boxing:** Society members trained in Chinese martial arts techniques, which included intense physical and mental discipline and meditation techniques. Essentially, they believed that their physical prowess enabled them to deflect bullets.

[2] **Great Qing Dynasty:** Chinese imperial family between 1644 and 1912. The Qing encouraged the Boxer uprising.

[3] **Yike:** The type of martial art practiced by the Boxers.

death to prevent his impeding our program. We especially do not want to punish anyone by death without warning him first. We cannot bear to see you suffer innocently. Don't disobey this special notice!

READING AND DISCUSSION QUESTIONS

1. What are the Boxers' complaints?
2. How do the Boxers characterize the distinction between the West and China?
3. How do you imagine Chinese citizens might have responded to the Boxers' proclamations?

26-3 | Gandhi Rejects British "Civilization"

MOHANDAS GANDHI, *Indian Home Rule* (1909)

In his seminal 1909 pamphlet entitled "Indian Home Rule," Mohandas Gandhi (1869–1948) introduced the world to the key ideas that would inform the rest of his career as an activist for Indian independence. In the pamphlet, Gandhi rejected political violence and made the case for passive resistance. He also took direct aim at the claims of British imperialists that they were bringing civilization to India. In the excerpt included below, Gandhi contrasted European civilization with the "true civilization" of India. As you read it, think about the values Gandhi associated with each society. Why did he reject European civilization? What did he value most in his own civilization?

Civilization

READER: . . . Now will you tell me something of what you have read and thought of this civilization?

EDITOR: Let us first consider what state of things is described by the word "civilization." Its true test lies in the fact that people living in it make bodily welfare the object of life. We will take some examples. The people of Europe today live in better-built houses than they did a hundred years ago. This is considered an emblem of civilization, and this is also a matter to promote bodily happiness. Formerly, they wore skins, and used spears as their weapons. Now, they wear long trousers, and, for embellishing their bodies, they wear a variety of clothing, and, instead of spears, they carry with them revolvers containing five or more chambers. If people of a certain country, who have hitherto not been in the habit of wearing much clothing, boots, etc., adopt European clothing, they are supposed to have become civilized out of savagery. Formerly, in Europe, people plowed their lands mainly by manual labor. Now, one man can plow a vast tract by means of steam engines and can thus amass great wealth. This is called a sign of civilization.

Homer A. Jack, ed., *The Gandhi Reader* (Bloomington: Indiana University Press, 1956), 105–109.

Formerly, only a few men wrote valuable books. Now, anybody writes and prints anything he likes and poisons people's minds. Formerly, men traveled in wagons. Now, they fly through the air in trains at the rate of four hundred and more miles per day. This is considered the height of civilization. It has been stated that, as men progress, they shall be able to travel in airships and reach any part of the world in a few hours. Men will not need the use of their hands and feet. They will press a button, and they will have their clothing by their side. They will press another button, and they will have their newspaper. A third, and a motor-car will be in waiting for them. They will have a variety of delicately dished up food. Everything will be done by machinery. Formerly, when people wanted to fight with one another, they measured between them their bodily strength; now it is possible to take away thousands of lives by one man working behind a gun from a hill. This is civilization. Formerly, men worked in the open air only as much as they liked. Now thousands of workmen meet together and for the sake of maintenance work in factories or mines. Their condition is worse than that of beasts. They are obliged to work, at the risk of their lives, at most dangerous occupations, for the sake of millionaires. Formerly, men were made slaves under physical compulsion. Now they are enslaved by temptation of money and of the luxuries that money can buy. There are now diseases of which people never dreamt before, and an army of doctors is engaged in finding out their cures, and so hospitals have increased. This is a test of civilization. Formerly, special messengers were required and much expense was incurred in order to send letters; today, anyone can abuse his fellow by means of a letter for one penny. True, at the same cost, one can send one's thanks also. Formerly, people had two or three meals consisting of home-made bread and vegetables; now, they require something to eat every two hours so that they have hardly leisure for anything else. What more need I say? All this you can ascertain from several authoritative books. These are all true tests of civilization. And if anyone speaks to the contrary, know that he is ignorant. This civilization takes note neither of morality nor of religion. Its votaries calmly state that their business is not to teach religion. Some even consider it to be a superstitious growth. Others put on the cloak of religion, and prate about morality. Even a child can understand that in all I have described above there can be no inducement to morality. Civilization seeks to increase bodily comforts, and it fails miserably even in doing so.

This civilization is irreligion, and it has taken such a hold on the people in Europe that those who are in it appear to be half mad. They lack real physical strength or courage. They keep up their energy by intoxication. They can hardly be happy in solitude. Women, who should be the queens of households, wander in the streets or they slave away in factories. For the sake of a pittance, half a million women in England alone are laboring under trying circumstances in factories or similar institutions. This awful fact is one of the causes of the daily growing suffragette movement.

This civilization is such that one has only to be patient and it will be self-destroyed. According to the teaching of Mahomed this would be considered a Satanic Civilization. Hinduism calls it the Black Age. I cannot give you an adequate conception of it. It is eating into the vitals of the English nation. It must be shunned. Parliaments are really emblems of slavery. If you will sufficiently think over this, you will entertain the same opinion and cease to blame the English. They rather deserve our sympathy. They are a shrewd nation and I therefore believe that they will cast off the evil. They are enterprising and industrious, and their mode of thought is not inherently immoral. Neither are they bad at heart. I therefore respect them. Civilization is not an incurable disease, but it should never be forgotten that the English people are at present afflicted by it.

What Is True Civilization?

READER: You have denounced railways, lawyers and doctors. I can see that you will discard all machinery. What, then, is civilization?

EDITOR: The answer to that question is not difficult. I believe that the civilization India has evolved is not to be beaten in the world. Nothing can equal the seeds sown by our ancestors. Rome went, Greece shared the same fate; the might of the Pharaohs was broken; Japan has become westernized; of China nothing can be said; but India is still, somehow or other, sound at the foundation. The people of Europe learn their lessons from the writings of the men of Greece or Rome, which exist no longer in their former glory. In trying to learn from them, the Europeans imagine that they will avoid the mistakes of Greece and Rome. Such is their pitiable condition. In the midst of all this India remains immovable and that is her glory. It is a charge against India that her people are so uncivilized, ignorant, and solid, that it is not possible to induce them to adopt any changes. It is a charge really against our merit. What we have tested and found true on the anvil of experience, we dare not change. Many thrust their advice upon India, and she remains steady. This is her beauty: it is the sheet-anchor of our hope.

Civilization is that mode of conduct which points out to man the path of duty. Performance of duty and observance of morality are convertible terms. To observe morality is to attain mastery over our mind and our passions. So doing, we know ourselves. The Gujarati equivalent for civilization means "good conduct."

If this definition be correct, then India, as so many writers have shown, has nothing to learn from anybody else, and this is as it should be. We notice that the mind is a restless bird; the more it gets the more it wants, and still remains unsatisfied. The more we indulge our passions, the more unbridled they become. Our ancestors, therefore, set a limit to our indulgences. They saw that happiness was largely a mental condition. A man is not necessarily happy because he is rich, or unhappy because he is poor. The rich are often seen to be unhappy, the poor to be happy. Millions will always remain poor. Observing all this, our ancestors dissuaded us from luxuries and pleasures. We have managed with the same kind of plow as existed thousands of years ago. We have retained the same kind of cottages that we had in former times and our indigenous education remains the same as before. We have had no system of life-corroding competition. Each followed his own occupation or trade and charged a regulation wage. It was not that we did not know how to invent machinery, but our forefathers knew that, if we set our hearts after such things, we would become slaves and lose our moral fiber. They, therefore, after due deliberation decided that we should only do what we could with our hands and feet. They saw that our real happiness and health consisted in a proper use of our hands and feet. They further reasoned that large cities were a snare and a useless encumbrance and that people would not be happy in them, that there would be gangs of thieves and robbers, prostitution and vice flourishing in them and that poor men would be robbed by rich men. They were, therefore, satisfied with small villages. They saw that kings and their swords were inferior to the sword of ethics, and they, therefore, held the sovereigns of the earth to be inferior to the Rishis and the Fakirs.[4] A nation with a constitution like this is fitter to teach others than to learn from others. This nation had courts, lawyers and doctors, but they were all within bounds. Everybody knew that these professions were not particularly superior; moreover, these vakils and vaids[5] did not rob people; they were considered people's dependents, not their masters. Justice was tolerably fair. The ordinary rule was to avoid courts. There were no touts to lure people into them. This evil, too, was noticeable only in and around capitals. The common people lived independently and followed their agricultural occupation. They enjoyed true Home Rule. . . .

Now you see what I consider to be real civilization. Those who want to change conditions such as I have described are enemies of the country and are sinners.

READING AND DISCUSSION QUESTIONS

1. What evils did Gandhi associate with industrialization? Why did he believe that economic progress had little to do with social and moral progress?

2. How did Gandhi define "true civilization"? In his view, what marked Indian civilization as truly great?

---

[4] **the Rishis and the Fakirs:** Seers and holy men.
[5] **vakils and vaids:** Doctors of Indian medicine.

VIEWPOINTS COMPARATIVE QUESTIONS

1. On what might Lin, the Boxers, and Gandhi have agreed? On what would they have disagreed?

2. How did each author seek to undermine the moral arguments in favor of imperialism?

3. What role did religion play in the Boxers' argument? What role did it play in Gandhi's?

4. How might a Western imperialist have responded to these documents? What counter-arguments might such a person have made to each?

26-4 | A British Officer Describes the Great Revolt of 1857

SIR HENRY MONTGOMERY LAWRENCE, *Letter to Lieutenant-Governor J. Colvin* (June 13, 1857)

Sir Henry Montgomery Lawrence (1806–1857) was an officer of the British army in India. Born in Ceylon to a British army officer, he was educated in Britain but posted to India in 1823, where he gained considerable military and political experience as part of the British colonial force. Appointed chief commissioner of the British territory of Awadh in 1857, Lawrence was nominated as the next governor-general of India by the British East India Company. Before he could fully assume that post, a popular revolt among Indian troops spread throughout India, and Lawrence was killed defending British control of the city of Lucknow (retaken by British and Nepalese forces in 1858). The rebellion marked the end of the East India Company's rule and the start of direct British state control of India. Lawrence's letters give an intimate account of how the British military saw the rebellion, the empire, and the indigenous people of India.

My dear Colvin,

I wrote a long letter yesterday telling you of the sad succession of misfortunes in this quarter. Today I have had confirmation of the fate of Sooltanpoor & Fyzabad.[6] A native letter bearing the stamp of truth tells that the troops rose & butchered the Europeans at Sooltanpoor. From Fyzabad Mr Bradford writes (no date, probably the 6th) that the officers & ladies had all been saved, that everything had been conducted with the utmost regularity, the native civil officer

---

Letters of Sir Henry Montgomery Lawrence: Selections from the Correspondence of Sir Henry Montgomery Lawrence (1806–1857), ed. Sheo Bahadur Singh (New Delhi: Sagar, 1978), 28–30.

[6] **Sooltanpoor & Fyzabad:** Sultanpur, Faizabad, Daryabad, Sikrara, Sitapur, and Kanpur are place-names in present-day Uttar Pradesh. All were rendered according to British spelling in these documents.

taking prominent places, & that the King of Delhi had been proclaimed. In all quarters we hear of similar method & regularity—at Duriabad, Secrora & Seetapoor individuals have been obliged to give up their plunder, & the treasure is carefully guarded. The quiet method bespeaks some [leading] influence. We cannot get certain tidings from Cawnpoor, altho' we have sent many messengers, but we have no reason to doubt that Gen. Wheeler still holds his grounds. The mutineers hold the river bank for many miles above & below Cawnpoor & search all papers. They at once seized all the boats and drew them to their own bank. Would that we could help the besieged, but our numbers, the distance and the heat forbid the thought—this is frightful weather for field operations for Europeans. Yesterday we lost two out of about 130 from exposure after 3 p.m. in our pursuit of the mutinous Police Battalions,[7] & yet Mr Gubbins would be continually sending 50 men on Elephants, 40, 50 and more miles off. He is perfectly insane on what he considers *energetic*, manly measures. His language has been so extravagant that were he not really useful I should be obliged to take severe measures against him. He is *the one* malcontent in the garrison—all others, I believe, are satisfied that as much energy has been evinced as circumstances permitted. Yesterday the mutineer police about 1000 strong were followed about 8 miles by 100 H.M. 32nd,[8] 2 guns, 50 Sikh horse & 20 European volunteers. It left for an hour the Residency Post[9] with only 100 Europeans, with the jail close by, over which these Policemen had held guard. Fortunately in an hour 100 Europeans came with Treasure from the Muchee Bawan[10] & were retained till the near return of the detached party. I had also instantly got up 2 companies of Irregulars[11] to the jail. All was quiet during the night, and the result of the pursuit has been good. This morning the zemindars [tax collectors] brought masses of musquets that the mutineers had thrown away. About 50 of them seem to have been killed. Our loss of 2 Europeans from the sun is a serious loss. 2 horsemen were killed, & Mr Thornhill, C.S, wounded. We have seen sad details of this butchery of officers & ladies who escaped from Jhaligshanpoor between Mohomdee and Seetapoor. Mr Thomason fell with them, Capt. Oor alone escaped, being protected by some men of his old Regiment. Of the Seetapoor party Sir M. Jackson, one of his sisters, Lt. Burn & a child of Mr Christians's escaped to the jungles beyond Seetapoor. Capt. Jester found his way here. All

---

[7] **Police Battalions:** Indian troops employed as a police force by the British East India Company.

[8] **100 H.M. 32nd:** 100 members of Her Majesty's 32nd regiment, an armed forces unit.

[9] **Residency Post:** The complex of buildings occupied by the British resident, a representative of the British East India Company, which ruled the region indirectly. After the annexation of the region, the position of resident was replaced by the direct rule of a commissioner who continued to occupy and use the residency.

[10] **Muchee Bawan:** Macchi Bhawan, an area in the Agra Fort complex in Uttar Pradesh.

[11] **Irregulars:** Unlike "regular" troops, "irregulars" were variably trained, equipped on an ad hoc basis, and usually drawn from local populations. "Regular" troops were, by contrast, the official or formal members of a standing military force.

our Regulars except about 200 have taken leave to their homes, where many will go, for I believe their numbers were well purged on the 30th & 31st May, but there was a frantic fancy of Mr Gubbins to get rid of them all including those who have evinced unmistakeable fidelity, and to trust implicitly the Police & Irregulars, who have all gone with the herd. To my mind the Police have behaved in some respects the worst of all. I should have preferred keeping 500 of those men as more likely to be true than any other, but under Mr. Gubbin's pressure an order was issued when I was ill, to encourage all the Sikhs to be off. I have saved a few. We have still about 1000 Irregular Infantry, 200 Cavalry, 200 Regular Infantry, 30 Regular Cavalry & the Town Police, few of which can be expected to stand any severe pressure. We however hold our ground & daily strengthen both our Tower positions, bearing in mind that the Residency is to be the final point of concentration. The health of the troops is good & the weather propitious as long as there is not exposure to the sun. The conduct of the Europeans is beautiful. By God's help we can hold our own for a month, but there should be no delay in sending succor. The appearance of 2 European Regiments would soon enable us to settle the Province, but if succor be lost & this force destroyed, the difficulty would be vastly increased.

I have the honor to be yours,
H. M. Lawrence.

READING AND DISCUSSION QUESTIONS

1. How desperate does Lawrence seem in this letter? What language does he use to describe the seriousness of his position?

2. How does Lawrence describe the indigenous people of India and their behavior?

3. How does he describe the British military?

26-5 | Sun Yatsen Calls on China to Take Its Rightful Place in the World

SUN YATSEN, *On the Three People's Principles and the Future of the Chinese People* (1906)

Trained as a Western physician in Hong Kong, Sun Yatsen (1866–1925) studied and traveled extensively and became an important revolutionary during the final years of the Qing Dynasty (1644–1912). While in exile after a failed coup, he formed the Tongmenghui revolutionary

Prescriptions for Saving China: Selected Writings of Sun Yat-sen, ed. Julie Lee Wei, Ramon H. Myers, and Donald G. Gillin (Palo Alto, Calif.: Hoover Institution Press, 1994). Translation copyright © 1994 by the Board of Trustees of the Leland Stanford Junior University. Reprinted with permission of the publisher, Hoover Institution Press.

organization and won support among Chinese expatriates through his "Three Principles of the People," presented in this excerpt from a 1906 speech in Tokyo. Although the 1911 revolution occurred in his absence, he was selected as provisional president of the new Republic of China, a post he occupied for less than three months. However, his legacy as founder of the Guomindang (Nationalist Party) and his position as an iconic figure of Chinese modernity remain strong.

Let us pause to consider for a moment: Where is the nation? Where is the political power? Actually, we are already a people without a nation! The population of the globe is only one billion, several hundred million; we Han,[12] being 400 million, comprise one-fourth of that population.

Our nation is the most populous, most ancient, and most civilized in the world, yet today we are a lost nation. Isn't that enormously bizarre? The African nation of the Transvaal has a population of only 200,000, yet when Britain tried to destroy it, the fighting lasted three years.[13] The Philippines have a population of only several million, but when America tried to subdue it, hostilities persisted for several years.[14] Is it possible that the Han will gladly be a lost nation?

We Han are now swiftly being caught up in a tidal wave of nationalist revolution, yet the Manchus continue to discriminate against the Han. They boast that their forefathers conquered the Han because of their superior unity and military strength and that they intend to retain these qualities so as to dominate the Han forever. . . . Certainly, once we Han unite, our power will be thousands of times greater than theirs, and the success of the nationalist revolution will be assured.

As for the Principle of Democracy, it is the foundation of the political revolution. . . . For several thousand years China has been a monarchical autocracy, a type of political system intolerable to those living in freedom and equality. A nationalist revolution is not itself sufficient to get rid of such a system. Think for a moment: When the founder of the Ming dynasty expelled the Mongols and restored Chinese rule, the nationalist revolution triumphed, but his political system was only too similar to those of the Han, Tang, and Song dynasties.[15] Consequently, after another three hundred years, foreigners again began to invade China. This is the result of the inadequacy of the political system, so that a political revolution is an absolute necessity. . . . The aim of the political revolution is to create a constitutional, democratic political system. . . .

* * *

---

[12] **Han:** The Chinese people.

[13] **The African nation . . . three years:** A reference to the South African War (1899–1902).

[14] **The Philippines . . . several years:** Between 1899 and 1901, Filipinos fought against the United States after the United States took over the Philippines from Spain at the end of the Spanish-American War.

[15] **When the founder . . . dynasties:** The Ming Dynasty ruled from 1368 to 1644 C.E.; the Han (206 B.C.E.–220 C.E.), Tang (618–907 C.E.), and Song (960–1279 C.E.) were earlier Chinese dynasties.

Now, let me begin by discussing the origins of the Principle of the People's Livelihood, a principle that began to flourish only in the latter part of the nineteenth century. . . . As civilization advanced, people relied less on physical labor and more on natural forces, since electricity and steam could accomplish things a thousand times faster than human physical strength. For example, in antiquity a single man tilling the land could harvest at best enough grain to feed a few people, notwithstanding his toil and trouble. Now, however, as a result of the development of scientific agriculture, one man can grow more than enough to feed a thousand people because he can use machinery instead of his limbs, with a consequent increase in efficiency. . . .

In view of this, everyone in Europe and America should be living in a state of plenty and happiness undreamed of in antiquity. If we look around, however, we see that conditions in those countries are precisely the opposite. Statistically, Britain's wealth has increased more than several thousandfold over the previous generation, yet poverty of the people has also increased several thousandfold over the previous generation. Moreover, the rich are extremely few, and the poor extremely numerous. This is because the power of human labor is no match for the power of capital. In antiquity, agriculture and industry depended completely on human labor; but now, with the development of natural forces that human labor cannot match, agriculture and industry have fallen completely into the hands of capitalists. The greater the amount of capital, the more abundant the resources that can be utilized. Unable to compete, the poor have naturally been reduced to destitution. . . .

Indeed, this constitutes a lesson for China. . . . Civilization yields both good and bad fruits, and we should embrace the good and reject the bad. In the countries of Europe and America, the rich monopolize the good fruits of civilization, while the poor suffer from its evil fruits. . . . Our current revolution will create a nation that not only belongs to the citizenry but is socially responsible. Certainly, there will be nothing comparable to it in Europe or America.

Why have Europe and America failed to solve their social problems? Because they have not solved their land problem. Generally speaking, wherever civilization is advanced, the price of land increases with each passing day. . . . In China capitalists have not yet emerged, so that for several thousand years there has been no increase in land prices. . . . After the revolution, however, conditions in China will be different. For example, land prices in Hong Kong and Shanghai are currently as much as several hundred times higher than those in the interior. This increment is the result of the advance of civilization and the development of communications. It is inevitable that, as the entire nation advances, land prices everywhere will rise accordingly. . . . Fifty years ago, land along the banks of the Huangpu River in Shanghai was worth up to a million dollars a *mou* [1.5 acres]. This is evidence of the clearest sort, from which we can see that in the future the rich will get richer every day, and the poor poorer. . . . Consequently, we must come up with a solution now. . . .

With respect to a solution, although the socialists have different opinions, the procedure I most favor is land valuation. For example, if a landlord has land worth 1,000 dollars, its price can be set at 1,000 or even 2,000 dollars. Perhaps in the future, after communications have been developed, the value of his land will rise to 10,000 dollars; the owner should receive 2,000, which entails a profit and no loss, and the 8,000 increment will go to the state. Such an arrangement will greatly benefit both the state and the people's livelihood. Naturally, it will also eliminate the shortcomings that have permitted a few rich people to monopolize wealth. This is the simplest, most convenient, and most feasible method. . . .

Once we adopt this method, the more civilization advances, the greater the wealth of the nation, and then we can be sure our financial problems will not become difficult to handle. After the excessive taxes of the present have been abolished, the price of consumer goods will gradually fall and the people will become increasingly prosperous. We will forever abolish the vicious taxation policies that have prevailed for several thousand years. . . . After China's social revolution is accomplished, private individuals will never again have to pay taxes. The collection of land revenues alone will make China the richest nation on earth. . . .

Obviously, . . . it is necessary to give considerable attention to what the constitution of the Republic of China should be. . . . The British constitution embodies the so-called separation of powers into executive, legislative, and judicial, all mutually independent. . . . The Frenchman[16] later embraced the British system and melded it with his own ideals to create his own school of thought. The American constitution was based on Montesquieu's theories but went further in clearly demarcating the separation of powers. . . . As to the future constitution of the Republic of China, I propose that we introduce a new principle, that of the "five separate powers."

Under this system, there will be two other powers in addition to the three powers just discussed. One is the examination power. . . . American officials are either elected or appointed. . . .

With respect to elections, those endowed with eloquence ingratiated themselves with the public and won elections, while those who had learning and ideals but lacked eloquence were ignored. Consequently, members of America's House of Representatives have often been foolish and ignorant people who have made its history quite ridiculous. As for appointees, they all come and go with the president. The Democratic and Republican parties have consistently taken turns holding power, and whenever a president is replaced, cabinet members and other officials, comprising no fewer than 60,000–70,000 people,

---

[16] **the Frenchman:** Montesquieu (1689–1755), a French political philosopher who argued that individual freedom is safest when the three powers of government—the judicial, executive, and legislative—are kept separate in a state.

including the postmaster general, are also replaced. As a result, the corruption and laxity of American politics are unparalleled among the nations of the world. . . . Therefore, the future constitution of the Republic of China must provide for an independent branch expressly responsible for civil service examinations. Furthermore, all officials, however high their rank, must undergo examinations in order to determine their qualifications. Whether elected or appointed, officials must pass those examinations before assuming office. This procedure will eliminate such evils as blind obedience, electoral abuses, and favoritism. . . .

The other power is the supervisory power, responsible for monitoring matters involving impeachment. For reasons that should be evident to all, such a branch is indispensable to any nation. The future constitution of the Republic of China must provide for an independent branch. Since ancient times, China had a supervisory organization, the Censorate,[17] to monitor the traditional social order. Inasmuch as it was merely a servant of the monarchy, however, it was ineffectual. . . .

With this added to the four powers already discussed, there will be five separate powers. That constitution will form the basis of the sound government of a nation that belongs to its own race, to its own citizens, and to its own society. This will be the greatest good fortune for our 400 million Han people. I presume that you gentlemen are willing to undertake and complete this task. It is my greatest hope.

READING AND DISCUSSION QUESTIONS

1. Sun presents his first principle only indirectly in the first three paragraphs of this speech. Describe what you think that principle is, based on your reading of the speech.

2. Sun mentions the Han and the Manchu. Why do you think he uses ethnic groups to describe the situation in China?

3. What are Sun's second and third principles? What distinction does he make between the third principle and socialism?

4. How does Sun invoke Western countries to strengthen the argument for his three principles?

---

[17] **the Censorate:** A unique feature of Chinese government during the Ming and Qing eras. Also called the Board of Censors, it was responsible for reviewing the conduct of officials and reporting any offenses to the emperor.

■ COMPARATIVE QUESTIONS ■

1. The documents in this chapter show different ways that Asian cultures engaged with Western modernity. Describe some of those forms of engagement.

2. Compare the attitudes of Lin Zexu, Gandhi, and Sun Yatsen toward the West. Compare also their approaches to both international and domestic affairs.

3. Several of the documents deal with the question of violence, either impending or ongoing. How does the position (or positions) taken in each document show a tolerance or distaste for violence? How is violence justified, and why? How and why is it condemned?

4. How might Gandhi have responded to the Great Revolt of 1857? Would he have sympathized with the rebels' goals? What about their methods for achieving those goals?

The Americas in the Age of Liberalism

1810–1917

During the nineteenth century, rebellions and revolutions overturned long-established patterns of European colonial rule throughout the Americas and in Australia. The newly independent countries focused on nation building and economic development and struggled to establish systems of government and new trade patterns and to address issues of land management, urbanization, and regional and racial differences. Their struggles produced markedly different results. The United States, Canada, and Australia created stable democratic societies, whereas Latin American countries grappled with ongoing political and economic instability. The United States transformed into an industrial power rivaling those of Europe, while Canada and Australia retained their largely agricultural economies. At the same time, social and economic inequality persisted across the Americas, sparking tensions in every nation.

27-1 | Bolívar Identifies the Challenges Latin America Faces

SIMÓN BOLÍVAR, *Jamaica Letter* (1815)

Simón Bolívar (1783–1830), the son of a wealthy colonial family whose ancestors had been in Venezuela since the sixteenth century, was educated in both Enlightenment ideals and military science. He rose to prominence during the 1810s, when American rebels took advantage of Napoleon's occupation of Spain and formed independent states in former Spanish colonies. Despite early revolutionary successes that earned him the title of *El Libertador*, or "the Liberator," Bolívar fled to Jamaica and then Haiti in 1815. Returning to Venezuela with Haitian support the following year, he launched the campaign that would liberate much of Latin

Guillermo A. Sherwell, *Simón Bolívar, El Libertador* (Washington, D.C.: Byron S. Adams, 1921), 89–92.

America from Spanish rule. Bolívar's goals of freedom and equality were compromised in their execution by Latin American political and economic interests, and Bolívar died disenchanted with the "ungovernable" continent. His famous Jamaica Letter outlines his grievances and hopes for American independence.

Europe itself, . . . by reasons of wholesome policies, should have prepared and carried out the plan of American independence, not only because it is so required for the balance of the world, but because this is a legitimate and safe means of obtaining commercial posts on the other side of the ocean. . . .

I consider the actual state of America as when, after the collapse of the Roman Empire, each member constituted a political system in conformity with its interests and position, but with this great difference: that these scattered members reestablished the old nationalities with the alterations required by circumstances or events. But we, who scarcely keep a vestige of things of the past, and who, on the other hand, are not Indians nor Europeans, but a mixture of the legitimate owners of the country and the usurping Spaniards; in short, we, being Americans by birth and with rights equal to those of Europe, have to dispute these rights with the men of the country, and to maintain ourselves against the possession of the invaders. Thus, we find ourselves in the most extraordinary and complicated predicament. . . .

Americans, under the Spanish system now in vigor, have in society no other place than that of serfs fit for work, and, at the most, that of simple consumers; and even this is limited by absurd restrictions, such as prohibition of the cultivation of European products; the monopoly of certain goods in the hands of the king; the prevention of the establishment in America of factories not possessed by Spain; the exclusive privileges of trade, even regarding the necessities of life; the obstacles placed in the way of the American provinces so that they may not deal with each other, nor have understandings, nor trade. In short, do you want to know what was our lot? The fields, in which to cultivate indigo, cochineal,[1] coffee, sugar cane, cocoa, cotton; the solitary plains, to breed cattle; the deserts, to hunt the wild beasts; the bosom of the earth, to extract gold, with which that avaricious country was never satisfied.

We were never viceroys or governors except by very extraordinary reasons; archbishops and bishops, seldom; ambassadors, never; military men, only as subordinates; nobles, without privileges; lastly, we were neither magistrates nor financiers, and hardly merchants. All this we had to accept in direct opposition to our institutions.

The Americans have risen suddenly and without previous preparation and without previous knowledge and, what is more deplorable, without experience in public affairs, to assume in the world the eminent dignity of legislators, magistrates, administrators of the public treasury, diplomats, generals and all the supreme and subordinate authorities which form the hierarchy of an organized state.

---

[1] **cochineal:** An insect from which valuable (and exportable) carmine dye is derived.

The events of the mainland have proved that perfectly representative institutions do not agree with our character, habits, and present state of enlightenment. . . . So long as our fellow citizens do not acquire the talents and the political virtues which distinguish our brothers of the North, who have a system of government altogether popular in character, I am very much afraid these institutions might lead to our ruin instead of aiding us. . . .

I desire more than anybody else to see the formation in America of the greatest nation in the world, not so much as to its extension and wealth as to its glory and freedom.

READING AND DISCUSSION QUESTIONS

1. As Bolívar describes it, what is the advantage of American independence for Europe?

2. How did Europe (especially Spain) treat its American holdings, according to Bolívar?

3. What are the problems that Bolívar predicts for American self-governance? What kind of a system does he propose?

27-2 | War and the Military in American Democracies

ALEXIS DE TOCQUEVILLE, From *Democracy in America* (1840)

French thinker Alexis de Tocqueville (1805–1859) spent much of the early 1800s touring the United States and writing about the uniqueness of the American democratic experiment. His incisive observations revealed the strengths and inherent weaknesses of a political and economic system based on the notion of equality. One area in which democracy seemed to contradict itself was military service and the quest for peace. Tocqueville's comments on this topic were published a decade after the wars for independence in Latin and South America left parts of those regions under military rule and other areas plagued by violence and the need to recruit armies by force.

Book III
Chapter XXII
Why Democratic Nations Naturally Desire Peace, and Democratic Armies, War

The same interests, the same fears, the same passions that deter democratic nations from revolutions deter them also from war; the spirit of military glory and the spirit of revolution are weakened at the same time and by the same causes. The ever increasing numbers of men of property who are lovers of peace,

Alexis de Tocqueville, *Democracy in America*, 3d ed., ed. Francis Bowen, trans. Henry Reeve (Cambridge: Sever and Francis, 1863), 2:326–332.

the growth of personal wealth which war so rapidly consumes, the mildness of manners, the gentleness of heart, those tendencies to pity which are produced by the equality of conditions, that coolness of understanding which renders men comparatively insensible to the violent and poetical excitement of arms, all these causes concur to quench the military spirit. I think it may be admitted as a general and constant rule that among civilized nations the warlike passions will become more rare and less intense in proportion as social conditions are more equal.

War is nevertheless an occurrence to which all nations are subject, democratic nations as well as others. Whatever taste they may have for peace, they must hold themselves in readiness to repel aggression, or, in other words, they must have an army. Fortune, which has conferred so many peculiar benefits upon the inhabitants of the United States, has placed them in the midst of a wilderness, where they have, so to speak, no neighbors; a few thousand soldiers are sufficient for their wants. But this is peculiar to America, not to democracy.

The equality of conditions and the manners as well as the institutions resulting from it do not exempt a democratic people from the necessity of standing armies, and their armies always exercise a powerful influence over their fate. It is therefore of singular importance to inquire what are the natural propensities of the men of whom these armies are composed. . . .

In democratic armies all the soldiers may become officers, which makes the desire of promotion general and immeasurably extends the bounds of military ambition. The officer, on his part, sees nothing that naturally and necessarily stops him at one grade more than at another; and each grade has immense importance in his eyes because his rank in society almost always depends on his rank in the army. Amongst democratic nations it often happens that an officer has no property but his pay and no distinction but that of military honors; consequently, as often as his duties change, his fortune changes and he becomes, as it were, a new man. What was only an appendage to his position in aristocratic armies has thus become the main point, the basis of his whole condition.

Under the old French monarchy officers were always called by their titles of nobility; they are now always called by the title of their military rank. This little change in the forms of language suffices to show that a great revolution has taken place in the constitution of society and in that of the army.

In democratic armies the desire of advancement is almost universal: it is ardent, tenacious, perpetual; it is strengthened by all other desires and extinguished only with life itself. But it is easy to see that, of all armies in the world, those in which advancement must be slowest in time of peace are the armies of democratic countries. As the number of commissions is naturally limited while the number of competitors is almost unlimited, and as the strict law of equality is over all alike, none can make rapid progress; many can make no progress at all. Thus the desire of advancement is greater and the opportunities of advancement fewer there than elsewhere. All the ambitious spirits of a democratic army are consequently ardently desirous of war, because war makes vacancies and warrants the violation of that law of seniority which is the sole privilege natural to democracy.

We thus arrive at this singular consequence, that, of all armies, those most ardently desirous of war are democratic armies, and of all nations, those most fond of peace are democratic nations; and what makes these facts still more extraordinary is that these contrary effects are produced at the same time by the principle of equality.

All the members of the community, being alike, constantly harbor the wish and discover the possibility of changing their condition and improving their welfare; this makes them fond of peace, which is favorable to industry and allows every man to pursue his own little undertakings to their completion. On the other hand, this same equality makes soldiers dream of fields of battle, by increasing the value of military honors in the eyes of those who follow the profession of arms and by rendering those honors accessible to all. In either case the restlessness of the heart is the same, the taste for enjoyment is insatiable, the ambition of success is great; the means of gratifying it alone are different. . . .

Moreover, as amongst democratic nations (to repeat what I have just remarked) the wealthiest, best-educated, and ablest men seldom adopt the military profession, the army, taken collectively, eventually forms a small nation by itself, where the mind is less enlarged and habits are more rude than in the nation at large. Now, this small uncivilized nation has arms in its possession and alone knows how to use them; for, indeed, the pacific temper of the community increases the danger to which a democratic people is exposed from the military and turbulent spirit of the army. Nothing is so dangerous as an army in the midst of an unwarlike nation; the excessive love of the whole community for quiet continually puts the constitution at the mercy of the soldiery.

It may therefore be asserted, generally speaking, that if democratic nations are naturally prone to peace from their interests and their propensities, they are constantly drawn to war and revolutions by their armies. Military revolutions, which are scarcely ever to be apprehended in aristocracies, are always to be dreaded among democratic nations. These perils must be reckoned among the most formidable that beset their future fate, and the attention of statesmen should be sedulously applied to find a remedy for the evil.

When a nation perceives that it is inwardly affected by the restless ambition of its army, the first thought which occurs is to give this inconvenient ambition an object by going to war. I do not wish to speak ill of war: war almost always enlarges the mind of a people and raises their character. In some cases it is the only check to the excessive growth of certain propensities that naturally spring out of the equality of conditions, and it must be considered as a necessary corrective to certain inveterate diseases to which democratic communities are liable.

War has great advantages, but we must not flatter ourselves that it can diminish the danger I have just pointed out. That peril is only suspended by it, to return more fiercely when the war is over; for armies are much more impatient of peace after having tasted military exploits. War could be a remedy only for a people who were always athirst for military glory.

I foresee that all the military rulers who may rise up in great democratic nations will find it easier to conquer with their armies than to make their armies live at peace after conquest. There are two things that a democratic people will always find very difficult, to begin a war and to end it.

Again, if war has some peculiar advantages for democratic nations, on the other hand it exposes them to certain dangers which aristocracies have no cause to dread to an equal extent. I shall point out only two of these.

Although war gratifies the army, it embarrasses and often exasperates that countless multitude of men whose minor passions every day require peace in order to be satisfied. Thus there is some risk of its causing, under another form, the very disturbance it is intended to prevent.

No protracted war can fail to endanger the freedom of a democratic country. Not indeed that after every victory it is to be apprehended that the victorious generals will possess themselves by force of the supreme power, after the manner of Sulla and Caesar;[2] the danger is of another kind. War does not always give over democratic communities to military government, but it must invariably and immeasurably increase the powers of civil government; it must almost compulsorily concentrate the direction of all men and the management of all things in the hands of the administration. If it does not lead to despotism by sudden violence, it prepares men for it more gently by their habits. All those who seek to destroy the liberties of a democratic nation ought to know that war is the surest and the shortest means to accomplish it. This is the first axiom of the science. . . .

The remedy for the vices of the army is not to be found in the army itself, but in the country. Democratic nations are naturally afraid of disturbance and of despotism; the object is to turn these natural instincts into intelligent, deliberate, and lasting tastes. When men have at last learned to make a peaceful and profitable use of freedom and have felt its blessings, when they have conceived a manly love of order and have freely submitted themselves to discipline, these same men, if they follow the profession of arms, bring into it, unconsciously and almost against their will, these same habits and manners. The general spirit of the nation, being infused into the spirit peculiar to the army, tempers the opinions and desires engendered by military life, or represses them by the mighty force of

---

[2] **Sulla and Caesar:** Sulla refers to Lucius Cornelius Sulla, a dictator who claimed power in Rome from 82 to 79 B.C.E.; Caesar is Julius Caesar, dictator of Rome from 45 to 44 B.C.E., when he was murdered by political leaders who feared his growing sense of self-importance.

public opinion. Teach the citizens to be educated, orderly, firm, and free and the soldiers will be disciplined and obedient.

Any law that, in repressing the turbulent spirit of the army, should tend to diminish the spirit of freedom in the nation and to overshadow the notion of law and right would defeat its object; it would do much more to favor than to defeat the establishment of military tyranny. After all, and in spite of all precautions, a large army in the midst of a democratic people will always be a source of great danger. The most effectual means of diminishing that danger would be to reduce the army, but this is a remedy that all nations are not able to apply.

READING AND DISCUSSION QUESTIONS

1. How is military rank determined in democratic countries? What is the effect of this system?

2. According to Tocqueville, the principle of equality inspires different motivations among the soldiers and citizens of a democracy. What are these motivations, and why might they be a source of conflict?

3. Tocqueville says that laws won't keep armies from seeking to wage war. What does he see as the key to a lasting peace?

VIEWPOINTS

Female Abolitionists Make the Case Against Slavery

From the abolitionist movement's beginnings in the eighteenth century, women played important roles in the fight against slavery. Despite discrimination from male abolitionists and social prohibitions against female activism, female abolitionists were in the forefront of the movement, writing antislavery literature, participating in abolitionist organizations, and speaking out against the evils of slavery. For many, participation in the abolitionist movement inspired an equally strong commitment to the cause of women's rights. It is no coincidence that the 1840s saw both the intensification of the struggle over slavery and the organization of the Seneca Falls women's rights convention. This feature includes excerpts from the writings of two of the most important female abolitionists: Angelina Grimke and Harriet Beecher Stowe. As you read them, ask yourself how their antislavery activism might have been shaped by their gender. What differences between Grimke and Stowe do you note in this context?

27-3 | Angelina Grimke Explains the Fundamental Principle of Abolitionism

ANGELINA GRIMKE, *Letters to Catherine E. Beecher* (1838)

Angelina Grimke (1805–1879) was the daughter of a prominent South Carolina slave owner. From a young age, Grimke demonstrated a strong will and the courage of her convictions. Her personal religious journey brought her into contact with antislavery activists, and she joined the movement, leaving her family and moving to Philadelphia in 1829 to pursue her new calling. In 1837, she and her sister Sarah became the first women to conduct a speaking tour on behalf of the American Anti-Slavery Society, scandalizing traditionalists by appearing before mixed-gender audiences. The excerpt included here was written by Grimke in response to a book by Catherine E. Beecher, the daughter of a prominent minister and an opponent of slavery. While Grimke wanted an immediate end to slavery through any means short of violence, Beecher was in favor of gradual emancipation through persuasion and compromise. As you read Grimke's letter, ask yourself why her argument was incompatible with Beecher's approach. What connection can you make between Grimke's position on slavery and her willingness to transgress conventional social mores?

The great fundamental principle of Abolitionists is, that man cannot rightfully hold his fellow man as property. Therefore, we affirm, that *every slaveholder is a man-stealer*. We do so, for the following reasons: to steal a man is to rob him of himself. It matters not whether this be done in Guinea, or Carolina; a man is a *man*, and *as* a man he has *inalienable* rights, among which is the right to personal *liberty*. Now if every man has an *inalienable* right to personal liberty, it follows, that he cannot rightfully be reduced to slavery. But I find in these United States, 2,250,000 men, women and children, robbed of that to which they have an *inalienable* right. How comes this to pass? Where millions are plundered, are there no *plunderers*? If, then, the slaves have been robbed of their liberty, *who* has robbed them? Not the man who stole their forefathers from Africa, but he who now holds them in bondage; no matter *how* they came into his possession, whether he inherited them, or bought them, or seized them at their birth on his own plantation. The only difference I can see between the original man-stealer, who caught the African in his native country, and the American slaveholder, is, that the former committed *one* act of robbery, while the other perpetrates the same crime *continually*. Slaveholding is the perpetrating of acts, all of the same kind, in a *series*, the first of which is technically called man-stealing. The *first* act robbed the man of himself; and the same state of mind that prompted *that act, keeps up the series*, having *taken* his all from him: it *keeps* his all from him, not only *refusing* to *restore*, but still robbing him of all he gets, and as fast as he gets it. Slaveholding, then, is *the constant or habitual perpetration of the act of man-stealing. To make* a slave is *man-stealing—the* act *itself—*to *hold* him such is man-stealing—the *habit*, the

Angelina Grimke, *Letters to Catherine E. Beecher* (Boston: Isaac Knapp, 1838), 4–5.

permanent state, made up of *individual* acts. In other words—to *begin* to hold a slave is man-stealing—to *keep on* holding him is merely a *repetition* of the first act—a doing the same identical thing *all the time*. A series of the same acts continued for a length of time is a *habit*—a *permanent state*. And the *first* of this series of the *same* acts that make up this *habit* or state is just like all the rest.

If every slave has a right to freedom, then surely the man who withholds that right from him to-day is a man-stealer, though he may not be the first person who has robbed him of it. Hence we find that Wesley says—"Men-*buyers* are *exactly on a level* with men-*stealers*." And again—"Much less is it possible that any child of man should ever be *born a slave*." Hear also Jonathan Edwards—"To hold a man in a state of slavery, is to be *every day guilty* of robbing him of his liberty, or of *man-stealing*." And Grotius says—"Those are men-stealers who abduct, *keep*, sell or buy *slaves* or freemen."

READING AND DISCUSSION QUESTIONS

1. According to Grimke, what is the fundamental principle of abolitionism?

2. Why does Grimke make no distinction between slave owners and those who participated in the slave trade?

3. What connections can you make between this letter and Grimke's uncompromising approach to the fight against slavery?

27-4 | A Slave Dealer Explains His Craft

HARRIET BEECHER STOWE, From *Uncle Tom's Cabin* (1852)

The 1852 publication of *Uncle Tom's Cabin* by Harriet Beecher Stowe (1811–1896) was a pivotal event in the American abolitionist movement. An instant success, the novel appealed to the sentimentalism of the mid-nineteenth-century reading public, humanizing the issue of slavery for many Northerners by presenting readers with sympathetic slave characters and then placing those characters in emotionally charged circumstances. The opening scene of the novel provides a good example of Stowe's approach. In it, Mr. Shelby, a slave owner, and Mr. Haley, a slave trader, negotiate the possible sale of a young boy and his mother. The boy, Harry, is innocent and charming; the mother, Eliza, beautiful, sincere, and virtuous. As the scene develops, an implicit contrast is created between the absence of feeling displayed by the slave trader and the depth of emotion the reader imagines the mother and child will experience if their parting comes to pass. As you read this excerpt, place yourself in the position of a nineteenth-century reader. How might such a reader have responded to the scene? Why?

Harriet Beecher Stowe, *Uncle Tom's Cabin* (London: John Cassell, 1852), 3–5.

"Hurrah! bravo! what a young 'un!" said Haley; "that chap's a case, I'll promise. Tell you what," said he, suddenly clapping his hand on Mr. Shelby's shoulder, "fling in that chap, and I'll settle the business—I will. Come, now, if that ain't doing the thing up about the rightest."

At this moment, the door was pushed gently open, and a young quadroon woman, apparently about twenty-five, entered the room.

There needed only a glance from the child to her, to identify her as its mother. There was the same rich, full, dark eye, with its long lashes; the same ripples of silky black hair. The brown of her complexion gave way on the cheek to a perceptible flush, which deepened as she saw the gaze of the strange man fixed upon her in bold and undisguised admiration. Her dress was of the neatest possible fit, and set off to advantage her finely-molded shape. A delicately formed hand, and a trim foot and ankle, were items of appearance that did not escape the quick eye of the trader, well used to run up at a glance the points of a fine female article.

"Well, Eliza?" said her master, as she stopped and looked hesitatingly at him.

"I was looking for Harry, please, sir;" and the boy bounded toward her, showing his spoils, which he had gathered in the skirt of his robe.

"Well, take him away, then," said Mr. Shelby; and hastily she withdrew, carrying the child on her arm.

"By Jupiter!" said the trader, turning to him in admiration, "there's an article now! You might make your fortune on that ar gal in Orleans, any day. I've seen over a thousand, in my day, paid down for gals not a bit handsomer."

"I don't want to make my fortune on her," said Mr. Shelby, drily; and, seeking to turn the conversation, he uncorked a bottle of fresh wine, and asked his companion's opinion of it.

"Capital, sir—first chop!" said the trader; then turning, and slapping his hand familiarly on Shelby's shoulder, he added: "Come, how will you trade about the gal? what shall I say for her? what 'll you take?"

"Mr. Haley, she is not to be sold," said Shelby; "my wife would not part with her for her weight in gold."

"Ay, ay, women always say such things, 'cause they ha'nt no sort of calculation. Just show 'em how many watches, feathers, and trinkets one's weight in gold would buy, and that alters the case, I reckon."

"I tell you, Haley, this must not be spoken of. I say no, and I mean no," said Shelby, decidedly.

"Well, you'll let me have the boy though?" said the trader; "you must own I've come down pretty handsomely for him."

"What on earth can you want with the child?" said Shelby.

"Why, I've got a friend that's going into this yer branch of the business— wants to buy up handsome boys to raise for the market. Fancy articles entirely— sell for waiters, and so on, to rich 'uns, that can pay for handsome 'uns. It sets off one of yer great places—a real handsome boy to open door, wait, and tend. They fetch a good sum; and this little devil is such a comical, musical concern, he's just the article."

"I would rather not sell him," said Mr. Shelby, thoughtfully; "the fact is, sir, I'm a humane man, and I hate to take the boy from his mother, sir."

"Oh, you do?—La! yes—something of that ar nature. I understand, perfectly. It is mighty onpleasant getting on with women sometimes. I al'ays hates these yer screechin,' screamin' times. They are *mighty* onpleasant; but, as I manages business, I generally avoids 'em, sir. Now, what if you get the girl off for a day, or a week, or so; then the thing's done quietly,—all over before she comes home. Your wife might get her some ear-rings, or a new gown, or some such truck, to make up with her."

"I'm afraid not."

"Lor bless ye, yes! These critters an't like white folks, you know; they gets over things, only manage right. Now, they say," said Haley, assuming a candid and confidential air, "that this kind o' trade is hardening to the feelings; but I never found it so. Fact is, I never could do things up the way some fellers manage the business. I've seen 'em as would pull a woman's child out of her arms, and set him up to sell, and she screechin' like mad all the time;—very bad policy—damages the article—makes 'em quite unfit for service sometimes. I knew a real handsome gal once, in Orleans, as was entirely ruined by this sort o' handling. The fellow that was trading for her didn't want her baby; and she was one of your real high sort, when her blood was up. I tell you, she squeezed up her child in her arms, and talked, and went on real awful. It kinder makes my blood run cold to think on't; and when they carried off the child, and locked her up, she jest went ravin' mad, and died in a week. Clear waste, sir, of a thousand dollars, just for want of management,—there's where 't is. It's always best to do the humane thing, sir; that's been *my* experience."

And the trader leaned back in his chair, and folded his arm, with an air of virtuous decision, apparently considering himself a second Wilberforce.[3]

The subject appeared to interest the gentleman deeply; for while Mr. Shelby was thoughtfully peeling an orange, Haley broke out afresh, with becoming diffidence, but as if actually driven by the force of truth to say a few words more.

"It don't look well, now, for a feller to be praisin' himself; but I say it jest because it's the truth. I believe I'm reckoned to bring in about the finest droves of niggers that is brought in—at least I've been told so; if I have once, I reckon I have a hundred times—all in good case—fat and likely, and I lose as few as any man in the business. And I lays it all to my management, sir; and humanity, sir, I may say, is the great pillar of *my* management."

Mr. Shelby did not know what to say, and so he said, "Indeed!"

"Now, I've been laughed at for my notions, sir, and I've been talked to. They an't pop'lar, and they an't common; but I stuck to 'em, sir; I've stuck to 'em, and

---

[3] **Wilberforce:** William Wilberforce (1759–1833), British politician and antislavery activist.

realized well on 'em; yes, sir, they have paid their passage, I may say"; and the trader laughed at his joke.

There was something so piquant and original in these elucidations of humanity, that Mr. Shelby could not help laughing in company. Perhaps you laugh too, dear reader; but you know humanity comes out in a variety of strange forms now-a-days, and there is no end to the odd things that humane people will say and do.

READING AND DISCUSSION QUESTIONS

1. What does the scene suggest about Eliza's morals? How does her reaction to Mr. Haley's evident lust help establish her as a sympathetic character?

2. What importance should we attach to Mr. Shelby's references to his wife's opposition to the sale of the family's slaves? What do these references suggest about Stowe's views on the moral and emotional differences between men and women?

3. How would you explain the popularity of *Uncle Tom's Cabin*? Why might a nineteenth-century audience have found it so moving and persuasive?

VIEWPOINTS COMPARATIVE QUESTIONS

1. Compare and contrast Grimke's and Stowe's arguments against slavery. How might each have responded to the other's work?

2. How did each author appeal to the basic assumptions and beliefs of their audience? How did they seek to change those assumptions and beliefs?

27-5 | Expansion and Economic Development in Canada
Advertisement for Rail Travel to Canada (1900)

In 1885, the Canadian Pacific Railway Company completed the first Canadian transcontinental railroad. The company was formed in 1881, in part to address the political scandals associated with lucrative rail contracts and to emphasize an all-Canada railroad. However, other railroad companies such as the St. Paul, Minneapolis and Manitoba Railway continued to build and maintain their own lines, many of which took advantage of established U.S. routes. This advertisement shows not only how Canadian railroads sought to attract "customers" from Canada and abroad to populate the huge tracts of land awarded to railroad companies, but also the international nature of Canadian railroad development. As you examine the advertisement, think about the role railroads played in facilitating Canada's westward expansion.

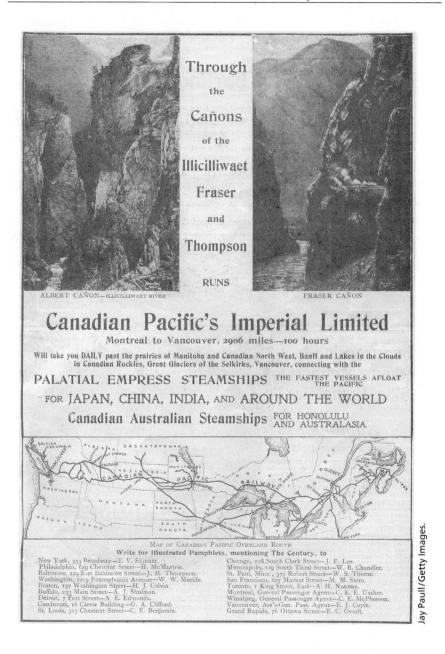

READING AND DISCUSSION QUESTIONS

1. To whom is the advertisement designed to appeal? What sort of person was the railroad expecting to make the journey west?

2. Why were the railroads crucial to the economic viability of the western provinces? Besides transporting settlers west, what other services did they provide?

■ COMPARATIVE QUESTIONS ■

1. How might de Tocqueville have analyzed the upheaval of nation building as it is presented in Bolívar's Jamaica Letter?

2. What light do the documents in this chapter shed on the persistence of economic inequality in the Americas? Which groups were in the best position to benefit from the opportunities the Americas presented? Which were in the worst position?

3. Compare and contrast Harriet Beecher Stowe's account of slavery with that of Olaudah Equiano (see Document 20-4). What techniques of persuasion did both authors employ?

4. How might Stowe and Grimke have responded to Anna Maria Falconbridge's description of life on board a slave ship (see Document 20-3)? What fault might they have found with her characterization of slavery, slaves, and slave owners?

World War and Revolution
1914–1929

World War I (1914–1918) changed the global balance of economic, military, and political power. Though the conflict started as a dispute between two small eastern European nations over a political assassination, a web of national alliances and long-suppressed hostilities over lost territory helped escalate it into four years of war that involved most major countries. The "Great War" led to a rise in Asian nationalism; the decline of Great Britain, France, and Germany as world powers and the ascent of the United States as a global force. People everywhere seized opportunities created by the war to effect change, and Russia was transformed by a social revolution at home. At the end of the war, the victors redrew the world map.

28-1 | Life at Home and on the Battlefield
Correspondence of Evelyn and Fred Albright (1917)

Even for the millions of civilians fortunate enough to live far from the front lines, the First World War presented dramatic interruptions to daily life at home. The correspondence of Evelyn and Fred Albright, two Canadian citizens, spanned the years from 1910 through 1917 and included over 550 letters. Fred, a lawyer, enlisted in 1916 and was sent to England for training in 1917. He shared vivid details of his overseas posting in letters to his wife. In letters back to her husband, Evelyn chronicled the challenges and triumphs of her life at home, including her work at Fred's law office. These excerpts show how the war touched lives far from Europe, capturing not only the Albrights' individual experiences but also their great love and, following Fred's death at the Second Battle of Passchendaele, Belgium, in late October 1917, Evelyn's grief.

An Echo in My Heart: The Letters of Elnora Evelyn (Kelly) Albright and Frederick Stanley Albright, comp. and ed. Lorna Brooks. www.echoinmyheart.ca. Letters and material pertaining to the Albright Collection are housed in The Archives and Research Collections Centre, Western University, London, ON, Canada.

Fred to Evelyn

France
Mon evening,
Oct. 1 1917

My darling wife,—

It is one of those beautiful clear evenings which have been our almost invariable portion since coming here. By daylight saving time, which still prevails with the army in France, it is 6.30 and a soft twilight haze has followed the setting of the sun. I went outside and stretched myself out on the bank, when before I started to write, I heard the distant hum of a German airplane and immediately after came the order "Get under cover," so we all hurried to our dugouts and now I am sitting at the entrance to the dugout which has been my home for the past 4 days and which we are leaving tonight for a while back of the lines.

We don't rush to cover from airplanes because of danger but because the aircraft are out for reconnaissance and the least movement on the ground is discernable. Naturally we don't want Heine[1] to know what positions we occupy. Of course he knows this and where most of the other trenches now held by us are, both because he can see them and because a large number of them were once occupied by him. But such matters are employed to conceal the guns, dispositions of troops etc. that Fritz[2] doesn't know where our strong points are, so on every available opportunity he sends over his airplanes for observation purposes, just as we do over Fritz's lines.

Later.

Since writing the above we had to put on our equipment and stand to, ready to move out. But as we have a wait of no one knows how long, I am back in the dugout writing by candle light. One has to snatch such odd moments if he would write at all. I haven't written any since last Friday. . . .

I haven't had any parcels from you since about a week prior to leaving Eng. I find that papers & boxes are sent up to the front line trenches however, when possible. Several of the fellows got parcels today. It really is wonderful to think that daily mail can be delivered even to the front line trenches. Yes—and hot tea and occasionally boiled rice or potatoes.

The grub here is remarkably good and there is no stint. Every night ration parties go out for the grub to the head of a narrow gauge railway about a mile away. Drinking water has to be carried rather farther. In some places it is almost impossible to get water for washing purposes at all but here we are unusually fortunate in having right at hand a spring well at the bottom of what Fritz had intended for a dugout before the water appeared.

---

[1] **Heine:** Slang for German.
[2] **Fritz:** Slang for German.

Wed. evening, Oct 3/17

Once again my abode has changed. On Monday night we came out of the line and while the battalion is still considered as being in support we are back 4 or 5 miles—quite beyond the range of all but the largest guns—and they rarely put a shell over this way except when firing at one of our captive balloons so we feel absolutely safe here.

Though freer from danger this place is in many respects less desirable than the line. There the grub is of the best & unstinted. Here we have a piece of bread a slice of bacon & tea for breakfast. Bully beef, bread jam & cheese for dinner & mulligan bread & tea for supper. There the quarters were much more commodious & comfortable. . . . The dugout from which I last wrote was about from 4 to 5 feet in height. The ceiling & walls were all carefully timbered and planked by Fritz and it was dry & quite comfortable. Of course there were lice—they are everywhere here—but they didn't trouble much. Most of the boys have already been attacked but as far as I know I am still free.

There were a few rats which we could plainly hear in the walls & ceiling but I never saw any inside. As for our present abode it is more a hut than a dugout for it is not really underground. Made of sandbags with a roof of loose sheets of corrugated iron it is situated on the side of a steep slope facing west. The floor is of chalk clay.

Rat holes in the sand bags abound and the rodents themselves can be seen scurrying all around at any time of day or night. The night before last when I was up for a visit to the latrine I saw 2 of the night cooks out on a rat hunting expedition. One wouldn't so much mind them outside, but when they play hide and seek around and over you while you are sleeping, and even nibble at one's toes, as they did the other night to the serj. maj. [sergeant major], they may truly be considered a pest.

Monday night I left a little bread & cheese in my mess tin for morning and as a result there are now 2 holes in the canvas cover and 2 distinct dents in the tin itself where Mr. Rat's teeth endeavored to punch a hole through the metal.

As for the mansion(?) itself—it is of such dimensions that when McKenzie, Edwards & I are in at night we have to put our packs & equipment outside. During the day we reverse the process. In plain figures, its inside dimensions are nearly 5' 10" long, 4½' wide & 3½' high—quite a snug little apartment for 3. Of course we sleep with our clothes on. We use our greatcoats for bedding, and the first night we each had a blanket over us but yesterday while we were out on a working party someone relieved us of 2 and now we have only 1 blanket for the 3 of us.

Fortunately the weather is mild, although the air becomes quite chilly before morning. However I always sleep warm. I haven't slept with my clothes off—I mean my outer clothes for 10 days. When we were in the line, of course we had to keep our puttees & boots on and wear our box respirators—and were supposed to keep all equipment on. In the front line everything is worn but in the support line where I was most of the fellows slept with their equipment off.

. . . I told you the night before we left the line we got back here about 3 a.m. had something to eat & got to bed about 3.30. Then 15 of us—among whom were McK. [McKenzie], Edwards & I had to get up at 6, breakfast at 6.30 & start at 7 on a working party. We marched back to within a mile of where we had been in the line—our work was under cover & needless to say we didn't work very hard. About 3.30 we quit & marched back—arriving here about 5.30. After supper I had a rub bath, & a shave and by the time I read your letter, & one from Don [Albright], I was ready for bed. Today we were on the same work and the same place.

It takes us about 2 hours each way going and coming, & the marching is all in trenches which wind and twist and turn. Nearly all the way the bottom is covered with trench matting—ie—a walk about 2 feet wide made of small slots laid crosswise on 2" x 4" scantling. This is a great boon in wet weather but makes hard walking in dry weather.

We have just been warned for the same working party tomorrow for which I am very glad. If we didn't go on the day party we'd be on a night one, and its nicer to work in the day and have the night for sleep. Don't worry about me darling. Though my time is full and I sometimes get tired, I'm hard as nails and never felt in better health in my life. I'm never too tired to sleep or rest and I'm sure I can hold up my end with the best of them.

Do you remember Mr. Lucas who was in the 191 & was with me at Sarcee? His son was killed last Thursday night. I wish you would see or phone Mrs. Lucas and assure her that her boy didn't suffer. He was killed instantaneously by a big shell which killed 1 other and wounded 2. This was the first night we were in the line. McKenzie helped to carry him out and he is buried near here in a little cemetery where the 50th now inter all their dead. If I get time I'll write the Lucases a short letter. Anyhow I know they would appreciate your telling them what I have just written.

Oh my darling, I am so glad you have been feeling better, and that you had a good visit at Beamsville. The other fellows have come in now and we must turn in so goodnight my own darling wife.

Your Ferd.[3]

Evelyn to Fred

Calgary,
Nov. 11 1917

Dearest Ferd:—

One year ago to-day was the Sunday when the gas was off. That was a memorable day, wasn't it? And to-day was so warm that I didn't even wear my little fur around my neck, much less carry my muff.

---

[3] **Ferd:** Fred's pet name, often used in their correspondence.

I took David to church this morning and Mr. and Mrs. Peters kindly brought us home. David kicked up a row, but I did not tell his parents as they would have felt very much humiliated, and I'm not sure that a spanking would have done him any good. I gave him a good talking to tonight when he was in bed. He needs a *very* firm hand, and he's just at a very saucy age.

Mr. Dagleish preached this morning about the halo on common things. It was a good enough sermon, freely interspersed with quotations from the poets, Ruskin, etc. I wonder why that stuff seems so academic to me now, whereas it used to appeal to me very much. The church was very well filled this morning and the music was good. Wilfred gave an Organ Recital yesterday afternoon, which I did not attend, but if he keeps them up all winter I hope to go often. . . .

Last night, in the night I woke up, and an utterable longing for you swept over me, and so dearest, I prayed for you, and then I went to sleep again. I had just received your letter telling me you were reading the 46th Psalm, the night we read the bad Russian news, and I read it and felt comforted. . . .

There are some things I'd like to tell Wray, yet I do not want to preach at him, and I can't say some of them without making him think we were discussing him at Beamsville, which as you very well know we were, so I had better keep my mouth shut.

Well dearie, I'll have a birthday this week. How funny you should think it was in October. . . .

Mr. Clarke told Miss Playter she was to get $40 after she had been there two months, the same as they gave me, but I was there 5 months before they gave me $40. And if she gets $40, then why shouldn't I get what Fitch, Roy and Bryenton have been getting? You don't think me mercenary, do you dear? Of course, I know I'm not worth very much to the office just now, but that's not my fault; I'll work if I get it to do.

I had a good story to tell you, but I've forgotten what it was. Maybe I'll remember it to tell you tomorrow. Goodnight dearest. I'm going up to get in bed now, and I'll write to my parents there. You seem far away tonight dearest. I wonder why. You are ever uppermost in my thoughts.

Your wife.

Evelyn to Fred, After His Death in Late October

Taber, Alta
Nov. 23, 1917

Dearest: —

It is not yet two weeks since I wrote my last letter to you, not two weeks since I read that awful telegram that told me you were gone from me.

I suppose it seems silly for me to write to you, but if you know, you'll understand, and nobody else need know. But it has come to me that time might dim your image and the knowledge of your dear companionship, and I cannot bear to think of that. Then too, my darling, oh my darling, I sometimes cannot believe that you are gone, and I go on pretending as I have ever since you went away last March, that you were coming home again. And if you should—why then you'd be glad of a link between the times. It is so easy, sweetheart, to lose myself in dreaming, for whenever hard unpleasant things have come, I have always made believe things were as I would have them. But in this case, the coming back to Earth is hard.

I think it has been like this, sweetheart. I could not, would not face the thought that you would not come back: I interpreted those psalms we read together, as meaning that you would be kept safe from accident, danger and death. When I knew that you were in the thick of things, I went calmly to sleep at night, believing that you were in God's hands and that He would keep you safe, for I could not, and do not yet believe that it is His will that any of you should fall. Some of the time, while I so calmly slept and went about my work, you were lying dead Dead! Oh my darling, as I have so often called you—the light of my life.

I have thought of late dear one, that I did not fully realize what it meant to you to go. I was so filled with my own grief, with the thought of my loneliness, and with the dread of what you would have to face, that I did not fully realize what it meant to you to give up all you did and to leave me, fearing that you might never come back. You have always said I wrote cheerful letters; I am glad if you thought they were, for I tried to make them so for you had enough to bear, without me making your lot harder.

The woman is coming up to sweep, so I'll stop. But my dear one, it almost seems as if you'll read this some day. Or is it that you are reading it over my shoulder as I write? In any case, you know I adore you, my sweetheart and my friend. Oh darling, I shall try to live on cheerfully and well, but it seems that I am like a tree, half killed my [sic] lightning. Such a tree, I suppose is not expected to give the shade of a whole one—but the question always comes, why should it have been marred and blighted? Do you know now?

Your wife, for wherever you are, my darling, I shall always be that.

READING AND DISCUSSION QUESTIONS

1. From the tone of their letters, how frequent do you imagine contact was between Fred and Evelyn? How might the frequency of contact affect the war experiences of those at the front and those at home?

2. What does the correspondence reveal about Evelyn's life without her husband? What had changed, and how had she adjusted to her new circumstances?

3. What is the role of religion in these letters? When is it mentioned, and how?

28-2 | War Brings Revolution to Russia

VLADIMIR ILYICH LENIN, *All Power to the Soviets!* (1917)

Vladimir Ilyich Ulyanov (1870–1924), better known by his nom de guerre Lenin, was a central intellectual and political force behind the uprisings that made up the Russian Revolution (1905–1917). Following years of exile and a triumphant return to Russia with the assistance of the German government, Lenin capitalized on the fall of the tsar by pushing for further revolution under the guidance of his Bolshevik faction of what would become the Russian Communist Party. In the months leading to the October 1917 revolution and Bolshevik power, Lenin took control of the popular newspaper *Pravda* (*Truth*) and used its editorial pages to powerful effect. The speech reproduced here demonstrates both the political infighting that marked the Russian Revolution and Lenin's relentless use of propaganda to outmaneuver his opponents.

"Drive nature out of the door and she will rush back through the window." It seems that the Socialist-Revolutionary and Menshevik parties[4] have to "learn" this simple truth time and again by their own experience. They under took to be "revolutionary democrats" and found themselves in the shoes of revolutionary democrats — they are now forced to draw the conclusions which every revolutionary democrat must draw.

Democracy is the rule of the majority. As long as the will of the majority was not clear, as long as it was possible to make it out to be unclear, at least with a grain of plausibility, the people were offered a counter-revolutionary bourgeois government disguised as "democratic." But this delay could not last long. During the several months that have passed since February 27[5] the will of the majority of the workers and peasants, of the overwhelming majority of the country's population, has become clear in more than a general sense. Their will has found expression in mass organizations — the Soviets of Workers', Soldiers' and Peasants' Deputies.

How, then, can anyone oppose the transfer of all power in the state to the Soviets? Such opposition means nothing but renouncing democracy! It means no

---

"All Power to the Soviets!" *Pravda*, no. 99 (July 18, 1917). Republished in *Lenin Collected Works*, 45 vols. (Moscow: Progress, 1977), 25:155–156.

[4] **Socialist-Revolutionary and Menshevik parties:** Russian political factions during the Russian Revolutions. The Mensheviks, with the Bolsheviks, made up the Russian Marxist Party; the Mensheviks were more inclusive and favored more compromise than did their Bolshevik counterparts. They were banned by the Bolsheviks in 1921. The Socialist-Revolutionary Party emphasized rural peasants more than either wing of the Russian Marxists did; despite success at the polls, they were outmaneuvered by the Bolsheviks and largely dissolved.

[5] **February 27:** This date marked the initial revolution that toppled the Russian tsar and brought the Provisional Government to power.

more no less than imposing on the people a government which *admittedly* can neither come into being nor hold its ground *democratically*, i.e., as a result of truly free, truly popular elections.

It is a fact, strange as it may seem at first sight, that the Socialist-Revolutionaries and Mensheviks have *forgotten* this perfectly simple, perfectly obvious and palpable truth. Their position is so false, and they are so badly confused and bewildered, that they are unable to "recover" this truth they have lost. Following the elections in Petrograd[6] and in Moscow, the convocation of the All-Russia Peasant Congress, and the Congress of Soviets,[7] the classes and parties throughout Russia have shown what they stand for so clearly and specifically that people who have not gone mad or deliberately got themselves into a mess simply cannot have any illusions on this score.

To tolerate the Cadet Ministers or the Cadet government or Cadet policies[8] means challenging democrats and democracy. This is the source of the political crises since February 27, and this also the source of the shakiness and vacillation of our government system. At every turn, daily and even hourly, appeals are being made to the people's revolutionary spirit and to their democracy on behalf of the most authoritative government institutions and congresses. Yet the government's policies in particular, are all departures from revolutionary principles, and breaches in democracy.

This sort of thing will not do.

It is inevitable that a situation like the present should show elements of instability now for one reason, now for another. And it is not exactly a clever policy of jib. Things are moving by fits and starts towards a point where power will be transferred to the Soviets, which is what our Party called for long ago.

READING AND DISCUSSION QUESTIONS

1. What is the main point of Lenin's speech, and how does he argue his point?

2. According to Lenin, who opposes his call for the transfer of power to the Soviets?

3. How does Lenin characterize those who are not directly in line with his thinking? To what end?

---

[6] **Petrograd:** Later Leningrad, and now St. Petersburg.

[7] **All-Russia Peasant Congress . . . Congress of Soviets:** Meetings in 1918 that codified and strengthened Bolshevik control of the Russian government.

[8] **Cadet Ministers . . . Cadet policies:** Members of the Constitutional Democratic (Konstitutionnaya Demokraticheskaya) Party prominent in the Provisional Government.

Competing Perspectives on the Treaty of Versailles

The peace conference that convened in Paris in 1919 was contentious from the start. Even among the victorious Allies, there was no consensus about the shape of the postwar world and thus no consensus on the terms of peace. France, Britain, and the United States each had its own agenda and its own expectations. President Woodrow Wilson's vision of a permanent peace seemed to many in France to be a recipe for French isolation and decline. Britain was more interested in strengthening its grip on its overseas empire than it was in the problems of France or the implementation of Wilson's lofty principles. Delegates from Asia, Africa, and the Middle East came to the conference hoping to share in Wilson's promise of self-determination, only to discover that, even before the war had ended, France and Britain had entered into secret agreements designed to perpetuate the imperialist system. Finally, Germany was forced to sit on the sidelines while the Allies reached compromises at its expense, ultimately producing a punitive treaty meant to prevent Germany from ever rejoining the ranks of the great powers.

28-3 | France, Britain, and the United States Remake the World

Les Trois Grands Ouvriers du Monde Nouveau (February 1, 1919)

This image, which appeared on the cover of a French magazine in early 1919, highlights a fundamental truth about the Paris Peace Conference. For all the talk about world peace and the need to include all nations in the negotiations, France, Britain, and the United States dominated the conference. They were "the three great creators of the new world," and it was their needs, ambitions, and fears that would determine the shape of that world. The image also reveals something of the tensions that existed between the Allies from the start, with the three Allied leaders appearing as anything but trusting friends. As you examine the image, consider what it reveals about French public opinion as the peace conference got under way. What hopes and fears does the image reveal?

READING AND DISCUSSION QUESTIONS

1. How did the artist characterize Georges Clemenceau of France (center), Lloyd George of Great Britain (left), and Woodrow Wilson (right)? What was the depiction of each leader meant to suggest about his agenda for the peace talks?

2. Which leader seems most confident? Which the least confident? Why?

28-4 | Germany Protests the Terms of Peace

GERMAN DELEGATION TO THE PARIS PEACE CONFERENCE, *On the Conditions of Peace* (October 1919)

The Treaty of Versailles, signed at the 1919 Paris Peace Conference, formally brought World War I to an end and set the conditions for peace. Orchestrated by the Allied powers—the United States, Great Britain, and France—the treaty blamed the war on Germany and ordered it to pay $33 billion in reparations, cede all of its colonies, dismantle its air force, and greatly reduce other military operations. It also established the League of Nations as an international peacekeeping organization. Russia did not attend the conference, and Germany—the nation most impacted by the treaty—was not permitted to contribute to the negotiations. Fearing invasion, Germany ultimately signed the treaty despite continued protests.

Although President Wilson, in his speech of October 20th, 1916, has acknowledged that "no single fact caused the war, but that in the last analysis the whole European system is in a deeper sense responsible for the war, with its combination of alliances and understandings, a complicated texture of intrigues and espionage that unfailingly caught the whole family of nations in its meshes," . . . Germany is to acknowledge that Germany and her allies are responsible for all damages which the enemy Governments or their subjects have incurred by her and her allies' aggression. . . . Apart from the consideration that there is no incontestable legal foundation for the obligation for reparation imposed upon Germany, the amount of such compensation[9] is to be determined by a commission nominated solely by Germany's enemies, Germany taking no part. . . . The commission is plainly to have power to administer Germany like the estate of a bankrupt.

As there are innate rights of man, so there are innate rights of nations. The inalienable fundamental right of every state is the right of self-preservation and self-determination. With this fundamental right the demand here made upon Germany is incompatible. Germany must promise to pay an indemnity, the amount of which at present is not even stated. The German rivers are to be placed under the control of an international body upon which Germany's delegates are always to be but the smallest minority. Canals and railroads are to be built on German territory at the discretion of foreign authorities.

These few instances show that that is not the just peace we were promised, not the peace "the very principle of which," according to a word of President Wilson, "is equality and the common participation in a common benefit. . . ."

"Comments of the German Delegation to the Paris Peace Conference on the Conditions of Peace, Oct., 1919," in *International Conciliation*, no. 143 (October 1919).

    [9] **amount of such compensation:** A reparations commission appointed by the Peace Conference determined the final sum to be $33 billion in 1921.

In such a peace the solidarity of human interests, which was to find its expression in a League of Nations, would have been respected. How often Germany has been given the promise that this League of Nations would unite the belligerents, conquerors as well as conquered, in a permanent system of common rights! . . .

But in contradiction to them, the Covenant of the League of Nations has been framed without the cooperation of Germany. Nay, still more. Germany does not even stand on the list of those States that have been invited to join the League of Nations. . . . What the treaty of peace proposes to establish, is rather a continuance of the present hostile coalition which does not deserve the name of "League of Nations." . . . The old political system based on force and with its tricks and rivalries will thus continue to thrive!

Again and again the enemies of Germany have assured the whole world that they did not aim at the destruction of Germany. . . .

In contradiction to this, the peace document shows that Germany's position as a world power is to be utterly destroyed. The Germans abroad are deprived of the possibility of keeping up their old relations in foreign countries and of regaining for Germany a share in world commerce, while their property, which has up to the present been confiscated and liquidated, is being used for reparation instead of being restored to them. . . .

In this war, a new fundamental law has arisen which the statesmen of all belligerent peoples have again and again acknowledged to be their aim: the right of self-determination. To make it possible for all nations to put this privilege into practice was intended to be one achievement of the war. . . .

Neither the treatment described above of the inhabitants of the Saar region[10] as accessories to the [coal] pits nor the public form of consulting the population in the districts of Eupen, Malmédy, and Prussian Moresnet[11] — which, moreover, shall not take place before they have been put under Belgian sovereignty — comply in the least with such a solemn recognition of the right of self-determination.

The same is also true with regard to Alsace-Lorraine. If Germany has pledged herself "to right the wrong of 1871," this does not mean any renunciation of the right of self-determination of the inhabitants of Alsace-Lorraine. A cession of the country without consulting the population would be a new wrong, if for no other reason, because it would be inconsistent with a recognized principle of peace.

On the other hand, it is incompatible with the idea of national self-determination for two and one-half million Germans to be torn away from their native land against their own will. By the proposed demarcation of the boundary,

---

[10] **inhabitants of the Saar region:** After fifteen years, Saar inhabitants would vote in a plebiscite to decide if they would stay under the administration of a League of Nations commission or become part of France or Germany. In 1935, they voted to join Germany.

[11] **Prussian Moresnet:** Moresnet was annexed outright by Belgium. In Eupen and Malmédy, those who objected to transferring the areas to Belgium could sign their names in a public registry. Both areas became Belgian.

unmistakably German territories are disposed of in favor of their Polish neighbors. Thus, from the Central Silesian districts of Guhrau and Militsch certain portions are to be wrenched away, in which, beside 44,900 Germans, reside at the utmost 3,700 Poles. . . .

This disrespect of the right of self-determination is shown most grossly in the fact that Danzig[12] is to be separated from the German Empire and made a free state. Neither historical rights nor the present ethnographical conditions of ownership of the Polish people can have any weight as compared with the German past and the German character of that city. . . . Likewise the cession of the commercial town of Memel, which is to be exacted from Germany, is in no way consistent with the right of self-determination. The same may be said with reference to the fact that millions of Germans in German-Austria are to be denied the union with Germany which they desire and that, further, millions of Germans dwelling along our frontiers are to be forced to remain part of the newly created Czecho-Slovakian State.

Even as regards that part of the national territory that is to be left to Germany, the promised right of self-determination is not observed. A Commission for the execution of the indemnity shall be the highest instance for the whole State. Our enemies claim to have fought for the great aim of the democratization of Germany. To be sure, the outcome of the war has delivered us from our former authorities, but instead of them we shall have in exchange a foreign, dictatorial power whose aim can and must be only to exploit the working power of the German people for the benefit of the creditor states.[13] . . .

The fact that this is an age in which economic relations are on a world scale, requires the political organization of the civilized world. The German Government agrees with the Governments of the Allied and Associated Powers in the conviction that the horrible devastation caused by this war requires the establishment of a new world order, an order which shall insure the "effective authority of the principles of international law," and "just and honorable relations between the nations." . . .

There is no evidence of these principles in the peace document which has been laid before us. Expiring world theories, emanating from imperialistic and capitalistic tendencies, celebrate in it their last horrible triumph. As opposed to these views, which have brought unspeakable disaster upon the world, we appeal to the innate sense of right of men and nations, under whose token the English State developed, the Dutch People freed itself, the North American nation established its independence, France shook off absolutism. The bearers of such hallowed traditions cannot deny this right to the German people, that now for the first time has acquired in its internal polities the possibility of living in harmony with its free will based on law.

---

[12] **Danzig:** Danzig was administered by the League of Nations.

[13] **Commission for the execution . . . states:** After the Germans fell behind in their payments in 1923, the French-controlled reparations commission sent French, Belgian, and Italian technicians into Germany's Ruhr region to collect coal to make up for the delinquent payments.

READING AND DISCUSSION QUESTIONS

1. What does the German delegation say is the real cause of the war?

2. What does the delegation mean when it invokes the "innate rights of nations"?

3. How does the peace proposed by the treaty differ from that which Germany expected and says it was promised, particularly by Wilson?

4. According to the Germans, in what ways does the treaty violate the right of self-determination?

28-5 | War and Peace from a Japanese Perspective

KONOE FUMIMARO, *Against a Pacifism Centered on England and America* (1918)

Konoe Fumimaro (1891–1945) held a range of political and diplomatic positions in modern Japan, including three terms as prime minister. As a member of the delegation to the Paris Peace Conference in 1918, Konoe argued for the inclusion of a "racial equality clause" in the charter of the League of Nations, a proposal that won majority support but was defeated through lack of support from Woodrow Wilson and active opposition from member states of the British Empire, such as Australia. Konoe's outspoken argument here, written before his departure for the Paris conference, foreshadows Japanese nationalist rhetoric against Anglo-British power during the Second World War.

In my view, the European war has been a conflict between established powers and powers not yet established, a conflict between countries that found upholding the status quo convenient and countries that found overthrowing the status quo convenient. The countries that found upholding the status quo convenient clamored for peace, while the countries that found overthrowing the status quo convenient cried out for war. Pacifism does not always serve justice and humanism, and militarism does not always violate justice and humanism. All depends on the nature of the status quo. If the prewar status quo was the best possible and was consonant with justice and humanism, he who would destroy it is the enemy of justice and humanism; but if the status quo did not meet the criteria of justice and humanism, its destroyer is not necessarily the enemy of justice and humanism. By the same token, the pacifist countries that would uphold this status quo are not necessarily qualified to pride themselves on being the champions of justice and humanity.

Although England and America may have regarded Europe's prewar status as ideal, an impartial third party cannot acknowledge it to have been ideal in terms of justice and humanism. As the colonial history of England and France

William Theodore de Bary, Carol Gluck, and Arthur E. Tiedemann, eds., *Sources of Japanese Tradition*, 2 vols. (New York: Columbia University Press, 2006), 2:291–293. Copyright © 2006 Columbia University Press. Reprinted with permission of the publisher.

attests, they long ago occupied the less civilized regions of the world, made them into colonies, and had no scruples about monopolizing them for their own profit. Therefore not only Germany but all late-developing countries were in the position of having no land to seize and being unable to find any room for expansion. This state of affairs contravenes the principle of equal opportunity for all humanity, jeopardizes all nations' equal right to survival, and is a gross violation of justice and humanity. Germany's wish to overthrow this order was quite justified; the means it chose, however, were unfair and immoderate, and because they were based on militarism, with its emphasis on armed might, Germany received the world's opprobrium. Nevertheless, as a Japanese, I cannot help feeling deep sympathy for what Germany has to do.

. . . At the coming peace conference, in joining the League of Nations Japan must insist at the very least, that repudiation of economic imperialism and nondiscriminatory treatment of Orientals and Caucasians be agreed upon from the start. Militarism is not the only thing injurious to justice and humanism. Although the world has been saved from the smoke of gunpowder and the hail of bullets by Germany's defeat, military might is not all that threatens nations' equal right to survival. We must realize that there is invasion through money, conquest through wealth. Just as we repudiate military imperialism, so in the same spirit we should naturally repudiate economic imperialism, which seeks to profit by monopolizing enormous capital and abundant natural resources and suppressing other nations' free growth without recourse to arms. I cannot avoid grave misgivings as to how far economic imperialism can be repudiated at the coming peace conference, led as it is by England and America, which I fear will unsheathe the sword of their economic imperialism after the war.

If we cannot subdue this rampant economic imperialism at the peace conference, England and America, which have profited most from the war, will promptly unify the world under their economic dominance and will rule the world, using the League of Nations and arms limitations to fix the status quo that serves their purpose. How will other countries endure this? Deprived of arms to express their revulsion and indignation, they will have no choice but to follow England and America, bleating in their wake like a flock of meek sheep. England has lost no time in trumpeting a policy of self-sufficiency, and many are advocating that other countries be denied access to its colonies. Such are the contradictions between what England and America say and what they do. This, indeed, is why I am wary of those who glorify England and America. If such a policy is carried out, needless to say it would be a great economic blow to Japan. Japan is limited in territory, [is] poor in natural resources, and has a small population and thus a meager market for manufactured products. If England closed off its colonies, how would we be able to assure the nation's secure survival? In such a case, the need to ensure its survival would compel Japan to attempt to overthrow the status quo as Germany did before the war. If this is the fate awaiting all late-developing countries with little territory and no colonies, not only for the sake of Japan but for the sake of establishing the equal right to life of all nations of the world on the basis of justice and human-ism, we must do away with economic imperialism and see that countries do not monopolize their colonies but accord other countries equal use of them both as markets for manufactured products and as suppliers of natural resources.

The next thing that the Japanese, especially, should insist upon is the elimi-nation of discrimination between Caucasians and Orientals. There is no need to dwell on the fact that the United States, along with the English colonies of Australia and Canada, opens its doors to Caucasians but looks down on the Japanese and on Orientals in general and rejects them. This is something at which the Japanese have long chafed. Not only are Orientals barred from employment and forbidden to lease houses and farmland, but still worse, it is reported that in some places an Oriental wishing to spend the night at a hotel is required to have a Caucasian guarantor. This is a grave humanitarian problem that no defender of justice, Oriental or otherwise, should overlook.

At the coming peace conference, we must see that the English and Americans show deep remorse for their past sins and change their arrogant and insulting attitude, and we must insist, from the standpoint of justice and humanism, that they revise all laws that call for discriminatory treatment of Orientals, including of course rescinding immigration restrictions against Orientals. I believe that the coming peace conference will be the great test of whether the human race can bring itself to reconstruct a world based on justice and humanism. If Japan does not rashly endorse a pacifism centered on England and America but steadfastly asserts its position from the standpoint of justice and humanism in the true sense, it will long be celebrated in history as the champion of justice.

READING AND DISCUSSION QUESTIONS

1. What arguments did Konoe make against British and American pacifism? How did he describe the "status quo" supported by this pacifism?

2. Whom did Konoe blame for the war? Why did he sympathize with Germany?

3. What role did race play in Konoe's vision of the postwar world? What racial divi-sions did he employ? Why?

VIEWPOINTS COMPARATIVE QUESTIONS

1. How might Konoe have responded to the French magazine cover? What impor-tance might he have attached to it?

2. On what might Konoe and the German delegates to the Paris Peace Conference have agreed? On what might they have disagreed?

■ COMPARATIVE QUESTIONS ■

1. The documents in this chapter range from intensely personal to geopolitical in nature. What connections can you draw between the emotions and experiences presented in the Albrights' letters and the political stances of the other authors?

2. How might Lenin have responded to the Paris peace talks? How would he have interpreted their course and outcome?

3. In your opinion, what were the most important problems with the treaties that formally ended World War I? What light do the documents included in this chapter shed on this question?

29

Nationalism in Asia
1914–1939

Though the First World War is often cast as a European conflict, it reflected and exacerbated tensions throughout the world. The global network of empires and colonies that had formed by the turn of the century drew Asian peoples into the conflict, and the rhetoric of freedom and democracy mobilized during the war inspired nationalist sentiments in many contexts. For some in Asia, the war was an opportunity to fight for national sovereignty against imperial control. For others, the war created an opportunity to link their own popular nationalist causes with the stated goals of the victors. For Asians, the material and human cost of the war and the ensuing geopolitical reorganization was manifest in new ways of thinking about national identity. The documents in this chapter present a range of personal and political views on nations and national identity in Asia, exploring the complex mix of fear, hope, disappointment, and resolve of Asians who sought to build national identities out of the chaos of the early twentieth century.

29-1 | An Eyewitness to Genocide

MARY L. GRAFFAM, *An Account of Turkish Violence Against Armenians* (1915)

As young Turkish revolutionaries rose to power in Turkey after 1908, they sought to enforce a narrowly defined national identity that erased the country's multiculturalism and instead focused on Turkish language, culture, and race. Their efforts to consolidate what was left of the Ottoman Empire led to genocide against the Armenians. During World War I, while the international community was distracted by the war, the Turks massacred thousands of Armenians and deported others. Mary Graffam, a missionary from Massachusetts, was among the hundreds of U.S. and European workers and diplomats in Turkey who recorded the

Mary L. Graffam, reprinted from the *Missionary Herald* (Boston), December 1915.

killings, starvation, and brutal deportations. These eyewitness accounts were later printed in newspapers around the world.

When we were ready to leave Sivas,[1] the Government gave forty-five ox-carts for the Protestant townspeople and eighty horses, but none at all for our pupils and teachers; so we bought ten ox-carts, two horse arabas [wagons], and five or six donkeys, and started out. In the company were all our teachers in the college, about twenty boys from the college and about thirty of the girls'-school. It was as a special favor to the Sivas people, who had not done anything revolutionary, that the Vali [provincial governor] allowed the men who were not yet in prison to go with their families.

The first night we were so tired that we just ate a piece of bread and slept on the ground wherever we could find a place to spread a yorgan [blanket]. It was after dark when we stopped, anyway. We were so near Sivas that the gendarmes [Armed Ottoman police] protected us, and no special harm was done; but the second night we began to see what was before us. The gendarmes would go ahead and have long conversations with the villagers, and then stand back and let them rob and trouble the people until we all began to scream, and then they would come and drive them away. Yorgans and rugs, and all such things, disappeared by the dozen, and donkeys were sure to be lost. Many had brought cows; but from the first day those were carried off, one by one, until not a single one remained.

We got accustomed to being robbed, but the third day a new fear took possession of us, and that was that the men were to be separated from us at Kangal. . . . Our teacher from Mandjaluk was there, with his mother and sisters. They had left the village with the rest of the women and children, and when they saw that the men were being taken off to be killed the teacher fled to another village, four hours away, where he was found by the police and brought safely with his family to Kangal, because the tchaoush [officer] who had taken them from Mandjaluk wanted his sister. I found them confined in one room. I went to the Kaimakam [district official] and got an order for them all to come with us.

At Kangal some Armenians had become Mohammedans, and had not left the village, but the others were all gone. . . . They said that a valley near there was full of corpses. At Kangal we also began to see exiles from Tokat. The sight was one to strike horror to any heart; they were a company of old women, who had been robbed of absolutely everything. At Tokat the Government had first imprisoned the men, and from the prison had taken them on the road. . . . After the men had gone, they arrested the old women and the older brides, perhaps about thirty or thirty-five years old. There were very few young women or children. All the younger women and children were left in Tokat. . . .

---

[1] **Sivas:** City in north-central Turkey, where Mary Graffam was the principal of a girls' school.

When we looked at them we could not imagine that even the sprinkling of men that were with us would be allowed to remain. We did not long remain in doubt; the next day we . . . had come to Hassan Tehelebi . . . and it was with terror in our hearts that we passed through that village about noon. But we encamped and ate our supper in peace, and even began to think that perhaps it was not so, when the Mudir [official in charge] came round with gendarmes and began to collect the men. . . .

The night passed, and only one man came back to tell the story of how every man was compelled to give up all his money, and all were taken to prison. The next morning they collected the men who had escaped the night before and extorted forty-five liras from our company, on the promise that they would give us gendarmes to protect us. One "company" is supposed to be from 1,000 to 3,000 persons. Ours was perhaps 2,000, and the greatest number of gendarmes would be five or six. In addition to these they sewed a red rag on the arm of a Kurdish villager and gave him a gun, and he had the right to rob and bully us all he pleased.[2]

Broken-hearted, the women continued their journey. . . .

As soon as the men left us, the Turkish drivers began to rob the women, saying: "You are all going to be thrown into the Tokma Su [river], so you might as well give your things to us, and then we will stay by you and try to protect you." Every Turkish woman that we met said the same thing. The worst were the gendarmes, who really did more or less bad things. One of our schoolgirls was carried off by the Kurds twice, but her companions made so much fuss that she was brought back. . . .

As we approached the bridge over the Tokma Su, it was certainly a fearful sight. As far as the eye could see over the plain was this slow-moving line of oxcarts. For hours there was not a drop of water on the road, and the sun poured down its very hottest. As we went on we began to see the dead from yesterday's company, and the weak began to fall by the way. The Kurds working in the fields made attacks continually, and we were half-distracted. I piled as many as I could on our wagons, and our pupils, both boys and girls, worked like heroes. One girl took a baby from its dead mother and carried it until evening. Another carried a dying woman until she died. We bought water from the Kurds, not minding the beating that the boys were sure to get with it. I counted forty-nine deaths, but there must have been many more. One naked body of a woman was covered with bruises. I saw the Kurds robbing the bodies of those not yet entirely dead. . . .

The hills on each side were white with Kurds, who were throwing stones on the Armenians, who were slowly wending their way to the bridge. I ran ahead and stood on the bridge in the midst of a crowd of Kurds, until I was used up

---

[2] **sewed a red rag . . . he pleased:** The "red rag" was an arm band that gave the Kurds special status.

[exhausted]. I did not see anyone thrown into the water, but they said, and I believe it, that a certain Elmas, who has done handwork for me for years, was thrown over the bridge by a Kurd. Our Badvelli's wife was riding on a horse with a baby in her arms, and a Kurd took hold of her to throw her over, when another Kurd said: "She has a baby in her arms," and they let her go. . . .

The police for the first time began to interfere with me here, and it was evident that something was decided about me. The next morning after we arrived at this bridge, they wanted me to go to Malatia; but I insisted that I had permission to stay with the Armenians. During the day, however, they said that [I had been ordered] to come to Malatia, and that the others were going to Kiakhta. Soon after we heard that they were going to Ourfa, there to build villages and cities, &c.

In Malatia I went at once to the commandant, a captain who they say has made a fortune out of these exiles. I told him how I had gone to Erzeroum last winter, and how we pitied these women and children and wished to help them, and finally he sent me to the Mutessarif [district official]. The latter is a Kurd, apparently anxious to do the right thing; but he has been sick most of the time since he came, and the "beys" [Kurdish chiefs] here have had things more or less their own way, and certainly horrors have been committed. . . .

My friends here are very glad to have me with them, for they have a very difficult problem on their hands and are nearly crazy with the horrors they have been through here. The Mutessarif and other officials here and at Sivas have read me orders from Constantinople again and again to the effect that the lives of these exiles are to be protected, and from their actions I should judge that they must have received such orders; but they certainly have murdered a great many in every city. Here there were great trenches dug by the soldiers for drilling purposes. Now these trenches are all filled up, and our friends saw carts going back from the city by night. A man I know told me that when he was out to inspect some work he was having done, he saw a dead body which had evidently been pulled out of one of these trenches, probably by dogs. . . . The Beledia Reis [village chief] here says that every male over ten years old is being murdered, that not one is to live, and no woman over fifteen. The truth seems to be somewhere between these two extremes.

READING AND DISCUSSION QUESTIONS

1. What happened to the men after Graffam's group left Tokat? In what ways were they treated differently than the women and children?

2. Where were the Armenian exiles sent (and for what purpose) after Graffam was separated from them?

3. What does Graffam's account suggest about how the Armenian genocide was carried out? What role did government officials, military officers, and the police play? What about ordinary people?

29-2 | The British Government Supports a Jewish State in Palestine

ARTHUR JAMES BALFOUR, *Debating the Balfour Declaration* (1917)

The decision to support a Jewish homeland in Palestine posed a diplomatic dilemma for Great Britain. Though Lord Balfour, the British foreign secretary (1916–1919), would ultimately be authorized to endorse a Jewish homeland, the behind-the-scenes discussions excerpted below illustrate the War Department's concern about the consequences of such support. On the one hand, England hoped its actions might enlist American Zionists to push the U.S. Congress to back Britain in the war and would help Britain retain control of the Suez Canal. On the other, it risked its alliance with Arab leaders, who saw a separate Jewish state as contradictory to its government by majority rule.

The Balfour Declaration, 1917

Foreign Office
November 2nd, 1917
Dear Lord Rothschild,[3]

I have much pleasure in conveying to you, on behalf of His Majesty's Government, the following declaration of sympathy with Jewish Zionist aspirations which has been submitted to, and approved by, the Cabinet.

"His Majesty's Government view with favor the establishment in Palestine of a national home for the Jewish people, and will use their best endeavors to facilitate the achievement of this object, it being clearly understood that nothing shall be done which may prejudice the civil and religious rights of existing non-Jewish communities in Palestine, or the rights and political status enjoyed by Jews in any other country."

I should be grateful if you would bring this declaration to the knowledge of the Zionist Federation.[4]

Yours sincerely,
Arthur James Balfour

Cambon Letter to Sokolow,[5] June 4, 1917

You were good enough to present the project to which you are devoting your efforts, which has for its object the development of Jewish colonization in Palestine. You consider that, circumstances permitting, and the independence of

---

"The Balfour Declaration," *Times* (London), November 9, 1917, p. 1.

[3] **Lord Rothschild:** Walter Lord Rothschild was a former member of Parliament (1899–1910) and an ardent English Zionist who was influential in shaping the Balfour Declaration.

[4] **Zionist Federation:** The British Federation of Zionists, an organization that lobbied the British government to support a Jewish homeland in Palestine.

[5] **Cambon . . . Sokolow:** Jules Cambon, secretary-general of the French Foreign Ministry; Nahum Sokolow, head of the Zionist Organization based in London.

the Holy Places being safeguarded on the other hand, it would be a deed of justice and of reparation to assist, by the protection of the Allied Powers, in the renaissance of the Jewish nationality in that Land from which the people of *Israel* were exiled so many centuries ago.

The French Government, which entered this present war to defend a people wrongfully attacked, and which continues the struggle to assure the victory of right over might, can but feel sympathy for your cause, the triumph of which is bound up with that of the Allies.

I am happy to give you herewith such assurance.

Official Zionist Formula, 18 July 1917

H. M. Government, after considering the aims of the Zionist Organization,[6] accepts the principle of recognizing Palestine as the National Home of the Jewish people and the right of the Jewish people to build up its National life in Palestine under a protection to be established at the conclusion of Peace, following upon the successful issue of the war.

H. M. Government regards as essential for the realization of this principle the grant of internal autonomy to the Jewish nationality in Palestine, freedom of immigration for Jews, and the establishment of a Jewish National Colonizing Corporation for the re-settlement and economic development of the country.

The conditions and forms of the internal autonomy and a charter for the Jewish National Colonizing Corporation should, in the view of H. M. Government, be elaborated in detail and determined with the representatives of the Zionist Organization.

Minutes of War Cabinet Meeting No. 227, Minute No. 2, 3 September 1917

The War Cabinet had under consideration correspondence which had passed between the Secretary of State for Foreign Affairs and Lord Rothschild on the question of the policy to be adopted towards the Zionist movement. In addition to the draft declaration of policy included in the above correspondence, they had before them an alternative draft prepared by Lord Milner. They had also before them a Memorandum by Mr. Montagu entitled "The Anti-Semitism of the present Government."

It was suggested that a question raising such important issues as to the future of Palestine ought, in the first instance, to be discussed with our Allies, and more particularly with the United States.

On the question of submitting Lord Milner's draft for the consideration of the United States Government, Mr. Montagu urged that the use of the phrase "the home of the Jewish people" would vitally prejudice the position of every

---

[6] **Zionist Organization:** An umbrella organization that merged Zionist groups in Europe and elsewhere to establish a Jewish state in Palestine.

Jew elsewhere and expand the argument contained in his Memorandum. Against this it was urged that the existence of a Jewish State or autonomous community in Palestine would strengthen rather than weaken the situation of Jews in countries where they were not yet in possession of equal rights, and that in countries like England, where they possessed such rights and were identified with the nation of which they were citizens, their position would be unaffected by the existence of a national Jewish community elsewhere. The view was expressed that, while a small influential section of English Jews were opposed to the idea, large numbers were sympathetic to it, but in the interests of Jews who wished to go from countries where they were less favorably situated, rather than from any idea of wishing to go to Palestine themselves.

With reference to a suggestion that the matter might be postponed, the Acting Secretary of State for Foreign Affairs pointed out that this was a question on which the Foreign Office had been very strongly pressed for a long time past. There was a very strong and enthusiastic organization, more particularly in the United States, who were zealous in this matter, and his belief was that it would be of most substantial assistance to the Allies to have the earnestness and enthusiasm of these people enlisted on our side. To do nothing was to risk a direct breach with them, and it was necessary to face this situation.

The War Cabinet decided that—

The views of [U.S.] President Wilson should be obtained before any declaration was made, and requested the Acting Secretary of State for Foreign Affairs to inform the Government of the United States that His Majesty's Government were being pressed to make a declaration in sympathy with the Zionist movement, and to ascertain their views as to the advisability of such a declaration being made.

Minutes of War Cabinet Meeting No. 245, Minute No. 18, 4 October 1917

With reference to War Cabinet 227, Minute 2, the Secretary of State for Foreign Affairs stated that the German Government were making great efforts to capture the sympathy of the Zionist Movement. This Movement, though opposed by a number of wealthy Jews in this country, had behind it the support of a majority of Jews, at all events in Russia and America, and possibly in other countries. He saw nothing inconsistent between the establishment of a Jewish national focus in Palestine and the complete assimilation and absorption of Jews into the nationality of other countries. Just as English emigrants to the United States became, either in the first or subsequent generations, American nationals, so, in future, should a Jewish citizenship be established in Palestine, would Jews become either Englishmen, Americans, Germans, or Palestinians. What was at the back of the Zionist Movement was the intense national consciousness held by certain members of the Jewish race. They regarded themselves as one of the great historic races of the world, whose original home was Palestine, and these Jews had a passionate longing to regain once more this ancient national home. Other Jews had become absorbed into the nations among whom they and their forefathers had dwelt for many generations. Mr. Balfour then read a very sympathetic declaration by the French Government which had been conveyed to the Zionists, and he stated that he knew that President Wilson was extremely favorable to the Movement.

Attention was drawn to the contradictory telegrams received from Colonel House and Justice Brandeis.

The Secretary was instructed to take the necessary action.

The War Cabinet further decided that the opinions received upon this draft declaration should be collated and submitted to them for decision.

Minutes of War Cabinet Meeting No. 259, Minute No. 12, 25 October 1917

With reference to War Cabinet 245, Minute 18, the Secretary mentioned that he was being pressed by the Foreign Office to bring forward the question of Zionism, an early settlement of which was regarded as of great importance.

Lord Curzon[7] stated that he had a Memorandum on the subject in course of preparation.

The question was adjourned until Monday, 29th October, or some other day early next week.

Minutes of War Cabinet Meeting No. 261, Minute No. 12, 31 October 1917

With reference to War Cabinet 245, Minute 18, the War Cabinet had before them a note by the Secretary, and also a memorandum by Lord Curzon on the subject of the Zionist movement.

The Secretary of State for Foreign Affairs stated that he gathered that everyone was now agreed that, from a purely diplomatic and political point of view, it was desirable that some declaration favorable to the aspirations of the Jewish nationalists should now be made. The vast majority of Jews in Russia and America, as, indeed, all over the world, now appeared to be favorable to Zionism. If we could make a declaration favorable to such an ideal, we should be able to carry on extremely useful propaganda both in Russia and America. He gathered that the main arguments still put forward against Zionism were twofold: —

(*a.*) That Palestine was inadequate to form a home for either the Jewish or any other people.

(*b.*) The difficulty felt with regard to the future position of Jews in Western countries.

With regard to the first, he understood that there were considerable differences of opinion among experts regarding the possibility of the settlement of any

---

[7] **Lord Curzon:** George Nathaniel Curzon served in the British War Cabinet as Lord President of the Council (1916–1919).

large population in Palestine, but he was informed that, if Palestine were scientifically developed, a very much larger population could be sustained than had existed during the period of Turkish misrule. As to the meaning of the words "national home," to which the Zionists attach so much importance, he understood it to mean some form of British, American, or other protectorate, under which full facilities would be given to the Jews to work out their own salvation and to build up, by means of education, agriculture, and industry, a real center of national culture and focus of national life. It did not necessarily involve the early establishment of an independent Jewish State, which was a matter for gradual development in accordance with the ordinary laws of political evolution.

With regard to the second point, he felt that, so far from Zionism hindering the process of assimilation in Western countries, the truer parallel was to be found in the position of an Englishman who leaves his country to establish a permanent home in the United States. In the latter case there was no difficulty in the Englishman or his children becoming full nationals of the United States, whereas, in the present position of Jewry, the assimilation was often felt to be incomplete, and any danger of a double allegiance or non-national outlook would be eliminated.

Lord Curzon stated that he admitted the force of the diplomatic arguments in favor of expressing sympathy, and agreed that the bulk of the Jews held Zionist rather than anti-Zionist opinions. He added that he did not agree with the attitude taken up by Mr. Montagu. On the other hand, he could not share the optimistic views held regarding the future of Palestine. These views were not merely the result of his own personal experiences of travel in that country, but of careful investigations from persons who had lived for many years in the country. He feared that by the suggested declaration we should be raising false expectations which could never be realized. He attached great importance to the necessity of retaining the Christian and Moslem Holy Places in Jerusalem and Bethlehem, and, if this were to be effectively done, he did not see how the Jewish people could have a political capital in Palestine. However, he recognized that some expression of sympathy with Jewish aspirations would be a valuable adjunct to our propaganda, though he thought that we should be guarded in the language used in giving expression to such sympathy.

READING AND DISCUSSION QUESTIONS

1. What do the various leaders envision will be the impact of creating a Jewish state on Jews living in other countries?

2. What reasons do the leaders give for the urgency to act on this matter and show support for Zionism?

3. What are their concerns about establishing a Jewish settlement within Palestine?

4. Why might some historians see the Balfour Declaration as the cause of later Palestinian-Jewish conflicts? Based on these excerpts, what might support that claim?

29-3 | An Indian Nationalist Condemns the British Government

SAROJINI NAIDU, *The Agony and Shame of the Punjab* (1920)

Despite British concerns, the First World War provoked strong support for Britain among the Indian population. Indians rallied around the British war effort, offering soldiers, food, and other essential resources. After the war, however, Indian nationalism grew rapidly, due in large part to disillusionment with Britain's continuing imperialist policies toward its colonies. In 1919, British troops were ordered to use live ammunition to disperse a peaceful crowd of men, women, and children celebrating a Sikh festival in the city of Amritsar. Hundreds were killed and more than a thousand wounded. Indian feminist and nationalist leader Sarojini Naidu (1879–1949) used this incident and other examples of British hypocrisy to justify Indian independence and self-rule.

I speak to you today as standing arraigned because of the blood-guiltiness of those who have committed murder in my country. I need not go into the details. But I am going to speak to you as a woman about the wrongs committed against my sisters. Englishmen, you who pride yourselves upon your chivalry, you who hold more precious than your imperial treasures the honor and chastity of your women, will you sit still and leave unavenged the dishonor, and the insult and agony inflicted upon the veiled women of the Punjab?

The minions of Lord Chelmsford, the Viceroy, and his martial authorities rent the veil from the faces of the women of the Punjab. Not only were men mown down as if they were grass that is born to wither; but they tore asunder the cherished Purdah,[8] that innermost privacy of the chaste womanhood of India. My sisters were stripped naked, they were flogged, they were outraged. These policies left your British democracy betrayed, dishonored, for no dishonor clings to the martyrs who suffered, but to the tyrants who inflicted the tyranny and pain. Should they hold their Empire by dishonoring the women of another nation or lose it out of chivalry for their honor and chastity? The Bible asked, "What shall it profit a man to gain the whole world and lose his own soul?" You deserve no Empire. You have lost your soul; you have the stain of blood-guiltiness upon you; no nation that rules by tyranny is free; it is the slave of its own despotism.

Sarojini Naidu, "The Agony and Shame of the Punjab" [speech], in Padmini Sengupta, *Sarojini Naidu: A Biography* (London: Asia Publishing House, 1966), 161–162.

[8] **Purdah:** Practice in which Indian women hide themselves from view behind veils or in special building enclosures.

READING AND DISCUSSION QUESTIONS

1. Why is Naidu angry?

2. According to Naidu, how does the treatment of Indian women by British officials differ from their treatment of English women?

3. Why does she say that the English "deserve no Empire"? What might this reveal about Indian values at the time?

VIEWPOINTS

Prescriptions for National Improvement in China and Siam

Nationalist movements across Asia were united by a common set of commitments: resistance to foreign domination, the necessity of social and political reform, and the importance of creating a new sense of identity that transcended local, religious, and familial loyalties. Nonetheless, the interpretation of these objectives and the means by which Asian nationalists sought to achieve them varied widely, depending on the history, culture, and circumstances of the people in question. The documents included in this feature illustrate this diversity. In China, nationalism was shaped by the failures of the imperial government in the face of Western incursions and by the political fragmentation that followed the collapse of imperial rule. In sharp contrast, nationalism in Siam was closely tied to the successful efforts of the Siamese monarchy to resist colonization. As you read the documents, compare and contrast the ways in which the Chinese nationalist Jiang Jieshi and King Vajiravudh of Siam tackle the nationalist objectives outlined above. How did each author seek to create and maintain national unity?

29-4 | A Chinese Nationalist Offers a Recipe for Progress

JIANG JIESHI, *The New Life Movement* (1934)

Following the death of Nationalist Party leader Sun Yatsen (see Document 26-5), his protégé Jiang Jieshi (known in the West as Chiang Kai-shek) (1887–1975) took control of the Nationalist movement. By 1927, Jiang had established control of a precariously unified China

---

Sources of Chinese Tradition, ed. William Theodore de Bary and Richard Lufrano, 2 vols. (New York: Columbia University Press, 2001), 2:341–344. Copyright © 2001 Columbia University Press. Reprinted with permission of the publisher.

by defeating or eliminating his opposition, including his former allies, the Communists. Jiang's rule focused on the unification and "education" of China, which he felt necessary before democracy could be practiced. To those ends, in 1934 Jiang gave a speech proclaiming his New Life Movement. Enforced with the help of Jiang's secret and quasi-Fascist Blue Shirt Society, the New Life Movement set forth tradition, anti-individualism, and personal morality and hygiene as the foundation for a stronger, better China.

The Object of the New Life Movement

Why Is a New Life Needed?

The general psychology of our people today can be described as spiritless. What manifests itself in behavior is this: lack of discrimination between good and evil, between what is public and what is private, and between what is primary and what is secondary. Because there is no discrimination between good and evil, right and wrong are confused; because there is no discrimination between public and private, improper taking and giving [of public funds] occur; and because there is no distinction between primary and secondary, first and last are not placed in the proper order. As a result, officials tend to be dishonest and avaricious, the masses are undisciplined and calloused, youth become degraded and intemperate, adults are corrupt and ignorant, the rich become extravagant and luxurious, and the poor become mean and disorderly. Naturally it has resulted in disorganization of the social order and national life, and we are in no position either to prevent or to remedy natural calamities, disasters caused from within, or invasions from without. The individual, society, and the whole country are now suffering. . . . In order to develop the life of our nation, protect the existence of our society, and improve the livelihood of our people, it is absolutely necessary to wipe out these unwholesome conditions and to start to lead a new and rational life.

The Content of the New Life Movement

The Principles of the New Life Movement

The New Life Movement aims at the promotion of a regular life guided by the four virtues, namely, *li, yi, lian,* and *chi.* Those virtues must be applied to ordinary life in the matter of food, clothing, shelter, and action. The four virtues are the essential principles for the promotion of morality. They form the major rules for dealing with men and human affairs, for cultivating oneself, and for adjustment to one's surroundings. Whoever violates these rules is bound to fail, and a nation that neglects them will not survive.

There are two kinds of skeptics:

First, some hold that the four virtues are merely rules of good conduct. No matter how good they may be, they are not sufficient to save a nation whose knowledge and technique are inferior to others.

Those who hold this view do not seem to understand the distinction between matters of primary and secondary importance. People need knowledge and technique because they want to do good. Otherwise, knowledge and technique can only be instruments of dishonorable deeds. *Li, yi, lian,* and *chi* are the principal rules alike for the community, the group, or the entire nation. Those who do not observe these rules will probably utilize their knowledge and ability to the detriment of society and ultimately to their own disadvantage. Therefore, these virtues not only can save the nation but also can rebuild the nation.

Second, there is another group of people who argue that these virtues are merely formal refinements that are useless in dealing with hunger and cold. . . . [Yet] when these virtues prevail, even if food and clothing are insufficient, they can be produced by human labor; or, if the granary is empty, it can be filled through human effort. On the other hand, when these virtues are not observed, if food and clothing are insufficient, they will not be made sufficient by fighting and robbing; or, if the granary is empty, it will not be filled by stealing and begging. The four virtues, which rectify the misconduct of men, are the proper methods of achieving abundance. Without them, there will be fighting, robbing, stealing, and begging among men. . . .

The Meaning of *Li, Yi, Lian,* and *Chi*

Although *li, yi, lian,* and *chi* have always been regarded as the foundations of the nation, yet the changing times and circumstances may require that these principles be given a new interpretation. As applied to our life today, they may be interpreted as follows:

Li means "regulated attitude."

Yi means "right conduct."

Lian means "clear discrimination."

Chi means "real self-consciousness."

The word *li* (decorum) means *li* (principle). It becomes natural law when applied to nature; it becomes a rule when applied to social affairs; and it signifies discipline when used in reference to national affairs. A man's conduct is considered regular if it conforms with the above law, rule, and discipline. When one conducts oneself in accordance with the regular manner, one is said to have the regulated attitude.

The word *yi* means "proper." Any conduct that is in accordance with *li*—i.e., natural law, social rule, and national discipline—is considered proper. To act improperly, or to refrain from acting when one knows it is proper to act, cannot be called *yi*.

The word *lian* means "clear." It denotes distinction between right and wrong. What agrees with *li* and *yi* is right, and what does not agree is wrong. To take what we recognize as right and to forgo what we recognize as wrong constitute clear discrimination.

The word *chi* means "consciousness." When one is conscious of the fact that his own actions are not in accordance with *li, yi, lian,* and *chi*, one feels ashamed.

From the above explanations, it is clear that *chi* governs the motive of action, that *lian* gives the guidance for it, that *yi* relates to the carrying out of an action, and that *li* regulates its outward form. The four are interrelated. They are dependent upon each other in the perfecting of virtue.

Conclusion

In short, the main object of the New Life Movement is to substitute a rational life for the irrational, and to achieve this we must observe *li, yi, lian,* and *chi* in our daily life.

1. By the observance of these virtues, it is hoped that rudeness and vulgarity will be got rid of and that the life of our people will conform to the standard of art. By art we are not referring to the special enjoyment of the gentry. We mean the cultural standard of all the people, irrespective of sex, age, wealth, and class. It is the boundary line between civilized life and barbarism. It is the only way by which one can achieve the purpose of man, for only by artistically controlling oneself and dealing with others can one fulfill the duty of mutual assistance. . . . A lack of artistic training is the cause of suspicion, jealousy, hatred, and strife that are prevalent in our society today. . . . To investigate things so as to extend our knowledge, to distinguish between the fundamental and the secondary, to seek the invention of instruments, to excel in our techniques—these are the essentials of an artistic life, the practice of which will enable us to wipe out the defects of vulgarity, confusion, crudity, and baseness.

2. By the observance of these virtues, it is hoped that beggary and robbery will be eliminated and that the life of our people will be productive. The poverty of China is primarily caused by the fact that there are too many consumers and too few producers. Those who consume without producing usually live as parasites or as robbers. They behave thus because they are ignorant of the four virtues. To remedy this we must make them produce more and spend less. They must understand that luxury is improper and that living as a parasite is a shame.

3. By the observance of these virtues, it is hoped that social disorder and individual weakness will be remedied and that people will become more military-minded. If a country cannot defend itself, it has every chance of losing its existence. . . . Therefore our people must have military training. As a preliminary, we must acquire the habits of orderliness, cleanliness, simplicity, frugality, promptness, and exactness. We must preserve order, emphasize organization, responsibility, and discipline, and be ready to die for the country at any moment.

READING AND DISCUSSION QUESTIONS

1. What is the aim of the New Life Movement? What are its four components?

2. What criticisms does Jiang predict, and how does he answer them?

3. How does art figure into Jiang's vision of "New Life"? How is the promotion of art—or any other individual activity or attitude—supposed to have an impact on the nation?

4. Do you find Jiang's prescriptions for social improvement compelling? Why or why not?

29-5 | The King of Siam Promotes Siamese Nationalism

KING VAJIRAVUDH, *On the Siamese Nation* (1914, 1917)

Vajiravudh (1881–1925) was king of Siam from 1910 until his death in 1925 and—like his father before him—a major reformer in Siamese or Thai history. He took great pains to avoid the colonization of Siam and to guide Siamese involvement in the First World War through deft political alliances with powerful European and Asian nations. He also continued his father's policy of nourishing modern, Western-style reforms. Perhaps most important, Vajiravudh was instrumental in fostering Siamese nationalism, which would form the seeds of Thai nationalism after the 1933 coup d'état that created the nation of Thailand. Vajiravudh produced a range of speeches, essays, plays, poems, and even cartoons instructing the Siamese populace on the meaning and merits of Siamese nationalism. The first excerpt that follows is from a 1914 play; the second is from a 1917 poem written to commemorate the national flag that Vajiravudh himself designed.

From *Phra Ruang* (1914)

I ask the Thai to join in love,
To join in fellowship,
So that when the enemy comes
We can fight him in full strength.
The Thai combining their power
Will be able to raise a staunch defense.
Even if a powerful foe comes,
He will be defeated.

I ask only that we Thai not destroy our nation.
Let us unite our state, unite our hearts, into a great whole.
Thai—do not harm or destroy Thai,
But combine your spirit and your strength to preserve the state
So that all foreign peoples
Will give us increasing respect.

Help one another to further our progress
So the name "Thai" will redound throughout the world.
Help one another to sustain
Both our nation and our faith
So they will last to the end of time.
Let us progress, Thai! Chaiyo![9]

Walter F. Vella, *Chaiyo! King Vajiravudh and the Development of Thai Nationalism* (Honolulu: University of Hawaii Press, 1978), 140, 211, 245. Copyright © 1978 University of Hawaii Press. Reprinted with permission.

   [9] **Chaiyo!:** A new exclamation designed and popularized by Vajiravudh, it roughly translates as "Olé!" or "Hurray!"

Poem on the Flag (1917)

Let me speak of the meaning
Behind the three colors.

White is for purity and betokens the three gems
And the laws that guard the Thai heart.

Red is for our blood, which we willingly give up
To protect our nation and faith.

Blue is the beautiful hue of the people's leader,
And is liked because of him.[10]

Arranged in stripes, these three colors form the flag
That we Thai love.

Our soldiers carrying it forth to victory
Raise up the honor of Siam.

READING AND DISCUSSION QUESTIONS

1. What themes does Vajiravudh use in the two excerpts to illustrate the virtues and importance of nationalism? What does Siamese/Thai nationalism mean to the king?

2. The three colors of the Thai flag (still in use today) are found in the flags of several prominent Western nations. How might these color choices have resonated on the international stage? What does the choice of these colors suggest about Vajiravudh's understanding of modern nationalism?

3. The idea of a head of state producing plays, poetry, and cartoons may seem foreign to twenty-first-century readers. What is your reaction to Vajiravudh's personal involvement with defining Siamese/Thai nationalism? What might his contributions suggest about early-twentieth-century nationalism in Asia, or nationalism in general?

VIEWPOINTS COMPARATIVE QUESTIONS

1. How did each author view his nation's people? What role did they imagine the people playing in the life of the nation?

---

[10] **Blue is the beautiful hue . . . liked because of him:** According to Thai folk belief, each day of the week has a specific color; Vajiravudh claimed his birthday to be on a Friday, the color of which is blue.

2. What did each author see as the key to national survival? What did they identify as the greatest threat to the nation?

3. How did each author's nationalist vision draw on his people's history and culture? What role did tradition play in their construction of a new national identity?

▪ COMPARATIVE QUESTIONS ▪

1. In each of the documents in this chapter, the question of national identity is addressed either implicitly or explicitly. How does the author of each document take up the question of nationalism? What national identities are mentioned or described, and how?

2. How is nationalism presented as a positive or negative force in each document? Who is commenting on the value of nation and nationalism in each document, and what relationship can you identify between the author's identity and his or her views on nationalism?

3. How is nationalism connected to modernity in each document? How is nationalism linked to Western identity or Western ideas?

4. In Documents 29-4 and 29-5, we see Asian political and intellectual leaders attempting to define national identity for their countries. Compare and contrast the writings of Jiang Jieshi and King Vajiravudh. How do the authors' identities, the themes used to define and promote nationalism, and the use of foreign or Western ideas converge or differ in each text?

5. Lord Balfour and Sarojini Naidu represent the United Kingdom and its colony India, respectively. How do their writings reflect their position as imperial power or colony? Does any commonality of theme or purpose link them? On what do Balfour and Naidu agree, if anything?

The Great Depression and World War II

1929–1945

The Great Depression may have had its origins in the economy of the United States, but its effects were rapidly experienced throughout most of the world, and the hardships it generated added stress to the already fragile social and political situations that existed after the First World War. In the United States, the depression exacerbated social tensions; in Europe and elsewhere, it helped radicalize the political landscape, as men and women sought to create and make sense of new visions of state and citizen. New expressions of nationalism emerged, including the chilling racism of Hitler's Nazi Germany, Stalin's totalitarian order in the Communist Soviet Union, and Mussolini's Fascist control of Italy. While the Soviet Union's planned economy was largely spared the effects of the depression, citizens there also struggled to understand how their lives fit new forms of state and society. Universally, these social and political developments helped fuel the Second World War, which claimed millions of lives, ushered in the age of nuclear conflict, and reshaped the geopolitical landscape for decades.

30-1 | The U.S. Government Responds to Mass Unemployment
Field Office of the Works Progress Administration
(ca. 1935)

The Great Depression sparked a profound shift in the role of the federal government in the U.S. economy. Convinced that the problems created by the depression were too large to be tackled by private organizations and local governments, President Franklin Delano Roosevelt (1882–1945) persuaded Congress to intervene aggressively in the economy. Among Roosevelt's many initiatives was the Works Progress Administration (WPA). Created in 1935, the WPA put millions of Americans to work repairing and improving the country's infrastructure. As this photograph of a WPA field office suggests, the program had an impact on even the remotest corners of the country. As you examine the document, ask yourself what message the photographer hoped to convey to viewers. What did he or she want to say about the relationship between individual Americans and their government?

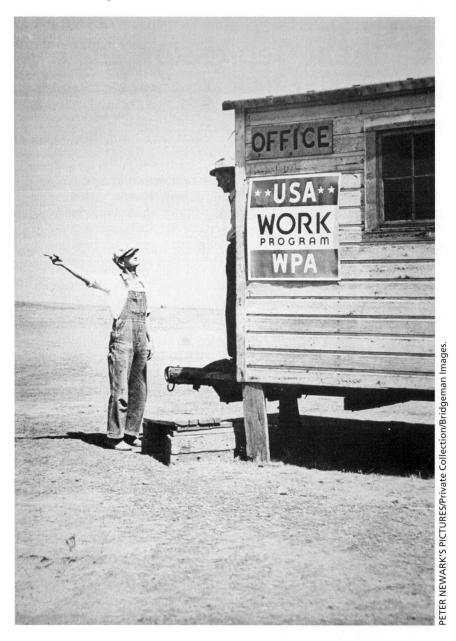

READING AND DISCUSSION QUESTIONS

1. How would you characterize the relationship between the two men in the photograph? What might their interaction have been meant to symbolize?

2. What connections might the photographer have meant to make between traditional American values and the WPA?

30-2 | Legislating Racial Purity

The Nuremberg Laws: The Centerpiece of Nazi Racial Legislation (1935)

Adolf Hitler's beliefs about Germanic racial superiority, first articulated in his 1925 book *Mein Kampf*, became the foundation for the Nuremberg Laws, enacted after Hitler (1889–1945) seized power as German chancellor in 1933. Designed to preserve the purity of the German race, the laws—which were a manifestation of Hitler's fierce anti-Semitism—deemed Jews inferior, defined who was a Jew, and prohibited intermarriage between Germans and non-Germans (especially Jews). In the end, Jews lost not only citizenship rights and jobs but also their freedom and lives; ultimately, six million perished in the Holocaust.

Article 5

1. A Jew is anyone who descended from at least three grandparents who were racially full Jews. Article 2, par. 2, second sentence will apply.

2. A Jew is also one who descended from two full Jewish parents, if: (a) he belonged to the Jewish religious community at the time this law was issued, or who joined the community later; (b) he was married to a Jewish person, at the time the law was issued, or married one subsequently; (c) he is the offspring from a marriage with a Jew, in the sense of Section 1, which was contracted after the Law for the Protection of German Blood and German Honor became effective . . . ; (d) he is the offspring of an extramarital relationship, with a Jew, according to Section 1, and will be born out of wedlock after July 31, 1936. . . .

Law for the Protection of German Blood and German Honor of September 15, 1935

Thoroughly convinced by the knowledge that the purity of German blood is essential for the further existence of the German people and animated by the

---

U.S. Chief of Counsel for the Prosecution of Axis Criminality, Nazi Conspiracy and Aggression (Washington, D.C.: U.S. Government Printing Office, 1946), vol. 4, doc. no. 1417-PS, 8–10; vol. 4, doc. no. 2000-PS, 636–638.

inflexible will to safe-guard the German nation for the entire future, the Reichstag[1] has resolved upon the following law unanimously, which is promulgated herewith:

Section 1

1. Marriages between Jews and nationals of German or kindred blood are forbidden. Marriages concluded in defiance of this law are void, even if, for the purpose of evading this law, they are concluded abroad. . . .

Section 2

Relation[s] outside marriage between Jews and nationals of German or kindred blood are forbidden.

Section 3

Jews will not be permitted to employ female nationals of German or kindred blood in their household.

Section 4

1. Jews are forbidden to hoist the Reich and national flag and to present the colors of the Reich. . . .

Section 5

1. A person who acts contrary to the prohibition of Section 1 will be punished with hard labor.
2. A person who acts contrary to the prohibition of Section 2 will be punished with imprisonment or with hard labor.
3. A person who acts contrary to the provisions of Sections 3 or 4 will be punished with imprisonment up to a year and with a fine or with one of these penalties. . . .

READING AND DISCUSSION QUESTIONS

1. What makes someone a Jew, according to the Nuremberg Laws?
2. Why do you think so much attention is paid to "relations" between Germans and Jews in these laws?
3. Within the laws, what restrictions render Jews different from and inferior to other Germans?
4. What do the laws suggest about the place of race in Nazi ideology?

---

[1] **Reichstag:** The German legislative assembly.

30-3 | The Place of Women in Stalin's Soviet Union
Letters to Izvestiya: *On the Issue of Abortion* (1936)

As Joseph Stalin (1879–1953) rose to absolute power in the Soviet Union between 1922 and 1927, he launched an ambitious and strict campaign to solidify socialism by placing all economic development under government control and promoting new cultural values. Women, who had gained greater equality after the 1917 Bolshevik Revolution, became a key focus. As birthrates dropped by up to 50 percent from 1930 to 1935, Stalin's government released propaganda celebrating women's traditional roles as wives and mothers and enacted legislation outlawing abortion except to save the mother's life. The public's thoughts on this legal change ran in newspapers such as *Pravda* and *Izvestiya*.

Letter from a Student [K.B.]

I have read in the press the draft law on the prohibition of abortion, aid to expectant mothers, etc., and cannot remain silent on this matter.

There are thousands of women in the same position as myself. I am a student reading the first course of the second Moscow Medical Institute. My husband is also a student reading the same course at our Institute. Our scholarships amount jointly to 205 rubles. Neither he nor I have a room of our own. Next year we intend to apply for admission to a hostel, but I do not know whether our application will be granted. I love children and shall probably have some in four or five years' time. But can I have a child now? Having a child now would mean leaving the Institute, lagging behind my husband, forgetting everything I have learnt and probably leaving Moscow because there is nowhere to live.

There is another married couple in our Institute, Mitya and Galya, who live in a hostel. Yesterday Galya said to me: "If I become pregnant I shall have to leave the Institute; one cannot live in a hostel with children."

I consider that the projected law is premature because the housing problem in our towns is a painful one. Very often it is the lack of living quarters that is the reason behind an abortion. If the draft included an article assuring married couples, who are expecting a baby, of a room — that would be a different matter.

In five years' time when I am a doctor and have a job and a room I shall have children. But at present I do not want and cannot undertake such a responsibility. . . .

Answer to the Student K.B.

Your paper recently published a letter from a student, K.B., in which she raised objections to the prohibition of abortions. I think the author of the letter . . . has not grasped the full significance of the projected law. The difficulties about which

K.B. writes and which, according to her, justify abortion are, she thinks, the difficulties of to-day which will have disappeared to-morrow. The writer of that letter completely ignored the fact that the government, by widening the network of child-welfare institutions, is easing the mother's task in looking after the child. The main mistake K.B. makes is, in my view, that she approaches the problem of childbearing as though it were a private matter. This would explain why she writes: "I shall have them (children) in four or five years' time." She hopes by that time to have completed her studies, obtained a medical diploma and found both a job and a room. But one must be logical! If during these years, K.B. intends to have recourse to abortions, who can vouch that by the time when she desires to have children she will still be able to do so? And for a normal woman to be deprived of the possibility of having children is as great a misfortune as the loss of a dear one.

I used to study in a factory and received a very small allowance while bringing up my small son whom I had to bring up on my own. (His father was dead.) It was a hard time. I had to go and unload trains or look for similar work that would bring in some money ... that was in 1923. Now my son is a good, rough Komsomol[2] and a Red Army[3] soldier in the Far East. How great are my joy and pride that I did not shun the difficulties and that I managed to bring up such a son.

Letter from an Engineer [E.T.]

I am non-party [not Communist], married, with a 5-year-old son. I work as an engineer and have been and still am in a responsible position. I regard myself as a good citizen of the U.S.S.R.

I cannot agree with the prohibition of abortions. And I am very glad that this law has not entered into force but has been submitted to the workers for discussion.

The prohibition of abortion means the compulsory birth of a child to a woman who does not want children. The birth of a child ties married people to each other. Not everyone will readily abandon a child, for alimony is not all that children need. Where the parents produce a child of their own free will, all is well. But where a child comes into the family against the will of the parents, a grim personal drama will be enacted which will undoubtedly lower the social value of the parents and leave its mark on the child.

A categorical prohibition of abortion will confront young people with a dilemma: either complete sexual abstinence or the risk of jeopardizing their studies or disrupting their life. To my mind any prohibition of abortion is bound to mutilate many a young life. Apart from this, the result of such a prohibition might be an increase in the death-rate from abortions because they will then be performed illegally.

---

[2] **Komsomol:** Member of the Communist Youth Organization.
[3] **Red Army:** The reconstituted Soviet army founded by Commissar of Military and Naval Affairs Leon Trotsky (1879–1940) after the 1917 Bolshevik Revolution.

Letter from Professor K. Bogorekov, Leningrad

Abortions are harmful. One cannot disagree with that. But situations in life do exist when this harmful remedy will allow a woman to preserve normal conditions of life.

If a single child already ties a woman down, two, three, or four children leave her no possibility at all of participating in social life and having a job. A man suffers less. He gives the family his salary irrespective of the number of children—and the whole burden falls upon the mother.

Sometimes abortion is an extreme but decisive means of averting the disruption of a young woman's life. It may become imperative, through the accident of an unlucky liaison for a young girl-student without means for whom a child would be a heavy penalty, or through bad heredity of the parents or a number of other contingencies which play an important part in life and can often lead to its mutilation. All this must be taken into account.

It must not be thought that the majority of abortions are the result of irresponsible behavior. Experience shows that a woman resorts to abortion as a last resource when other methods of safeguard against pregnancy have failed and the birth of a child threatens to make her life more difficult.

Simple statistics show that in spite of this the birth-rate of our country is increasing rapidly.[4] And what is needed is not pressure, but a stimulation of the birth-rate by means of financial assistance, improved housing conditions, legal action against those who fail to pay alimony, etc. . . .

Abortions will become obsolete by themselves when knowledge of human anatomy spreads, methods of birth-control are more widely used and—last but not least—when housing conditions are improved. . . .

Letter from Professor M. Malinovsky

Performing an abortion is an operation undoubtedly involving great risks. There are few operations so dangerous as the cleaning out of the womb during pregnancy. Under the best of conditions and in the hands of the most experienced specialist this operation still has a "normal" percentage of fatal cases. It is true that the percentage is not very high. Our surgeons have brought the technique of performing abortions to perfection. The foreign doctors who have watched operations in our gynæcological hospitals have unanimously testified that their technique is irreproachable. And yet . . . here are still cases in which it is fatal. This is understandable. The operation is performed in the dark and with instruments which, so far as their effect on so tender an organ as the womb is concerned, remind one of a crowbar. And even the most gifted surgeons, virtuosi at their job, occasionally cause great and serious injuries for which the woman often pays with her life. . . .

---

[4] **Birth-rate . . . increasing rapidly:** From what is known, this is a false statement.

The slave-like conditions of hired labor, together with unemployment and poverty, deprive women in capitalist countries of the impulse for childbearing. Their "will to motherhood" is paralyzed. In our country all the conditions for giving birth to and bringing up a healthy generation exist. The "fear of motherhood," the fear of the morrow, the anxiety over the child's future are gone.

The lighthearted attitude towards the family, the feeling of irresponsibility which is still quite strong in men and women, the disgusting disrespect for women and children—all these must come before our guns. Every baseness towards women and every form of profligacy [extravagance] must be considered as serious antisocial acts. . . .

READING AND DISCUSSION QUESTIONS

1. Why does K.B. argue that abortion must remain legal? What solution for reducing the number of abortions does she propose? What generational differences do you notice between K.B.'s position and that of the woman who responds to her?

2. Why does E.T. oppose the ban on abortion?

3. Professor K. Bogorekov says that abortion will cease when what happens? Why does he think this is the case?

4. What comparison does Professor Malinovsky make between socialist and capitalist countries?

VIEWPOINTS

Hiroshima and Nagasaki

By the summer of 1945, Germany had surrendered and it was clear that the Allies would prevail against the Japanese in the Pacific. What was not clear was how long victory would take and how many lives it would cost. As they made plans for the invasion of the Japanese mainland, American commanders estimated that this final stage of the war would produce a million American casualties and result in the deaths of 10 to 20 million Japanese. It was in this context that President Harry Truman and his advisers decided to drop nuclear weapons on the Japanese cities of Hiroshima and Nagasaki. The decision was not reached without debate, and it remains controversial to this day. Some scholars believe that Japan was close to surrender even before the bombs were dropped. Others point out that American leaders could have taken a number of intermediate steps before resorting to the use of nuclear weapons. Still others argue that racial animus played a significant role in the decision to use nuclear weapons against Japan. As you read the documents included in this feature, formulate your opinion on this controversy. Were American leaders right to use nuclear weapons against Japan when they did? If so, why? If not, what should they have done instead?

30-4 | Truman Describes the Creation and Use of Nuclear Weapons

HARRY S. TRUMAN, *White House Press Release on Hiroshima* (August 6, 1945)

After the death of U.S. President Franklin Delano Roosevelt in April 1945, his vice president, Harry S. Truman (1884–1972), became president and inherited command of the Second World War. The U.S. government had engaged in nuclear weapons research since 1939, when notable scientists (including Albert Einstein) had signed a letter to the president warning of the possible military applications of atomic energy. The following press release, although formally issued after the August 6 nuclear attack on Hiroshima, was written by the War Department and submitted to President Truman on July 30, a full week earlier. In effect, Truman's approval of this press release was a final go-ahead for the first military nuclear strike in history. The release itself was the first official notice to the American people—and the world—of the age of atomic weapons.

Sixteen hours ago an American airplane dropped one bomb on [Hiroshima] and destroyed its usefulness to the enemy.[5] That bomb had more power than 20,000 tons of T.N.T. It had more than two thousand times the blast power of the British "Grand Slam" which is the largest bomb ever yet used in the history of warfare.

The Japanese began the war from the air at Pearl Harbor.[6] They have been repaid many fold. And the end is not yet. With this bomb we have now added a new and revolutionary increase in destruction to supplement the growing power of our armed forces. In their present form these bombs are now in production and even more powerful forms are in development.

It is an atomic bomb. It is a harnessing of the basic power of the universe. The force from which the sun draws its power has been loosed against those who brought war to the Far East.

"Statement by the President of the United States" [White House press release], August 6, 1945 (Harry S. Truman Library and Museum, Ayers Papers), www.trumanlibrary.org/whistlestop/study_collections/bomb/large/documents/index.php?documentdate=1945-08-06&documenti d=59&studycollectionid=abomb&pagenumber=1.

[5] **[Hiroshima] . . . enemy:** While Hiroshima was an important port and military center, it was also a thriving city. In the original release, the city's name is withheld.

[6] **Pearl Harbor:** The U.S. Navy base in Hawaii and the site of the 1941 Japanese attack on U.S. forces.

Before 1939, it was the accepted belief of scientists that it was theoretically possible to release atomic energy. But no one knew any practical method of doing it. By 1942, however, we knew that the Germans were working feverishly to find a way to add atomic energy to the other engines of war with which they hoped to enslave the world. But they failed. We may be grateful to Providence that the Germans got the V-1's and V-2's[7] late and in limited quantities and even more grateful that they did not get the atomic bomb at all.

The battle of the laboratories held fateful risks for us as well as the battles of the air, land and sea, and we have now won the battle of the laboratories as we have won the other battles.

Beginning in 1940, before Pearl Harbor, scientific knowledge useful in war was pooled between the United States and Great Britain, and many priceless helps to our victories have come from that arrangement. Under that general policy the research on the atomic bomb was begun. With American and British scientists working together we entered the race of discovery against the Germans.

The United States had available the large number of scientists of distinction in the many needed areas of knowledge. It had the tremendous industrial and financial resources necessary for the project and they could be devoted to it without undue impairment of other vital war work. In the United States the laboratory work and the production plants, on which a substantial start had already been made, would be out of reach of enemy bombing, while at that time Britain was exposed to constant air attack and was still threatened with the possibility of invasion. For these reasons Prime Minister Churchill and President Roosevelt agreed that it was wise to carry on the project here. We now have two great plants and many lesser works devoted to the production of atomic power. Employment during peak construction numbered 125,000 and over 65,000 individuals are even now engaged in operating the plants. Many have worked there for two and a half years. Few know what they have been producing. They see great quantities of material going in and they see nothing coming out of these plants, for the physical size of the explosive charge is exceedingly small. We have spent two billion dollars on the greatest scientific gamble in history—and won.

But the greatest marvel is not the size of the enterprise, its secrecy, nor its cost, but the achievement of scientific brains in putting together infinitely complex pieces of knowledge held by many men in different fields of science into a workable plan. And hardly less marvellous has been the capacity of industry to design, and of labor to operate, the machines and methods to do things never done before so that the brain child of many minds came forth in physical shape and performed as it was supposed to do. Both science and industry worked under the direction of the United States Army, which achieved a unique success in managing so diverse a problem in the advancement of knowledge in an

---

[7] **V-1's and V-2's:** Guided missiles used by Germany against targets in Great Britain during the Second World War.

amazingly short time. It is doubtful if such another combination could be got together in the world. What has been done is the greatest achievement of organized science in history. It was done under high pressure and without failure.

We are now prepared to obliterate more rapidly and completely every productive enterprise the Japanese have above ground in any city. We shall destroy their docks, their factories, and their communications. Let there be no mistake; we shall completely destroy Japan's power to make war.

It was to spare the Japanese people from utter destruction that the ultimatum of July 26 was issued at Potsdam.[8] Their leaders promptly rejected that ultimatum. If they do not now accept our terms they may expect a rain of ruin from the air, the like of which has never been seen on this earth. Behind this air attack will follow sea and land forces in such numbers and power as they have not yet seen and with the fighting skill of which they are already well aware.

The Secretary of War, who has kept in personal touch with all phases of this project, will immediately make public a statement giving further details.

His statement will give facts concerning the sites of Oak Ridge near Knoxville, Tennessee, and at Richland near Pasco, Washington, and an installation near Santa Fe, New Mexico. Although the workers at the sites have been making materials to be used in producing the greatest destructive force in history they have not themselves been in danger beyond that of many other occupations, for the utmost care has been taken of their safety.

The fact that we can release atomic energy ushers in a new era in man's understanding of nature's forces. Atomic energy may in the future supplement the power that now comes from coal, oil, and falling water, but at present it cannot be produced on a basis to compete with them commercially. Before that comes there must be a long period of intensive research.

It has never been the habit of the scientists of this country or the policy of this Government to withhold from the world scientific knowledge. Normally, therefore, everything about the work with atomic energy would be made public.

But under present circumstances it is not intended to divulge the technical processes of production or all the military applications, pending further examination of possible methods of protecting us and the rest of the world from the danger of sudden destruction. I shall recommend that the Congress of the United States consider promptly the establishment of an appropriate commission to control the production and use of atomic power within the United States. I shall give further consideration and make further recommendations to the Congress as to how atomic power can become a powerful and forceful influence towards the maintenance of world peace.

---

[8] **The ultimatum of July 26 . . . at Potsdam:** The Potsdam Declaration of July 26, 1945, called for the "unconditional surrender" of Japanese military forces, warning of "prompt and utter destruction" unless Japan complied.

READING AND DISCUSSION QUESTIONS

1. Historians disagree about the U.S. motivation for using atomic weapons. How does Truman characterize Hiroshima and Japan in order to defend the use of the atomic bomb?

2. What points about the nuclear strike on Hiroshima does Truman emphasize? What details does he leave out?

3. What does Truman's press release suggest about the growth of Big Science? How did the Los Alamos project foreshadow postwar developments in the relationship between government and scientific research?

30-5 | The Impact of a Nuclear Weapon

TOSHIKO SAEKI, *Interview with a Survivor of Hiroshima* (1986)

On August 6, 1945, the U.S. military attacked the Japanese city of Hiroshima with a nuclear weapon. Casualty estimates range from slightly below to well over 100,000 deaths caused by the immediate attack, with many more deaths linked to radiation and other long-term injuries. Although the firebombing of Tokyo, Dresden, and other cities had produced similarly high death tolls, the shocking destructive power of the atomic weapon was unprecedented. The experiences of survivors—known by the Japanese term *hibakusha*—have been chronicled in many media and for a variety of reasons, including U.S. government studies on the effects of nuclear weapons on human populations. Here, a 1986 interview with a survivor by representatives of the Hiroshima Peace Cultural Center presents a firsthand account of the attack.

Ms. Toshiko Saeki, then 26. She was exposed to the atomic bomb when she entered the city to return to her parents' home in Yasufuruichi. She arrived in the city on the afternoon of August 6th and searched for members of her family every day after that. Thirteen people in her family, including her parents, perished as a result of the atomic bomb.

SAEKI: One of my older sisters lived about 12 kilometers from my house in Hiroshima and I had asked her to take care of my children. It was safer in the countryside. I was at my sister's house on August 5th, but when I moved to leave, my children started crying. My sister said it would be better if I spent the night, so I did.

INTERVIEWER: Where were you?

SAEKI: My sister's house was in present-day Numata-cho, about 12 kilometers from Hiroshima. After spending the night there, I was planning to return to

From the "Voice of Hibakusha" eyewitness accounts aired as part of *Hiroshima Witness*, produced by the Hiroshima Peace Cultural Center and NHK, the public broadcasting company of Japan. Translated into English and posted as "Testimony of Toshiko Saeki," AtomicArchive.com. Published in a limited edition by Andrew Mossberg. Reprinted by permission of Andrew Mossberg.

Hiroshima the next morning on the 7:00 bus. But I ended up missing the bus so I would have to return to Hiroshima on foot. I went back to my sister's house and was chatting with her when an air-raid alert sounded. This warning was soon lifted, though. I then saw an airplane, a B-29, flying toward us from the mountains to the left of the house. It seemed strange that the anti-aircraft artillery on Hijiyama Hill wasn't firing at it. I watched the airplane fly off until it disappeared. But then another airplane flew in from the same direction. Suddenly, there was an eerie flash and I felt engulfed in heat—it was incredibly hot. I hit the floor, and as I heard a tremendous explosion, some sliding doors inside the house came flying in my direction. I looked up to see what had happened and discovered that the ceiling had collapsed and my sister and my children were buried beneath it. My sister called out for everyone to run to the safety of the storeroom, but I was frozen there on the floor. I was still in shock from seeing that flash in the sky—it's a sight I'll never forget. An enormous fireball then rose into the air, gradually becoming a great cloud of smoke. I burst into tears and cried out, "Hiroshima has been destroyed! Our mother is dead!" My sister came out of the storeroom and told me to stop crying. "Kure was attacked," she said, "not Hiroshima!" But I didn't think so, because smoldering debris was now falling from the sky, confirming a closer distance.

INTERVIEWER: Which part of Hiroshima did you live in?

SAEKI: I was living in Hirosemotomachi, only about a kilometer from the hypocenter. So I had a sense of the distance from my sister's house and that's why, when I saw the flash, I was afraid Hiroshima had been attacked. I asked my sister to pack some food for me so I could head back to Hiroshima to help our family. In the meantime, it started raining. At first, I welcomed the rain as I thought it would put out the fire. But the rain was black and it was pouring down. Some of the drops stuck to my hand and I tried to wipe them off, but they were really sticky. I didn't think it was rain, but I had no idea what it was. I smelled it, then licked it, but I still wasn't sure. Finally, I gulped some of it down to make sure it wasn't oil.

INTERVIEWER: You swallowed some of it?

SAEKI: Yes, because if it had been oil, I would have had to flee right away. I had a friend who lived in Kure and she had written me a letter at the end of July. In the letter, she told me that enemy aircraft had sprayed oil on the city and then dropped incendiary bombs. Actually, if the police had seen the text of this letter, we could have gotten into trouble—mention of Japan's losses during the war was forbidden. There were no air-raid shelters in the countryside, so I knew I would have to flee quickly if it was oil.

INTERVIEWER: Then what did you do?

SAEKI: I was convinced that it was rain after all, not oil. So I went to catch a bus back to Hiroshima to help my family. On the way, I ran into 50 or 60 people fleeing Hiroshima. They looked frightful, far worse than the figures in the

Peace Memorial Museum.[9] I shouted at them to tell me what part of Hiroshima had been bombed. But they would only reply that something terrible had happened there. As I ran on, I encountered a man who was naked. I hesitated for a moment, but then I called out to him to stop. When I asked him what part of Hiroshima had been bombed, he stared at me for a long moment. "You're Toshiko, aren't you?" he said. The man's face was so swollen that I couldn't recognize him right away. He continued, "It's me, Toshiko! Can't you recognize me?" And then I finally realized that he was one of my older brothers. He was in a terrible state—his whole body was badly burned. Just after my mother woke him up, the bomb exploded and he lost consciousness. When he came to, he heard an old woman shrieking for help as flames began to engulf her. My brother crawled frantically through the fire and managed to escape. If he had hesitated, he surely would have been burned to death. He told me that my mother went up to the third floor after waking him up and she was likely hit hard by the blast. He had to assume that she was killed. He also told me that my younger sister, 18 years old, had gone to the hospital in Hatchobori that morning. I asked him which part of the city had been bombed and he replied that the area west of Honkawa had been totally destroyed.

INTERVIEWER: How long did it take you to reach Hiroshima?

SAEKI: I'm not sure what time I left my sister's house, but it was probably about 10:00 that morning. I had to go on foot, and in addition to running into my brother, I spent some time helping the wounded along the way, so it took about two hours. I finally arrived in Hiroshima at about noon.

INTERVIEWER: And what did you experience then?

SAEKI: In Koi, everyone was being evacuated to the elementary school. When I got there, the school was full of victims, crying out for help. People who weren't injured were carrying out the bodies of the dead. I started to look for my parents, but it was hard to recognize people's misshapen faces, so I tried to identify them by their clothing. Out in the schoolyard were piles of bodies and I wondered if my parents were among them. But I was at a loss as to how I might find them within these piles. When I was crossing Fukushima Bridge, I saw a lot of cattle in the river—evidently, they had escaped from a slaughterhouse. This picture tries to capture that moment. After all, humans weren't the only victims of the bomb. The victims included birds, cats, and dogs—but there aren't really words to describe the awful sight of those cattle. Like the human victims, their bodies were burned and bloated. They were horribly disfigured.

INTERVIEWER: How long did you look for the missing members of your family?

SAEKI: I searched for them almost every day after the bombing.

INTERVIEWER: Did you find out what happened to your mother?

---

[9] **Peace Memorial Museum:** A museum in Hiroshima, Japan, established in 1955 to preserve artifacts and testimony from the U.S. nuclear attack, its aftermath, and related issues.

SAEKI: Despite my efforts, I could find no clues. But on September 6th, my older brother called us all together. He placed something on the table before us—it was wrapped up in a piece of cloth. He told me that I should be the one to open it since I had been looking for her so hard. I unwrapped the bundle, expecting to find some bones, but I found her skull instead, half of it charred black. Her skull had no eyes or nose, but a bit of skin and hair was still on the back. And some glasses were still stuck to it.

INTERVIEWER: How did you know it was your mother?

SAEKI: I could tell by the glasses—they had thick lenses, like my mother's pair of glasses.

INTERVIEWER: What happened to your older brother?

SAEKI: After my mother's skull was found, he had a mental breakdown. He told me to wrap his whole body up in white cloth, leaving only his eyes and mouth uncovered. He said he wanted to conduct an experiment designed to discharge the radiation that had accumulated in his body. He couldn't be dissuaded, so we wrapped him up in some cloth. Then he told me to place a bucket, half-full of water, between his legs, with a tube running to his mouth so he could drink from the bucket. We used a tube from a bicycle tire pump and we placed it in his mouth. He then started sucking sugar water from the bucket. He wasn't really drinking much, though—it was spilling out of his mouth and his nose. When I checked on him a little while later, I found that he had stripped off all the cloth and he was now lying naked on the floor. I thought he was dead and I started shouting at him. "You can't die!" I cried. "You have to go on!" At that point, he got up, claimed that his experiment was a failure, then began sobbing. I told him it didn't matter and he didn't need to cry. But he called me a fool. He said that he had hoped to treat all the people of Hiroshima—starting with me—if the experiment had been successful.

INTERVIEWER: What about your younger sister? Where was she when the bomb exploded?

SAEKI: She was at the hospital in Hatchobori. She wasn't seriously injured in the blast and one of the doctors then accompanied her to Kyobashi. But on August 9th or 10th, she began vomiting blood, her stools were bloody, and her hair was coming out in clumps. My brother started complaining about the foul smells and about becoming infected from her illness. Up to that point, I had always believed that love and compassion among family members couldn't be shaken, even in an emergency. The war not only wiped out human lives, it ravaged human hearts.

INTERVIEWER: How many family members did you lose?

SAEKI: Six members of my immediate family were killed. If relatives are included, I lost a total of 13 people. They all died a different death. When I reflect on what they might have been thinking when they died, or their last word, I feel guilty for having survived. In fact, I've wondered many times if it wouldn't have been better if I had died with them. But the fact that I survived would lose all meaning if I didn't go on living, if I didn't live for the members of my family who died. My hope is that, by telling my story, the tragedy of Hiroshima won't be forgotten and it might help prevent another war. The things we believed in at that time were turned upside-down by the bombing, but I didn't know where to direct my rage. As I staggered through the living hell that Hiroshima had become, I was aghast at the utter waste of war. This is why I continue to speak out and tell my story.

READING AND DISCUSSION QUESTIONS

1. Toshiko Saeki gives a disturbingly personal account of the nuclear attack on Hiroshima. What is the value of her testimony, if any, in evaluating the history of atomic warfare?

2. Conventional weapons killed millions of people in the Second World War. What aspect of Saeki's testimony, if any, makes the atomic attacks on Hiroshima and Nagasaki unique in the war's long history of carnage?

3. Saeki refers to the Peace Memorial Museum. What is the effect of bringing up the museum in her narrative? How does she compare or contrast the preservation of history with her own experiences? What does this suggest for your understanding of Saeki's experience and of the event?

VIEWPOINTS COMPARATIVE QUESTIONS

1. How might Saeki have responded to Truman's press release? How might he have responded to her account?

2. In your opinion, what lessons should be taken from the bombing of Hiroshima and Nagasaki?

▪ COMPARATIVE QUESTIONS ▪

1. The documents in this chapter present varying perspectives on individual lives and government policies during the Great Depression and the Second World War. What comparisons or contrasts can you draw among the documents based on the perspective of each author? Which documents present an "official" version, and which a more personal version? How does the author's perspective affect your reading of each document?

2. Both the Nuremberg Laws and Truman's press release reflect the efforts of very different governments to explain themselves or to further their own interests. Compare and contrast these two documents.

3. The press release on Hiroshima and the interview with Toshiko Saeki present two very different accounts of the nuclear strike on the city of Hiroshima. How is the atomic bomb described in each document? Compare and contrast the descriptions.

4. In what ways does each document in this chapter quantify human suffering? When they cite numbers, what effect do those numbers give? Are numbers more or less powerful than other forms of description? Cite examples.

31

Decolonization, Revolution, and the Cold War

1945–1968

Almost immediately following the end of the Second World War, the competing economic and social systems of the United States and its European allies, on the one hand, and the Soviet Union and its allies, on the other, spawned the Cold War. This period of heightened military tension and mutual suspicion lasted more than four decades, as each side struggled to expand its influence—and limit that of its rival—through economic, political, and occasionally military activity. The postwar decades were also times of revolutionary change outside the West. The war weakened the grip of European nations on their overseas colonies, and nationalist movements in Asia, the Middle East, and Africa won independence for former colonies. In many cases, decolonization proceeded relatively peacefully. In others, the struggle for independence produced violent clashes. In all cases, however, the process of decolonization and subsequent efforts at nation building were shaped by the battle between the United States and the Soviet Union for global influence.

VIEWPOINTS

Decolonization and Dependence

The 1950s and 1960s saw widespread re-evaluation and contestation of the relationship between the industrialized West and the developing nations of the world. The most direct manifestation of this phenomenon was decolonization, the dismantling of the overseas empires Western powers had built over the course of the previous centuries. The Allies had cast World War II as a fight for freedom; with the war won, the peoples of Asia, Africa, and the Middle East demanded freedom for themselves. At the same time, many in the developing world came to understand that winning political independence was only part of the battle. They would also need to unravel the relationships and practices that kept the developing world economically and technologically dependent on Europe. As you read the documents included in this feature, think about the connections between decolonization and the fight against economic dependence. Why did many observers believe that true independence had both political and economic components?

31-1 | The United Nations Calls for an End to the Age of Empires

UNITED NATIONS GENERAL ASSEMBLY, *Declaration on the Granting of Independence to Colonial Countries and Peoples* (December 14, 1960)

After centuries of empire building and colonization, European countries began to move toward decolonization in the decades after World War II. Many former colonies obtained their freedom after 1945, driven in large part by the increasing quest for self-government in Africa and Asia. In 1960, the United Nations formalized the gradual process of granting independence to these once-colonized peoples, outlining basic assumptions about human rights and self-rule that would guide much of the decolonization process. Most UN member nations voted in favor of the declaration; the nine that abstained, however, were all imperialist nations, including the United States, Great Britain, France, Spain, and Portugal.

General Assembly Resolution 1514 (XV) of 14 December 1960

The General Assembly,

> Mindful of the determination proclaimed by the peoples of the world in the Charter of the United Nations to reaffirm faith in fundamental human rights, in the dignity and worth of the human person, in the equal rights of men and women and of nations large and small and to promote social progress and better standards of life in larger freedom,

> Conscious of the need for the creation of conditions of stability and well-being and peaceful and friendly relations based on respect for the principles of equal rights and self-determination of all peoples, and of universal respect for, and observance of, human rights and fundamental freedoms for all without distinction as to race, sex, language, or religion,

> Recognizing the passionate yearning for freedom in all dependent peoples and the decisive role of such peoples in the attainment of their independence,

General Assembly of the United Nations, Resolution 1514 (XV), December 14, 1960.

Aware of the increasing conflicts resulting from the denial of or impediments in the way of the freedom of such peoples, which constitute a serious threat to world peace,

Considering the important role of the United Nations in assisting the movement for independence in Trust and Non-Self-Governing Territories,

Recognizing that the peoples of the world ardently desire the end of colonialism in all its manifestations,

Convinced that the continued existence of colonialism prevents the development of international economic co-operation, impedes the social, cultural, and economic development of dependent peoples and militates against the United Nations ideal of universal peace,

Affirming that peoples may, for their own ends, freely dispose of their natural wealth and resources without prejudice to any obligations arising out of international economic co-operation, based upon the principle of mutual benefit, and international law,

Believing that the process of liberation is irresistible and irreversible and that, in order to avoid serious crises, an end must be put to colonialism and all practices of segregation and discrimination associated therewith,

Welcoming the emergence in recent years of a large number of dependent territories into freedom and independence, and recognizing the increasingly powerful trends towards freedom in such territories which have not yet attained independence,

Convinced that all peoples have an inalienable right to complete freedom, the exercise of their sovereignty, and the integrity of their national territory,

Solemnly proclaims the necessity of bringing to a speedy and unconditional end colonialism in all its forms and manifestations;

And to this end

Declares that:

1. The subjection of peoples to alien subjugation, domination, and exploitation constitutes a denial of fundamental human rights, is contrary to the Charter of the United Nations, and is an impediment to the promotion of world peace and co-operation.
2. All peoples have the right to self-determination; by virtue of that right they freely determine their political status and freely pursue their economic, social, and cultural development.
3. Inadequacy of political, economic, social or educational preparedness should never serve as a pretext for delaying independence.
4. All armed action or repressive measures of all kinds directed against dependent peoples shall cease in order to enable them to exercise peacefully and

freely their right to complete independence, and the integrity of their national territory shall be respected.

5. Immediate steps shall be taken, in Trust and Non-Self-Governing Territories or all other territories which have not yet attained independence, to transfer all powers to the peoples of those territories, without any conditions or reservations, in accordance with their freely expressed will and desire, without any distinction as to race, creed, or color, in order to enable them to enjoy complete independence and freedom.

6. Any attempt aimed at the partial or total disruption of the national unity and the territorial integrity of a country is incompatible with the purposes and principles of the Charter of the United Nations.

7. All States shall observe faithfully and strictly the provisions of the Charter of the United Nations, the Universal Declaration of Human Rights and the present Declaration on the basis of equality, non-interference in the internal affairs of all States, and respect for the sovereign rights of all peoples and their territorial integrity.

READING AND DISCUSSION QUESTIONS

1. According to this declaration, what goals do the peoples of the world share?
2. What problems would continued colonialism pose?
3. According to the declaration, what constitutes basic human rights?
4. How does the General Assembly describe its role in decolonization?

31-2 | A Poet Reflects on Economic Exploitation

PABLO NERUDA, From *Canto General:* "Standard Oil Co." and "United Fruit Co." (1950)

The Chilean poet, politician, and Nobel laureate Pablo Neruda (1904–1973) was a champion of left-wing political and social causes. He became politically active during the Spanish Civil War (1936–1939) and worked on behalf of the Chilean government to assist Spanish émigrés to Chile fleeing fascism in their native country. His membership in the Chilean Communist Party and his support for Soviet leader Joseph Stalin (which he later recanted) won him as many enemies as supporters. Similarly, his support for the 1970 election of Marxist Salvador Allende as president of Chile earned him political persecution when Allende died in a coup d'état supported by the U.S. government and corporate interests. The two poems here, taken from his epic collection *Canto General*, present his attack on the multinational corporations that, along with U.S. government policy, played a major role in modern Latin American history.

Pablo Neruda, *Canto General*, trans. Jack Schmitt (Berkeley: University of California Press, 1991), 176–179. Copyright © Fundación Pablo Neruda, 2014. Reprinted by permission of Agencia Carmen Balcells, S.A.

Standard Oil Co.[1]

When the drill bored down
toward the stony fissures
and plunged its implacable intestine
into the subterranean estates,
and dead years, eyes
of the ages, imprisoned
plants' roots
and scaly systems
became strata of water,
fire shot up through the tubes
transformed into cold liquid,
in the customs house of the heights,
issuing from its world
of sinister depth,
it encountered a pale engineer
and a title deed.

However entangled the petroleum's
arteries may be, however the layers
may change their silent site
and move their sovereignty
amid the earth's bowels,
when the fountain gushes
its paraffin foliage,
Standard Oil arrived beforehand
with its checks and its guns,
with its governments and its prisoners.

Their obese emperors
from New York are suave
smiling assassins
who buy silk, nylon, cigars,
petty tyrants and dictators.

They buy countries, people, seas,
police, county councils,
distant regions where
the poor hoard their corn
like misers their gold:

---

[1] **Standard Oil Co.:** A major U.S. oil and energy company at the end of the nineteenth century, considered a prime example of monopoly capitalism.

Standard Oil awakens them,
clothes them in uniforms, designates
which brother is the enemy.
The Paraguayan fights its war,
and the Bolivian wastes away[2]
in the jungle with its machine gun.

A President assassinated
for a drop of petroleum,
a million-acre
mortgage, a swift
execution on a morning
mortal with light, petrified,
a new prison camp for
subversives, in Patagonia,
a betrayal, scattered shots
beneath a petroliferous moon,
a subtle change of ministers
in the capital, a whisper
like an oil tide,
and zap, you'll see
how Standard Oil's letters
shine above the clouds,
above the seas, in your home,
illuminating their dominions.

United Fruit Co.[3]

When the trumpet blared everything
on earth was prepared
and Jehovah [God] distributed the world
to Coca-Cola Inc., Anaconda,
Ford Motors and other entities:
United Fruit Inc.
reserved for itself the juiciest,
the central seaboard of my land,
America's sweet waist.
It rebaptized its lands

---

[2] **Paraguayan fights . . . Bolivian wastes away:** Neruda refers to the Chaco War (1932–1935) between Paraguay and Bolivia and the role oil exploration and oil companies played therein.

[3] **United Fruit Co.:** An American producer of bananas, founded in 1899, that became a massive commercial and political presence in Central and South America. The company's influence on host governments — sometimes in cooperation with the U.S. government — inspired American author H. L. Mencken to coin the term "banana republic."

the "Banana Republics,"[4]
and upon the slumbering corpses,
upon the restless heroes
who conquered renown,
freedom and flags,
it established the comic opera:
it alienated self-destiny,
regaled Caesar's crowns,
unsheathed envy, drew
the dictatorship of flies:
Trujillo flies, Tacho flies,
Carías flies, Martínez flies,
Ubico flies,[5] flies soaked
in humble blood and jam,
drunk flies that drone
over the common graves,
circus flies, clever flies
versed in tyranny.

Among the bloodthirsty flies
the Fruit Co. disembarks,
ravaging coffee and fruits
for its ships that spirit away
our submerged lands' treasures
like serving trays.

Meanwhile, in the seaports'
sugary abysses,
Indians collapsed, buried
in the morning mist:
a body rolls down, a nameless
thing, a fallen number,
a bunch of lifeless fruit
dumped in the rubbish heap.

---

[4] **"Banana Republics"**: Countries that are heavily dependent on foreign capital and the production of one or a few exports. They are usually characterized by a corrupt government and exploitative labor practices.

[5] **Trujillo . . . Ubico:** Rafael Trujillo (1891–1961), Anastasio ("Tacho") Somoza García (1896–1956), Tiburcio Carías Andino (1876–1969), Maximiliano Hernández Martínez (1882–1966), and Jorge Ubico (1878–1946) were all mid-twentieth-century Central American dictators who symbolized corruption, collusion with foreign business interests, brutal suppression of dissent, and often mass killings of citizens perceived to be a threat to their political interests.

READING AND DISCUSSION QUESTIONS

1. How does Neruda portray the representatives of the two companies? How does he portray the companies themselves?

2. How does the poet present citizens of Latin American countries? What about Latin American leaders?

3. How might Neruda's political affiliations color his presentation of foreign investment in Latin American economies? Does he seem to be writing from a political or a regional point of view—as a Communist, as a Latin American citizen, or both?

VIEWPOINTS COMPARATIVE QUESTIONS

1. How is the relationship between "dependent" and "independent" nations characterized in each document? What evils are associated with "dependence"?

2. How might Neruda have modified the UN declaration? What might he have added that its authors left out?

31-3 | Truman Vows to Contain Communism

HARRY S. TRUMAN, *The Truman Doctrine* (March 12, 1947)

Not long after World War II ended, tensions heated up between leaders of the United States and the Soviet Union. Each country feared the other's influence on smaller nations and world politics. Joseph Stalin, who ruled the Soviet Union from 1927 to 1953, renewed efforts to spread communism, prompting U.S. fears that if one nation fell to communism, others would surely follow. As the Soviet Union intensified its efforts to spread communism to countries such as Greece, Turkey, and Iran, President Harry S. Truman (in office 1945–1953) urged congressional approval for financial and military assistance to those same countries and others that sought to maintain free and democratic forms of government. This policy of containing communism became known as the Truman Doctrine.

Mr. President, Mr. Speaker, Members of the Congress of the United States:

The gravity of the situation which confronts the world today necessitates my appearance before a joint session of the Congress. The foreign policy and the national security of this country are involved. . . .

The very existence of the Greek state is today threatened by the terrorist activities of several thousand armed men, led by Communists, who defy the

President Harry S. Truman, Address Before a Joint Session of Congress, March 12, 1947.

government's authority at a number of points, particularly along the northern boundaries. A Commission appointed by the United Nations Security Council is at present investigating disturbed conditions in northern Greece and alleged border violations along the frontier between Greece on the one hand and Albania, Bulgaria, and Yugoslavia on the other.

Meanwhile, the Greek Government is unable to cope with the situation. The Greek army is small and poorly equipped. It needs supplies and equipment if it is to restore the authority of the government throughout Greek territory. Greece must have assistance if it is to become a self-supporting and self-respecting democracy.

The United States must supply that assistance. We have already extended to Greece certain types of relief and economic aid but these are inadequate.

There is no other country to which democratic Greece can turn.

No other nation is willing and able to provide the necessary support for a democratic Greek government. . . .

Greece's neighbor, Turkey, also deserves our attention.

The future of Turkey as an independent and economically sound state is clearly no less important to the freedom-loving peoples of the world than the future of Greece. The circumstances in which Turkey finds itself today are considerably different from those of Greece. Turkey has been spared the disasters that have beset Greece. And during the war, the United States and Great Britain furnished Turkey with material aid.

Nevertheless, Turkey now needs our support.

Since the war Turkey has sought financial assistance from Great Britain and the United States for the purpose of effecting that modernization necessary for the maintenance of its national integrity.

That integrity is essential to the preservation of order in the Middle East.

The British government has informed us that, owing to its own difficulties, it can no longer extend financial or economic aid to Turkey.

As in the case of Greece, if Turkey is to have the assistance it needs, the United States must supply it. We are the only country able to provide that help.

I am fully aware of the broad implications involved if the United States extends assistance to Greece and Turkey, and I shall discuss these implications with you at this time.

One of the primary objectives of the foreign policy of the United States is the creation of conditions in which we and other nations will be able to work out a way of life free from coercion. This was a fundamental issue in the war with Germany and Japan. Our victory was won over countries which sought to impose their will, and their way of life, upon other nations.

To ensure the peaceful development of nations, free from coercion, the United States has taken a leading part in establishing the United Nations. The United Nations is designed to make possible lasting freedom and independence for all its members. We shall not realize our objectives, however, unless we are willing to help free peoples to maintain their free institutions and their national integrity against aggressive movements that seek to impose upon them totalitarian regimes. This is no more than a frank recognition that totalitarian regimes imposed on free peoples, by direct or indirect aggression, undermine the foundations of international peace and hence the security of the United States.

The peoples of a number of countries of the world have recently had totalitarian regimes forced upon them against their will. The Government of the United States has made frequent protests against coercion and intimidation, in violation of the Yalta agreement,[6] in Poland, Rumania, and Bulgaria. I must also state that in a number of other countries there have been similar developments.

At the present moment in world history nearly every nation must choose between alternative ways of life. The choice is too often not a free one.

One way of life is based upon the will of the majority, and is distinguished by free institutions, representative government, free elections, guarantees of individual liberty, freedom of speech and religion, and freedom from political oppression.

The second way of life is based upon the will of a minority forcibly imposed upon the majority. It relies upon terror and oppression, a controlled press and radio, fixed elections, and the suppression of personal freedoms.

I believe that it must be the policy of the United States to support free peoples who are resisting attempted subjugation by armed minorities or by outside pressures.

I believe that we must assist free peoples to work out their own destinies in their own way.

I believe that our help should be primarily through economic and financial aid which is essential to economic stability and orderly political processes.

It is necessary only to glance at a map to realize that the survival and integrity of the Greek nation are of grave importance in a much wider situation. If Greece should fall under the control of an armed minority, the effect upon its neighbor, Turkey, would be immediate and serious. Confusion and disorder might well spread throughout the entire Middle East.

Moreover, the disappearance of Greece as an independent state would have a profound effect upon those countries in Europe whose peoples are struggling against great difficulties to maintain their freedoms and their independence while they repair the damages of war.

It would be an unspeakable tragedy if these countries, which have struggled so long against overwhelming odds, should lose that victory for which they

---

[6] **Yalta agreement:** The 1945 accord reached by U.S. president Franklin Roosevelt, British prime minister Winston Churchill, and Soviet premier Joseph Stalin containing agreements to divide the peacetime world into three zones of occupation, to require an unconditional surrender from Germany, and to force Germany to make reparations to the Soviet Union.

sacrificed so much. Collapse of free institutions and loss of independence would be disastrous not only for them but for the world. Discouragement and possibly failure would quickly be the lot of neighboring peoples striving to maintain their freedom and independence.

Should we fail to aid Greece and Turkey in this fateful hour, the effect will be far reaching to the West as well as to the East.

We must take immediate and resolute action.

I therefore ask the Congress to provide authority for assistance to Greece and Turkey in the amount of $400,000,000 for the period ending June 30, 1948. In requesting these funds, I have taken into consideration the maximum amount of relief assistance which would be furnished to Greece out of the $350,000,000 which I recently requested that the Congress authorize for the prevention of starvation and suffering in countries devastated by the war.

In addition to funds, I ask the Congress to authorize the detail of American civilian and military personnel to Greece and Turkey, at the request of those countries, to assist in the tasks of reconstruction, and for the purpose of supervising the use of such financial and material assistance as may be furnished. . . .

This is a serious course upon which we embark.

I would not recommend it except that the alternative is much more serious. The United States contributed $341,000,000,000 toward winning World War II. This is an investment in world freedom and world peace.

The seeds of totalitarian regimes are nurtured by misery and want. They spread and grow in the evil soil of poverty and strife. They reach their full growth when the hope of a people for a better life has died. We must keep that hope alive.

The free peoples of the world look to us for support in maintaining their freedoms.

If we falter in our leadership, we may endanger the peace of the world — and we shall surely endanger the welfare of our own nation.

Great responsibilities have been placed upon us by the swift movement of events.

I am confident that the Congress will face these responsibilities squarely.

READING AND DISCUSSION QUESTIONS

1. What reasons does Truman give to convince Congress to provide aid to Greece and Turkey? What consequences does he fear will result from not helping them?

2. How does Truman reconcile his proposal to Turkey and Greece with U.S. foreign policy goals?

3. What forms of government does he say people around the world must now choose between?

4. What conditions does Truman believe make the world ripe for totalitarian regimes?

31-4 | A Soviet Leader Repudiates Stalin

NIKITA KHRUSHCHEV, *On the Personality Cult and Its Consequences* (1956)

Following the end of the Second World War, the Soviet Union under Joseph Stalin directed its efforts toward rebuilding its infrastructure and, through military and economic means, competing with capitalist-aligned nations for global influence during the Cold War. Stalin's death in 1953 signaled the end of an era and occasioned a flurry of political repositioning. Nikita Khrushchev (1894–1971) emerged as leader of the Communist Party and, later, premier of the Soviet Union's government. During the February 1956 Communist Party Congress, Khrushchev gave his famous "Secret Speech," a dramatic repudiation of Stalin and his "cult of personality." The speech, excerpted here, indicated not only a shift in domestic Soviet policy, but also a tacit break with Communist countries like China that had followed the USSR's Stalinist example.

Comrades! In the Party Central Committee's report to the 20th Congress, in a number of speeches by delegates to the Congress, and earlier at plenary sessions of the Party Central Committee, quite a lot has been said about the cult of the individual leader and its harmful consequences.

After Stalin's death the Party Central Committee began to implement a policy of explaining concisely and consistently that it is impermissible and foreign to the spirit of Marxism-Leninism to elevate one person, to transform him into a superman possessing supernatural characteristics akin to those of a god. Such a man supposedly knows everything, sees everything, thinks for everyone, can do anything, is infallible in his behavior.

Such a belief about a man—specifically about Stalin—was cultivated among us for many years.

The objective of the present report is not a thorough evaluation of Stalin's life and work. Concerning Stalin's merits, an entirely sufficient number of books, pamphlets and studies had already been written in his lifetime. Stalin's role in the preparation and execution of the socialist revolution, in the Civil War, and in the fight for the construction of socialism in our country is universally known. Everyone knows this well. At present we are concerned with a question which has immense importance for the Party now and in the future—[we are concerned] with how the Stalin cult gradually grew, the cult which became at a certain specific stage the source of a whole series of exceedingly serious and grave perversions of Party principles, of Party democracy, of revolutionary legality.

Because not all as yet realize fully the practical consequences resulting from the cult of the individual leader, the great harm caused by the violation of the principle of collective direction of the Party, and because immense and limitless power was gathered in the hands of one person, the Party Central

Khrushchev Speaks: Selected Speeches, Articles, and Press Conferences, 1949–1961 (Ann Arbor: University of Michigan Press, 1963), 207–265.

Committee considers it absolutely necessary to make the material pertaining to this matter available to the 20th Congress of the Communist Party of the Soviet Union.

Allow me first of all to remind you how severely the founders of Marxism-Leninism denounced every manifestation of the cult of the individual leader. In a letter to the German political worker Wilhelm Bloss, Marx stated: "Because of my antipathy to any cult of the individual, I never made public during the existence of the International the numerous addresses from various countries which recognized my merits, and which annoyed me. I did not even reply to them, except sometimes to rebuke their authors. Engels and I first joined the secret society of Communists on the condition that everything making for superstitious worship of authority would be deleted from its statutes. [Ferdinand] Lassalle subsequently did quite the opposite."

Some time later Engels wrote: "Both Marx and I have always been against any public manifestation with regard to individuals, with the exception of cases when it had an important purpose; and we most strongly opposed such manifestations as during our lifetime concerned us personally." . . .

Stalin acted not through persuasion, explanation and patient cooperation with people, but by imposing his concepts and demanding absolute submission to his opinion. Whoever opposed this concept or tried to prove his viewpoint and the correctness of his position was doomed to removal from the leading collective and to subsequent moral and physical annihilation. This was especially true during the period following the 17th Party Congress, when many prominent Party leaders and rank-and-file Party workers, honest and dedicated to the cause of communism, fell victim to Stalin's despotism. . . .

Stalin originated the concept "enemy of the people." This term automatically rendered it unnecessary that the ideological errors of a man or men engaged in a controversy be proved; this term made possible the use of the most cruel repression, violating all norms of revolutionary legality, against anyone who in any way disagreed with Stalin, against those who were only suspected of hostile intent, against those who had bad reputations. This concept, "enemy of the people," actually eliminated the possibility of any kind of ideological fight or the making of one's views known on this or that issue, even issues of a practical nature. In the main, and in actuality, the only proof of guilt used, contrary to all norms of current law, was the "confession" of the accused himself; and, as subsequent investigation has proved, "confessions" were obtained through physical pressures against the accused.

This led to glaring violations of revolutionary legality, and to the fact that many entirely innocent persons, who in the past had defended the Party line, became victims.

We must assert that, in regard to those persons who in their time had opposed the Party line, there were often no sufficiently serious reasons for their physical annihilation. The formula "enemy of the people" was specifically introduced for the purpose of physically annihilating such individuals. . . .

Stalin . . . used extreme methods and mass repressions at a time when the revolution was already victorious, when the Soviet state was strengthened, when the exploiting classes were already liquidated and socialist relations were rooted solidly in all phases of national economy, when our party was politically consolidated and had strengthened itself both numerically and ideologically. It is clear that here Stalin showed in a whole series of cases his intolerance, his brutality and his abuse of power. Instead of proving his political correctness and mobilizing the masses, he often chose the path of repression and physical annihilation, not only against actual enemies, but also against individuals who had not committed any crimes against the Party and the Soviet government. . . .

[Khrushchev details the purging and execution of members of government in the 1930s and 1940s, using secret police archives to argue for Stalin's murderous misuse of power.]

All the more monstrous are the acts, initiated by Stalin, which are gross violations of the basic Leninist principles of the nationalities policy of the Soviet state. We refer to the mass deportations from their native territory of whole nations, including all [their] Communists and Young Communists, without any exception; this deportation action was not dictated by any military considerations.

Thus, already at the end of 1943, when there occurred a permanent breakthrough on the fronts of the great patriotic war benefiting the Soviet Union, a decision was taken and carried out concerning deportation of all the Karachai from the lands on which they lived. In the same period, at the end of December 1943, the same lot befell the whole population of the Kalmyk Autonomous Republic. In March 1944, all the Chechen and Ingush people were deported and the Chechen-Ingush Autonomous Republic was liquidated. In April 1944, all Balkars were deported to faraway places from the territory of the Kabardino-Balkar Autonomous Republic and the republic itself was renamed the Kabardian Autonomous Republic. The Ukrainians avoided this fate only because there were too many of them and there was no place to which to deport them. Otherwise, he would have deported them too. . . .

Not only no Marxist-Leninist, but also no man of common sense can grasp how it is possible to make whole nations responsible for inimical activity, including women, children, old people, Communists and Young Communists, to use mass repression against them and to expose them to misery and suffering for the hostile acts of individual persons or groups of persons. . . .

Comrades! The cult of the individual caused the employment of faulty principles in Party work and in economic activity; it brought about gross violation of inner-Party and Soviet democracy, sterile administration by fiat, deviations of all sorts, covering up of shortcomings, and varnishing of reality. Our country gave birth to many flatterers and specialists in false optimism and deceit. . . .

Stalin's reluctance to consider life's realities and the fact that he was not aware of the real state of affairs in the provinces can be illustrated by his direction of agriculture.

All those who interested themselves even a little in the national situation saw the difficult situation in agriculture, but Stalin never even noted it. Did we tell Stalin about this? Yes; we told him; but he did not support us. Why? Because Stalin never traveled anywhere, did not meet city and collective farm workers; he did not know the actual situation in the provinces.

He knew the countryside and agriculture only from films. And these films had dressed up and beautified the existing situation in agriculture.

Many films pictured collective farm life as if the tables bent under the weight of turkeys and geese. Evidently Stalin thought that it was actually so. . . .

Stalin cut himself off from the people and never went anywhere. This lasted tens of years. The last time he visited a village was in January 1928, when he visited Siberia in connection with grain deliveries. How then could he have known the situation in the provinces?

And when he was once told during a discussion that our situation on the land was a difficult one and that the livestock situation was especially bad, . . . Stalin proposed that the taxes paid by the collective farms and by the collective farmers should be raised by 40,000,000,000 rubles. According to him, the peasants were well-off and the collective farmer would need to sell only one more chicken to pay his tax in full.

Imagine what this would have meant. Certainly 40,000,000,000 rubles is a sum which the collective farmers did not realize for all the products which they sold to the government. In 1952, for instance, the collective farms and the collective farmers received 26,280,000,000 rubles for all their products delivered and sold to the government.

Did Stalin's position rest, then, on data of any sort whatever? Of course not.

In such cases facts and figures did not interest him. If Stalin said anything, it meant it was so—after all, he was a "genius," and a genius does not need to count, he only needs to look and can immediately tell how it should be. When he expresses his opinion, everyone has to echo it and to admire his wisdom. . . .

Comrades! If today we sharply criticize the cult of the individual leader which was so widespread during Stalin's lifetime and if we speak about the many negative phenomena generated by this cult which is so alien to the spirit of Marxism-Leninism, various persons may ask: How could it be? Stalin headed the Party and the country for 30 years, and many victories were gained during his lifetime. Can we deny this? In my opinion, the question can be asked in this manner only by those who are blinded and hopelessly hypnotized by the cult of the individual leader, only by those who do not understand the essence of the revolution and of the Soviet state, only by those who do not understand in a Leninist manner the role of the Party and of the people in the development of Soviet society.

The socialist revolution was accomplished by the working class and the poor peasantry, with the partial support of the middle peasants. It was accomplished by the people under the leadership of the Bolshevist party. Lenin's great service consisted in that he created a militant party of the working class; he was armed with Marxist understanding of the laws of social development and with the science of proletarian victory in the struggle with capitalism, and he steeled this party in the crucible of the revolutionary struggle of the masses of the people. During this struggle the Party consistently defended the interests of the people, became their experienced leader, and led the working masses to power, to the creation of the first socialist state.

You remember well Lenin's wise words that the Soviet state is strong because of the awareness of the masses, because history is created by the millions and tens of millions of people.

Our historic victories were attained thanks to the organizational work of the Party, to the many local organizations, and to the self-sacrificing work of our great people. These victories are the result of the great drive and activity of the people and Party as a whole; they are not at all the fruit of Stalin's leadership, as was pictured during the period of the cult of the individual leader.

If we are to consider this matter as Marxists and as Leninists, then we must state unequivocally that the leadership practice which came into being during the last years of Stalin's life became a serious obstacle in the path of the development of Soviet society.

Stalin often failed for months to take up exceedingly important problems— the solution of which could not be postponed—concerning the life of the Party and state. During Stalin's leadership our peaceful relations with other nations were often threatened because one-man decisions could and often did cause great complications. . . .

Comrades! We must resolutely abolish the cult of the individual leader once and for all; we must draw the proper conclusions concerning both ideological-theoretical and practical work.

It is necessary for this purpose:

First, in a Bolshevist manner to condemn and to eradicate the cult of the individual leader as alien to Marxism-Leninism and not consonant with the principles of Party leadership and the norms of Party life, and to fight inexorably all attempts at bringing back this practice in one form or another.

To return to and actually practice in all our ideological work the very important Marxist-Leninist theses about the people as the maker of history and the creator of all mankind's material and spiritual benefits, about the decisive role of the Marxist party in the revolutionary struggle to change society, about the victory of communism.

In this connection we shall be obliged to do much to examine critically from the Marxist-Leninist viewpoint and to correct the widespread, erroneous views connected with the cult of the individual leader in the spheres of history, philosophy, economics and other sciences, as well as in literature and the fine arts. It is especially necessary that in the immediate future we compile a serious textbook of the history of our party, edited in accordance with scientific Marxist objectivism, a textbook of the history of Soviet society, a book pertaining to the events of the Civil War and the great patriotic war.

Secondly, to continue systematically and consistently the work done by the Party Central Committee during the past years, work characterized by scrupulous observance—in all Party organizations, from bottom to top—of the Leninist principles of Party leadership; characterized above all by the main principle, collective leadership; characterized by observance of the norms of Party life described in the Statutes of our party; and, finally, characterized by wide practice of criticism and self-criticism.

Thirdly, to restore completely the Leninist principles of Soviet, socialist democracy, expressed in the Constitution of the Soviet Union; to fight willfulness of individuals abusing their power. The evil caused by acts violating revolutionary socialist legality which accumulated over a long period as a result of the negative influence of the cult of the individual leader must be completely corrected.

Comrades! The 20th Congress of the Communist Party of the Soviet Union has manifested with new strength the unshakable unity of our party, its cohesiveness around the Central Committee, its resolute will to accomplish the great task of building communism.

READING AND DISCUSSION QUESTIONS

1. How does Khrushchev's speech challenge or support Soviet communism?

2. How does Khrushchev support his critique of Stalin, the leader of the Soviet Union for three decades? Why do you suppose he used the justification that he did?

3. Although Khrushchev gave the "secret speech" in a closed session, it was quickly reproduced and transmitted throughout the USSR and eastern Europe and printed in Western media shortly thereafter. What do you imagine Khrushchev hoped to accomplish with his speech? How might it have been received by ordinary Russians? How might readers in the West have interpreted it?

31-5 | Revolutionary Brothers-in-Arms
Erich Honecker and Fidel Castro (1974)

The Cuban Revolution (1953–1959) provides a good example of the pervasive influence of the Cold War competition between the United States and the Soviet Union. Fidel Castro (1926–2016) and his fellow revolutionaries did not set out to create a Communist state. They wanted to level the economic playing field, but this desire was not driven by ideology or pursued in concert with the Soviet Union. Nonetheless, when the revolution finally succeeded in toppling the U.S.-backed dictator Fulgencio Batista (1901–1973), the United States, acting on Cold War imperatives, immediately launched a campaign to undermine the new government and depose Castro. These policies gave Castro little choice but to form an alliance with the Soviet Union, an alliance that only grew stronger over the course of the 1960s and 1970s. This photograph of Fidel Castro embracing East German leader Erich Honecker (1912–1994) illustrates the close ties that had developed by the mid-1970s between the Soviet Union and Cuba.

ddrbildarchiv.de/Newscom/Picture Alliance/Havana, Cuba.

READING AND DISCUSSION QUESTIONS

1. How might this photograph have been interpreted by the majority of Americans in the mid-1970s? By the Cuban people? By the Soviet people?

2. Compare and contrast Cuba's relationship with the Soviet Union to the relationship between East Germany and the Soviet Union. What similarities and differences do you note? Did either Cuba or East Germany have much say in its own social and political development?

▪ COMPARATIVE QUESTIONS ▪

1. How do Neruda's poems complicate your understanding of the Cold War? Was the Cold War an ideological struggle, as President Truman claimed, or were other forces at work as well?

2. What factors were most important in shaping U.S. policy in Latin America in the 1950s and 1960s? What light do Neruda's poems and developments in Castro's Cuba shed on this question?

3. How might Bolívar (Document 27-1) have responded to the UN Declaration on the Granting of Independence to Colonial Countries and Peoples? Would he have agreed, for example, that "inadequacy of political, economic, social or educational preparedness should never serve as a pretext for delaying independence"?

4. Compare and contrast the documents relating to decolonization and dependence in this chapter with those relating to nineteenth-century imperialism in Chapters 25 and 26. What similarities and differences do you note?

32

Liberalization
1968–2000s

By the early 1970s, the postwar period of decolonization had come to an end. A host of new nations had been created, and the imperial order that had reached its apex in the late nineteenth and early twentieth centuries had been almost completely dismantled. This did not mean, however, that the unequal relationship between developing and developed nations had been fundamentally altered. Developing nations in Africa, Asia, the Middle East, and Latin America faced enormous political and economic challenges. These challenges were, in many cases, exacerbated by the actions and policies of the world's wealthiest and most powerful nations. Cold War competition prompted both the United States and the Soviet Union to intervene in the domestic politics of nations around the world, often in ways that ran counter to the interests of the nations involved. Moreover, starting in the 1970s, liberal political and economic ideology experienced a resurgence in the West. The United States in particular championed liberal economic policies and global free trade. Proponents of such policies argued that they would ultimately benefit all peoples because they would stimulate global economic growth. Opponents, including the leaders of a number of developing countries, saw liberalization as just the latest Western strategy to perpetuate global inequality.

32-1 | Remembering Argentina's "Dirty War"
Museo de la Memoria, Córdoba, Argentina (ca. 2000)

Between 1976 and 1983, Argentina's military junta waged a "Dirty War" against its political opponents, killing between 14,000 and 30,000 Argentines and imprisoning and torturing many thousands more. The Museo de la Memoria in Córdoba, Argentina, commemorates the victims of this dark period. As the museum's name suggests, its primary purpose is to counter the efforts of the junta to erase its victims from history by preserving their memory. The museum is housed in a building that was a center for the activities of a special division of the junta's Department of Intelligence. The division specialized in the kidnapping and torture of the regime's opponents and the "reassignment" of their children to families of regime supporters.

Museo de la Memoria, Cordoba, Argentina (photo)/AA World Travel Library/Bridgeman Images.

READING AND DISCUSSION QUESTIONS

1. What purposes do museums such as this one serve? Why is it important to preserve historical memory, particularly of tragic events?

2. In your opinion, what made the Dirty War possible? What group or groups should be held responsible for the political violence of the 1970s and early 1980s?

VIEWPOINTS

Race and Power in South Africa

The 1950s and 1960s saw the end of colonization and the establishment of new and independent nations across Africa. For the most part, this process was a peaceful one. In regions with large numbers of white settlers, however, decolonization was often accompanied by considerable violence. In French Algeria, for example, the large European population pressured the French government to resist calls for Algerian independence, sparking a long and bitter war between France and Algerian anticolonial forces (see Chapter 31). In South Africa, an even more entrenched European population made the preservation of the colonial racial hierarchy its highest priority, organizing the government, economy, and legal system of South Africa around that goal. As you read the documents included here, ask yourself if the racial policies of the South African government in the decades following World War II made political violence inevitable. How would Nelson Mandela have responded to this question? What about the leaders of the South African government under apartheid?

32-2 | The South African Government Justifies Apartheid

NATIONAL PARTY OF SOUTH AFRICA, *The National Party's Color Policy* (March 29, 1948)

When the Union of South Africa was established as a quasi-autonomous dominion of the British Empire in 1910, its legal and political system embraced the policies of segregation and disenfranchisement of nonwhites that had flourished in colonial times. Not until the 1948 South African parliamentary election, however, did the formal system of apartheid, or "separation," become official state policy. Inhabitants of South Africa were strictly defined according to government racial criteria that determined where they could live, whom they could marry or have sexual relationships with, what they could study, and whether they were in fact citizens. The resulting system of white supremacy emphasized the threat of decolonization and the need for unity among the white minority. Several points in the government's policy are laid out here in this 1948 government proclamation, as catalogued by the United Nations.

From U.N. General Assembly, Eighth Session. Supplement No. 16. *Report of the United Nations Commission on the Racial Situation in the Union of South Africa*, 1953. (A/2505 and A/2505/ADD.1). Official Record.

There are two sections of thought in South Africa in regard to the policy affecting the non-European community.[1] On the one hand there is the policy of equality, which advocates equal rights within the same political structure for all civilized and educated persons, irrespective of race or color, and the gradual granting of the franchise to non-Europeans as they become qualified to make use of democratic rights.

On the other hand there is the policy of separation (*apartheid*) which has grown from the experience of established European population of the country, and which is based on the Christian principles of Justice and reasonableness.

Its aim is the maintenance and protection of the European population of the country as a pure White race, the maintenance and protection of the indigenous racial groups as separate communities, with prospects of developing into self-supporting communities within their own areas, and the stimulation of national pride, self-respect, and mutual respect among the various races of the country.

We can act in only one of two directions. Either we must follow the course of equality, which must eventually mean national suicide for the White race, or we must take the course of separation (*apartheid*) through which the character and the future of every race will be protected and safeguarded with full opportunities for development and self-maintenance in their own ideas, without the interests of one clashing with the interests of the other, and without one regarding the development of the other as undermining or a threat to himself.

The party therefore undertakes to protect the White race properly and effectively against any policy, doctrine or attack which might undermine or threaten its continued existence. At the same time the party rejects any policy of oppression and exploitation of the non-Europeans by the Europeans as being in conflict with the Christian basis of our national life and irreconcilable with our policy.

The party believes that a definite policy of separation (*apartheid*) between the White races and the non-White racial groups, and the application of the policy of separation also in the case of the non-White racial groups, is the only basis on which the character and future of each race can be protected and safeguarded and on which each race can be guided so as to develop his own national character, aptitude and calling.

All marriages between Europeans and non-Europeans will be prohibited.

In their areas the non-European racial groups will have full opportunities for development in every sphere and will be able to develop their own institutions and social services whereby the forces of the progressive non-Europeans can be harnessed for their own national development (*volkeepbou*). The policy of the country must be so planned that it will eventually promote the ideal of complete separation (*algehele apartheid*) in a national way.

---

[1] **non-European community:** As used in this report, *European* loosely means "white," and *non-European* is approximately the same as "Colored" or "Native." South Asians in Africa are also nonwhite, but not native.

A permanent advisory body of experts on non-European affairs will be established.

The State will exercise complete supervision over the molding of the youth. The party will not tolerate interference from without or destructive propaganda from the outside world in regard to the racial problems of South Africa.

The party wishes all non-Europeans to be strongly encouraged to make the Christian religion the basis of their lives and will assist churches in this task in every possible way. Churches and societies which undermine the policy of *apartheid* and propagate doctrines foreign to the nation will be checked.

The Colored community takes a middle position between the European and the Natives. A policy of separation (*apartheid*) between the Europeans and Coloreds and between Natives and Coloreds will be applied in the social, residential, industrial and political spheres. No marriage between Europeans and Coloreds will be permitted. The Coloreds will be protected against unfair competition from the Natives in so far as where they are already established.

The Colored community will be represented in the Senate by a European representative to be appointed by the Government by reason of his knowledge of Colored affairs.

The present unhealthy system which allows Coloreds in the Cape to be registered on the same voters' roll as Europeans and to vote for the same candidate as Europeans will be abolished and the Coloreds will be represented in the House of Assembly by three European representatives.

These Colored representatives will be elected by a Colored representative council. They will not vote on:

(1) Votes on confidence in the Government.
(2) A declaration of war, and
(3) A change in the political rights of non-Europeans.

A State Department of Colored Affairs will be established.

The Colored community will be represented in the Cape Provincial Council by three Europeans elected by the Colored representative council.

A Colored representative council will be established in the Cape Province consisting of representatives elected by the Colored community, divided into constituencies with the present franchise qualifications, the head of the Department of Colored Affairs and representatives nominated by the Government. In their own areas the Colored community will have their own councils with their own public services which will be managed by themselves within the framework of the existing councils with higher authority.

Attention will be given to the provision of social, medical and welfare services in which the efforts of the Colored themselves can be harnessed, and in which they will be taught as far as possible to be self-supporting.

READING AND DISCUSSION QUESTIONS

1. Does this document represent the voice of Europeans or Africans? Who wrote this document?

2. What rationale does the national government present for the institution of apartheid?

3. How is religion used in this document, and to what end? What limitations, if any, are placed on religion?

4. What rights are given to "Colored" people, and what rights are denied them? What can you imagine to be the probable outcomes of such restrictions?

32-3 | Mandela Explains the Need for Armed Struggle Against Apartheid

NELSON MANDELA, *The Rivonia Trial Speech to the Court* (April 20, 1964)

The white Afrikaner government that came to power in South Africa following World War II enacted extreme forms of legal segregation (apartheid) that relegated blacks to the lowest-paid jobs and the poorest regions of the country. In the 1950s and 1960s, the African National Congress (ANC), led by young attorney Nelson Mandela (1918–2013), protested these racist policies first peacefully and later violently. The organization was outlawed in 1961, but Mandela continued to run the ANC while in hiding for seventeen months before he was arrested, tried, and found guilty of treason. He was imprisoned until 1990. Mandela first presented this defense following the 1963 arrest of ANC leaders at Liliesleaf Farm, Rivonia, and later included it in reports he released after becoming the first democratically elected president of South Africa in 1994.

In my youth . . . I listened to the elders of my tribe telling stories of the old days. Amongst the tales they related to me were those of wars fought by our ancestors in defense of the father-land. . . . I hoped then that life might offer me the opportunity to serve my people and make my own humble contribution to their freedom struggle. This is what has motivated me in all that I have done in relation to the charges made against me in this case. . . .

I have already mentioned that I was one of the persons who helped to form Umkonto.[2] I, and the others who started the organization, did so for two reasons. Firstly, we believed that as a result of Government policy, violence by the African people had become inevitable, and that unless responsible leadership was given to canalize and control the feelings of our people, there would be outbreaks of

---

Nelson Mandela, *No Easy Walk to Freedom*, ed. Ruth First (New York: Basic Books, 1965), 163–168. Used by permission of The Nelson Mandela Foundation.

[2] **Umkonto:** Short for "Umkonto we Sizwe," or Spear of the Nation, a militant subgroup of the African National Congress that Mandela founded while in hiding in 1961.

terrorism which would produce an intensity of bitterness and hostility between the various races of this country which is not produced even by war. Secondly, we felt that without violence there would be no way open to the African people to succeed in their struggle against the principle of White supremacy. All lawful modes of expressing opposition to this principle had been closed by legislation, and we were placed in a position in which we had either to accept a permanent state of inferiority, or to defy the Government. . . .

But the violence which we chose to adopt was not terrorism. We who formed Umkonto were all members of the African National Congress, and had behind us the ANC tradition of non-violence and negotiation as a means of solving political disputes. We believed that South Africa belonged to all the people who lived in it, and not to one group, be it Black or White. We did not want an interracial war, and tried to avoid it to the last minute. . . .

The African National Congress was formed in 1912 to defend the rights of the African people. . . . For thirty-seven years—that is until 1949—it adhered strictly to a constitutional struggle. It put forward demands and resolutions; it sent delegations to the Government in the belief that African grievances could be settled through peaceful discussion and that Africans could advance gradually to full political rights. But White Governments remained unmoved, and the rights of Africans became less instead of becoming greater. . . .

Even after 1949, the ANC remained determined to avoid violence. At this time, however, there was a change from the strictly constitutional means of protest which had been employed in the past. The change was embodied in a decision which was taken to protest against apartheid legislation by peaceful, but unlawful, demonstrations against certain laws. Pursuant to this policy the ANC launched the Defiance Campaign, in which I was placed in charge of volunteers. This campaign was based on the principles of passive resistance.[3] More than 8,500 people defied apartheid laws and went to jail. Yet there was not a single instance of violence in the course of this campaign on the part of any defier. . . .

In 1960 there was the shooting at Sharpeville,[4] which resulted in the proclamation of a state of emergency and the declaration of the ANC as an unlawful organization. My colleagues and I, after careful consideration, decided that we would not obey this decree. The African people were not part of the Government and did not make the laws by which they were governed. We believed in the words of the Universal Declaration of Human Rights,[5] that "the will of the people shall be the basis of authority of the Government," and for us to accept the banning was equivalent to accepting the silencing of the

---

[3] **passive resistance:** A form of nonviolent political protest used and popularized by Indian leader Mohandas Gandhi (1869–1948).

[4] **shooting at Sharpeville:** The Sharpeville Massacre of 1960, in which police killed 69 and wounded 178 anti-apartheid demonstrators.

[5] **Universal Declaration of Human Rights:** A declaration of the rights of every human being, adopted by the United Nations on December 10, 1948.

Africans for all time. The ANC refused to dissolve, but instead went underground. . . .

Each disturbance pointed clearly to the inevitable growth among Africans of the belief that violence was the only way out—it showed that a Government which uses force to maintain its rule teaches the oppressed to use force to oppose it. . . .

The avoidance of civil war had dominated our thinking for many years, but when we decided to adopt violence as part of our policy, we realized that we might one day have to face the prospect of such a war. . . . We did not want to be committed to civil war, but we wanted to be ready if it became inevitable.

Four forms of violence were possible. There is sabotage, there is guerrilla warfare, there is terrorism, and there is open revolution. We chose to adopt the first method and to exhaust it before taking any other decision.

In the light of our political background the choice was a logical one. Sabotage did not involve loss of life, and it offered the best hope for future race relations. Bitterness would be kept to a minimum and, if the policy bore fruit, democratic government could become a reality. . . .

Attacks on the economic lifelines of the country were to be linked with sabotage on Government buildings and other symbols of apartheid. These attacks would serve as a source of inspiration to our people. In addition, they would provide an outlet for those people who were urging the adoption of violent methods and would enable us to give concrete proof to our followers that we had adopted a stronger line and were fighting back against Government violence. . . .

Another of the allegations made by the State is that the aims and objects of the ANC and the Communist Party are the same. . . .

It is true that there has often been close cooperation between the ANC and the Communist Party. But cooperation is merely proof of a common goal—in this case the removal of White supremacy—and is not proof of a complete community of interests. . . .

It is perhaps difficult for White South Africans, with an ingrained prejudice against communism, to understand why experienced African politicians so readily accept communists as their friends. But to us the reason is obvious. Theoretical differences amongst those fighting against oppression is a luxury we cannot afford at this stage. What is more, for many decades communists were the only political group in South Africa who were prepared to treat Africans as human beings and their equals; who were prepared to eat with us, talk with us, live with us, and work with us. They were the only political group which was prepared to work with the Africans for the attainment of political rights and a stake in society. Because of this, there are many Africans who, today, tend to equate freedom with communism. . . .

Our fight is against real, and not imaginary, hardships or, to use the language of the State prosecutor, "so-called hardships." Basically, we fight against two features which are the hallmarks of African life in South Africa and which are entrenched by legislation which we seek to have repealed. These features are poverty and lack of human dignity. . . .

South Africa is the richest country in Africa, and could be one of the richest countries in the world. But it is a land of extremes and remarkable contrasts. The Whites enjoy what may well be the highest standard of living in the world, whilst Africans live in poverty and misery. Forty percent of the Africans live in hopelessly overcrowded and, in some cases, drought-stricken Reserves, where soil erosion and the overworking of the soil make it impossible for them to live properly off the land. Thirty percent are laborers, labor tenants, and squatters on White farms and work and live under conditions similar to those of the serfs of the Middle Ages. The other 30 percent live in towns where they have developed economic and social habits which bring them closer in many respects to White standards. Yet most Africans, even in this group, are impoverished by low incomes and [the] high cost of living. . . .

The lack of human dignity experienced by Africans is the direct result of the policy of White supremacy. White supremacy implies Black inferiority. Legislation designed to preserve White supremacy entrenches this notion. Menial tasks in South Africa are invariably performed by Africans. When anything has to be carried or cleaned the White man will look around for an African to do it for him, whether the African is employed by him or not. Because of this sort of attitude, Whites tend to regard Africans as a separate breed. They do not look upon them as people with families of their own; they do not realize that they have emotions—that they fall in love like White people do; that they want to be with their wives and children like White people want to be with theirs; that they want to earn enough money to support their families properly, to feed and clothe them and send them to school. And what "house-boy" or "garden-boy" or laborer can ever hope to do this? . . .

Poverty and the breakdown of family life have secondary effects. Children wander about the streets of the townships because they have no schools to go to, or no money to enable them to go to school, or no parents at home to see that they go to school, because both parents (if there be two) have to work to keep the family alive. This leads to a breakdown in moral standards, to an alarming rise in illegitimacy, and to growing violence which erupts, not only politically, but everywhere. Life in the townships is dangerous. There is not a day that goes by without somebody being stabbed or assaulted. And violence is carried out of the townships in the White living areas. People are afraid to walk alone in the streets after dark. Housebreakings and robberies are increasing, despite the fact that the death sentence can now be imposed for such offenses. Death sentences cannot cure the festering sore. . . .

During my lifetime I have dedicated myself to this struggle of the African people. I have fought against White domination, and I have fought against Black domination. I have cherished the ideal of a democratic and free society in which all persons live together in harmony and with equal opportunities. It is an ideal which I hope to live for and to achieve. But if needs be, it is an ideal for which I am prepared to die.

READING AND DISCUSSION QUESTIONS

1. What reason does Mandela give for the ANC's decision to defy the government decree that outlawed the group?

2. What form of violence did the formerly nonviolent ANC adopt, and how does Mandela justify this decision?

3. How does Mandela describe the experience of blacks under apartheid? Why did he believe that apartheid contributed to a host of social problems?

VIEWPOINTS COMPARATIVE QUESTIONS

1. According to the South African government, what were the intended consequences of apartheid? According to Mandela, what were the actual consequences of apartheid?

2. In your opinion, who bore the greater responsibility for the violence that rocked South Africa in the 1970s and 1980s: the South African government or the ANC? Why?

32-4 | Deng Xiaoping Places China on a New Path

DENG XIAOPING, *Build Socialism with Chinese Characteristics* (June 30, 1984)

Following the death of Mao Zedong in 1976, the longtime Chinese Communist Party leader Deng Xiaoping (1904–1997) gained control of the party and of the Chinese government. Espousing the Four Modernizations of agriculture, industry, military, and science and technology, Deng sought to move China away from the upheaval of Mao's radical leadership and toward a reconciliation with Western modernity. This transition laid the foundation for China's rapid economic growth, while retaining its distinctly authoritarian political structures. Deng Xiaoping delivered the following speech to a group of Japanese delegates in 1984, using classical Marxist theory to explain the necessity of a more open economy for the ultimate realization of socialist values.

People may ask, If China had taken the capitalist instead of the socialist road, could the Chinese people have liberated themselves and could China have finally stood up? The Nationalists took that road for more than twenty years and proved that it does not work. By contrast, the Chinese Communists, by adhering to

Sources of Chinese Tradition, ed. William Theodore de Bary and Richard Lufrano, 2 vols. (New York: Columbia University Press, 2000), 2:507–510. Copyright © 2001 Columbia University Press. Reprinted with permission of the publisher.

Marxism and integrating Marxism with actual conditions in China in accordance with Mao Zedong Thought, took their own road and succeeded in the revolution by encircling the cities from the countryside. Conversely, if we had not been Marxists, or if we had not integrated Marxism with Chinese conditions and followed our own road, China would have remained fragmented, with neither independence nor unity. China simply had to adhere to Marxism. If we had not fully believed in Marxism, the Chinese revolution would never have succeeded. That belief was the motive force. After the founding of the People's Republic, if we had taken the capitalist rather than the socialist road, we would not have ended the chaos in the country or changed its conditions—inflation, unstable prices, poverty, and backwardness. We started from a backward past. There was virtually no industry for us to inherit from old China, and we did not have enough grain for food. Some people ask why we chose socialism. We answer that we had to, because capitalism would get China nowhere. We must solve the problems of feeding and employing the population and of reunifying China. That is why we have repeatedly declared that we shall adhere to Marxism and keep to the socialist road. But by Marxism we mean Marxism that is integrated with Chinese conditions, and by socialism we mean socialism that is tailored to Chinese conditions and has Chinese characteristics.

What is socialism and what is Marxism? We were not quite clear about this before. Marxism attaches utmost importance to developing the productive forces. We advocate communism. But what does that mean? It means the principle of from each according to his ability, to each according to his needs, which calls for highly developed productive forces and overwhelming material wealth. Therefore, the fundamental task for the socialist stage is to develop the productive forces. The superiority of the socialist system is demonstrated by faster and greater development of the productive forces than under the capitalist system. One of our shortcomings since the founding of the People's Republic was that we neglected the development of the productive forces. Socialism means eliminating poverty. Pauperism is not socialism, still less communism. The superiority of the socialist system lies above all in its ability to increasingly develop the productive forces and to improve the people's material and cultural life. The problem facing us now is how China, which is still backward, is to develop the productive forces and improve the people's living standard. This brings us back to the point of whether to continue on the socialist road or to stop and turn onto the capitalist road. The capitalist road can only enrich less than 10 percent of the Chinese population; it can never enrich the 90 percent. That is why we must adhere to socialism. The socialist principle of distribution to each according to his work will not create an excessive gap in wealth. Consequently, no polarization will occur as our productive forces become developed over the next twenty to thirty years.

The minimum target of our Four Modernizations is to achieve a comparatively comfortable standard of living by the end of the century. . . . By a "comfortable standard" we mean that per capita GNP [gross national product] will reach U.S. $800. That is a low level for you, but it is really ambitious for us. China has a population of 1 billion now and it will reach 1.2 billion by then. If, when the GNP reached $1,000 billion, we applied the capitalist principle of distribution, it would not amount to much and could not help to eliminate poverty and backwardness. Less than 10 percent of the population would enjoy a better life, while more than 90 percent remained in poverty. But the socialist principle of distribution can enable all the people to become relatively comfortable. This is why we want to uphold socialism. Without socialism, China can never achieve that goal.

However, only talking about this is not enough. The present world is an open one. China's past backwardness was due to its closed-door policy. After the founding of the People's Republic, we were blockaded by others, and so the country remained closed to some extent, which created difficulties for us. Some "left" policies and the Cultural Revolution in particular were disastrous for us. In short, the experience of the past thirty years or more proves that a closed-door policy would hinder construction and inhibit development. . . . Our political line focuses on the four modernizations, on continuing to develop the productive forces. Nothing short of world war would make us release our grip on this essential point. Even should world war break out, we would engage in reconstruction after the war. A closed-door policy would not help construction. There are two kinds of exclusion: one is directed against other countries; the other is directed against China itself, with one region or department closing its doors to the others. We are suggesting that we should develop a little faster—just a little, because it would be unrealistic to go too fast. To do this, we have to invigorate the domestic economy and open up to the outside. We must first of all solve the problem of the countryside, which contains 80 percent of the population. China's stability depends on the stability of the countryside with this 80 percent—this is the reality of China from which we should proceed. No matter how successful our work in the cities is, it will not mean much without the stable base of the countryside. Therefore, we must first of all solve the problem of the countryside by invigorating the economy and adopting an open policy so as to bring the initiative of 80 percent of the population into full play. We adopted this policy at the end of 1978, and after several years in operation it has produced the desired results. . . .

As for our relations with foreign countries, we shall pursue the policy of opening up still wider to the outside world. We have opened fourteen medium and large coastal cities. We welcome foreign investment and advanced techniques. Management is also a kind of technique. Will they undermine our socialism? Not likely, because the socialist economy is our mainstay. Our socialist economic base is so huge that it can absorb tens and hundreds of billions of dollars' worth of foreign funds without shaking the socialist foundation. Besides, we adhere to the socialist principle of distribution and do not tolerate economic polarization. Thus, foreign investment will doubtless serve as a major supplement to the building of socialism in our country. And as things stand now, this supplement is indispensable. Naturally, some problems will arise in the wake of foreign investment. But the negative aspects are far less significant than the positive use we can make of it to accelerate our development. It may entail a slight risk, but not much.

Well, those are our plans. We shall accumulate experience and try new solutions as new problems arise. In general, we believe the road we have chosen—building socialism with Chinese characteristics—is the right one and will work. We have followed this road for five and a half years and have achieved satisfactory results. We want to quadruple China's GNP by the end of the century. The pace of development so far exceeded our projections. And so I can tell our friends that we are even more confident now.

READING AND DISCUSSION QUESTIONS

1. How does Deng justify more open markets as a part of socialism?

2. How are international affairs connected to Deng's plan? How does Deng plan to change China's stance toward the world?

3. What aspects of Deng's argument convinces you? What aspects do you find unconvincing?

32-5 | Building a Meaningful Life in Contemporary Japan
MALE JAPANESE CITIZENS, *"Ikigai"* (2003)

Following Japan's cataclysmic defeat in the Second World War, the American-led occupation forces worked closely with Japanese political and industrial leaders to rebuild the war-torn country and, during the Cold War, to make Japan a bulwark against communism in East Asia. Close relationships between industry and government, a hallmark of the prewar economy, continued to drive Japan's postwar economic recovery, though in slightly different forms. Within the corporate world, a highly gendered Japanese workforce also depended on long-term relationships, and lifetime employment at a single company became the norm for Japanese men. After the collapse of the economic "bubble" in the early 1990s, however, Japanese men began to question their relationship with Japan's economy and society. The selections here present a range of contemporary Japanese male voices on the changing definition of *ikigai*—that which makes life worth living.

Corporate Executive

For the past thirty years, my *ikigai* has been the companies I've worked for; they've been more important to me than my family. I don't expect much from my family; they don't expect me to be at home on weekends anymore. Yes, I can't say that I'm a family man. I have more human communication with the young girls . . . in my office than I do with my own daughters. . . .

There are fewer and fewer company men like me these days; there are many more "my home" types — these kind of people aren't at all happy if I tell them to

Gordon Mathews, "Can a Real Man Live for His Family? *Ikigai* and Masculinity in Today's Japan," in James Roberson and Nobue Suzuki, eds., *Men and Masculinities in Contemporary Japan* (New York: RoutledgeCurzon, 2003), 109–225. Reprinted by permission of Gordon Mathews.

come to the office on Sunday! I've never said no to any of my job assignments — I was always there when they needed me. I like men who do that: manly men . . . , like Western cowboys! Men living for their companies are better than those who live for their families; that's why Japan's developed! I get upset when I see a young man with dyed hair driving around in a fancy car with a pretty girl. Fifty years ago, people his age all died in the war; they didn't have the chance to enjoy their youth! I want to drag that young man out of his car and put a judo hold on him, teach him a lesson!

High School Teacher

Maybe Americans can separate business and private life, but I can't, and most Japanese can't. If you don't have business, you can't have any private life. . . . In my house, my wife was like a widow; I was busy, even on Sundays, with my school clubs. So now, if I'm not home, everyone feels more relaxed! . . .

Young people today overwhelmingly value being with their families. They calmly say, "My child's sick. I'll take the day off." Nobody ever did that when I was young! Today's young people don't have any fighting spirit! They relax with their families before they think about work!

Sarariman (White-Collar Worker) 1

The problem was that we worked too hard, generated too much money, that had to be plowed back into the system, into stocks and land, creating "the bubble economy." . . . If only Japanese hadn't worked so hard, maybe the economic downturn would never have happened.

Sarariman 2

If you ask my coworkers whether they find *ikigai* in work for this company, they might say they do. But they'd be lying. . . . But, then, maybe they really do find *ikigai* here. If you don't have time to do anything but work, then isn't that your *ikigai*?

Retired Railroad Worker

You know how work is. The husband has to be subservient to his boss, and so when he comes home, he wants to boss around his wife and children: "Turn off the TV! Put the kids to bed!" And communication between husband and wife, father and children, goes bad.

Self-Employed Repairman

I believe that the husband's the boss of the family. A wife should know what her husband is thinking by looking at his face. She should properly send him off to work in the morning; and when he comes home at night, there should be a drink and some good food waiting for him. A husband should educate his wife to do that. . . . When I got married, my wife fell in love with me; I didn't care whether I married her or not. She works part-time at the supermarket as a cashier — she's a little overbearing now, since she's got her own money.

Sarariman 3

Early in our marriage, my wife was always angry because I came home late from work, and because I wasn't *yasashii* (affectionate); I didn't take her anywhere on weekends, I didn't convey to her that I loved her. We came very close to divorce several times. Once my wife left with the kids and didn't come home for three days; I still don't know where they went. I wasn't thinking much about my family then; that's why my wife got so upset. I realized that I'd have to change. My wife made me promise that, unless I was out of town on business, I'd have breakfast with the family no matter how late I came home the previous night. I also spend every Sunday — at least half the day — with my family. Saturdays I use for myself: I go fishing. . . . I feel exhausted because of the stress on my job — that's why I need Saturdays for myself. When I'm with my family, I just can't get rid of stress.

Bank Worker

I don't like my work — I really hate it — but I wouldn't want to stay at home either, taking care of my children. Maybe that's my pride — maybe I don't want to deviate from the ideal image of a man. A man is supposed to work outside the home. In Japan, if a man says his child rather than his work is his *ikigai*, he'll be considered a sissy. . . . I could never say that. . . . In Japan women are discriminated against in the workplace, but at the same time they have less obligation; they have more time to follow their own pursuits. Do I wish I could be a woman instead of a man? Well . . . I could never say that; but it's possible that it's true.

Junior High School Teacher

I want to be with my wife when she gives birth; I'll need to take three days off from school for that. When I told that to the mothers in the PTA, they said, "That's great — go ahead!" I thought they were going to say, "What? Why so long a vacation!" But they didn't. They really appreciate me! . . . I usually get home by 7:30 or 8:00; sometimes not until 9:00 or 10:00. All I can do after I come home so late is bathe, eat and sleep; that's tough on my wife. I'm really tired. Sometimes it's just too much trouble to listen to her, to be honest. I'd really like more free time. . . . My family — my wife and child to be — is more important than my work. I'd quit my work, if I had to, for my family. My family is my *ikigai*. I just wish I had more time to be with my family.

Construction Worker and Former Rock Musician

I like myself now because I'm working hard for my family, but I hate myself because I gave up music. I'm not a bad father — I'm supporting my family — but maybe it'd be better for my two kids if I showed them a father who's pursuing his dream. Life isn't only a matter of making money; that's why I half regret my life now. I want to quit my job and play music again. But it'd be hard. The older you get, the less courage you've got. Compared to five years ago, I'm much more of a coward than I used to be. Maybe I've become a better husband and father to the extent that I've grown chicken-hearted! . . . I live for my dream of music, but I also live for my wife: she too is my *ikigai*. But yeah, I guess that my real *ikigai* is music. I don't play the guitar much these days, but I have that desire — I'll have that for the rest of my life.

READING AND DISCUSSION QUESTIONS

1. How do these accounts of *ikigai* present Japan's economic success in the postwar era?

2. Some of these accounts deal explicitly with Japanese history, including the Second World War. How does history inform each of these accounts? Why might history play a larger role in some accounts than in others?

3. How does each of these accounts talk about gender? What women's roles are described here? Based on these accounts, what can you say about gender roles in contemporary Japan?

■ COMPARATIVE QUESTIONS ■

1. What connections can you make between the military governments that took power in South America in the 1970s (see Document 32-1) and the caudillos who rose to power in the nineteenth century (see Chapter 27)?

2. Compare and contrast the place of East Asia in the global economy today (see Documents 32-4 and 32-5) with the place it occupied in the first half of the twentieth century (see Chapter 29). What has changed? Why?

3. How might Gandhi (see Chapters 26 and 29) have responded to Mandela's defense of violent struggle in South Africa (see Documents 32-2 and 32-3)? What differences might Mandela have identified between India and South Africa to justify his position?

4. What similarities and differences do you see between the civil rights movement in the United States in the 1950s and 1960s and the fight against apartheid in South Africa (see Documents 32-2 and 32-3)? How did the civil rights movement shape American public opinion about apartheid in the 1970s and 1980s?

5. Compare and contrast the National Party's Color Policy with the Nazis' Nuremberg Laws (Document 30-2). In what ways are the two policies similar?

33

The Contemporary World in Historical Perspective

The 1990s marked the beginning of a new era in world history. The Cold War was over, new human rights initiatives were springing up in long-repressed countries, and the so-called age of globalization was under way. By the early twenty-first century, the political and economic systems of all countries were more intricately linked and interdependent than ever before. Booms and busts, environmental issues, terrorism, war, and the spread of multinational corporations had become concerns for all nation-states. The United Nations emerged as an important voice in the global political arena. Western corporations reached into developing nations promising economic improvement on the one hand, and seeking new and cheaper sources of labor on the other. For some, the global economy has led to growth, technological development, and the promise of social and political reform. For others, the greater worldwide interconnectedness has exposed vast differences in values and wealth. One international constant remains—the struggle of people to be responsible global citizens.

33-1 | Defining and Defending Torture
JOHN YOO, *Memoranda Regarding U.S. Military Interrogations* (2002, 2003)

Following the attacks of September 11, 2001, the United States' most visible responses were military action against and invasion of Afghanistan (2001) and Iraq (2003). Domestically, President George W. Bush's administration moved to clarify the legal and political grounds for

John Yoo, Deputy Assistant Attorney General of the United States, to Alberto R. Gonzales, Counsel to the President, August 1, 2002, Office of Legal Counsel, U.S. Department of Justice, Washington, D.C. John Yoo, Deputy Assistant Attorney General of the United States, to William J. Haynes II, General Counsel of the Department of Defense, March 14, 2003, Office of Legal Counsel, U.S. Department of Justice, Washington, D.C.

what was termed the war on terrorism, an effort that involved the detention and interrogation of both U.S. citizens and aliens. Deputy Assistant Attorney General of the United States John Yoo was asked by then-Counsel to the President Alberto R. Gonzalez, and later by General Counsel of the Department of Defense William J. Haynes II, to provide a legal opinion on the power of the president to interrogate prisoners and whether such interrogation was prosecutable as torture. His responses, excerpted here from fifty- and eighty-page letters, respectively, were widely understood to condone interrogation techniques such as waterboarding, adding to the controversy surrounding the U.S. response to the attacks of September 11.

Memorandum for Alberto R. Gonzales, Counsel to the President

August 1, 2002

Re: Standards of Conduct for Interrogation
Under 18 U.S.C. 2340–2340A

You have asked for our Office's views regarding the standards of conduct under the Convention Against Torture and Other Cruel, Inhuman and Degrading Treatment or Punishment as implemented by Sections 2340–2340A of title 18 of the United States Code.[1] As we understand it, this question has arisen in the context of the conduct of interrogations outside of the United States. We conclude . . . that Section 2340A proscribes acts inflicting, and that are specifically intended to inflict, severe pain or suffering, whether mental or physical. Those acts must be of an extreme nature to rise to the level of torture within the meaning of Section 2340A and the Convention. We further conclude that certain acts may be cruel, inhuman, or degrading, but still not produce pain and suffering of the requisite intensity to fall within Section 2340A's proscription against torture. . . .

We conclude that for an act to constitute torture as defined in Section 2340, it must inflict pain that is difficult to endure. Physical pain amounting to torture must be equivalent in intensity to the pain accompanying serious physical injury, such as organ failure, impairment of bodily function, or even death. For purely mental pain or suffering to amount to torture under Section 2340, it must result in significant psychological harm of significant duration, e.g., lasting for months or even years. We conclude that the mental harm also must result from one of the predicate acts listed in the statute, namely: threats of imminent death; threats of infliction of the kind of pain that would amount to physical torture; infliction of such physical pain as a means of psychological torture; use of drugs or other procedures designed to deeply disrupt the senses, or fundamentally alter an individual's personality; or threatening to do any of these things to a third party. The legislative history simply reveals that Congress intended for the statute's definition to track the Convention's definition of torture and the reservations, understandings, and declarations that the United States submitted with its ratification. We conclude that the statute, taken as a whole, makes plain that it prohibits only extreme acts. . . .

---

[1] **Sections 2340–2340A . . . United States Code:** United States Code Title 18, Part I, Chapter 113C, Sections 2340 and 2340A define torture and make it illegal both within and beyond the United States.

We conclude that the treaty's text prohibits only the most extreme acts by reserving criminal penalties solely for torture and declining to require such penalties for "cruel, inhuman, or degrading treatment or punishment." This confirms our view that the criminal statute penalizes only the most egregious conduct. . . .

We examine international decisions regarding the use of sensory deprivation techniques. These cases make clear that while many of these techniques may amount to cruel, inhuman or degrading treatment, they do not produce pain or suffering of the necessary intensity to meet the definition of torture. From these decisions, we conclude that there is a wide range of such techniques that will not rise to the level of torture.

. . . We discuss whether Section 2340A may be unconstitutional if applied to interrogations undertaken of enemy combatants pursuant to the President's Commander-in-Chief powers. We find that in the circumstances of the current war against al Qaeda and its allies, prosecution under Section 2340A may be barred because enforcement of the statute would represent an unconstitutional infringement of the President's authority to conduct war.

Memorandum for William J. Haynes II, General Counsel of the Department of Defense

March 14, 2003

Re: Military Interrogation of Alien Unlawful Combatants
Held Outside the United States

You have asked our Office to examine the legal standards governing military interrogations of alien unlawful combatants held outside the United States. . . .

We conclude that the Fifth and Eighth Amendments,[2] as interpreted by the Supreme Court, do not extend to alien enemy combatants held abroad. . . . Federal criminal laws of general applicability do not apply to properly-authorized interrogations of enemy combatants, undertaken by military personnel in the course of an armed conflict. Such criminal statutes, if they were misconstrued to apply to the interrogation of enemy combatants, would conflict with the Constitution's grant of the Commander in Chief power solely to the President. . . .

Given the ongoing threat of al Qaeda attacks, the capture and interrogation of al Qaeda operatives is imperative to our national security and defense. Because of the asymmetric nature of terrorist operations, information is perhaps the most critical weapon for defeating al Qaeda. Al Qaeda is not a nation-state, and has no single country or geographic area as its base of operations. It has no fixed, large-scale military or civilian infrastructure. It deploys personnel, material, and finances covertly and attacks without warning using unconventional

---

[2] **Fifth and Eighth Amendments:** U.S. constitutional amendments guaranteeing citizens protection against government abuse in legal procedures and prohibiting the federal government from imposing cruel and unusual punishments, respectively.

weapons and methods. As the September 11, 2001 attacks and subsequent events demonstrate, it seeks to launch terror attacks against purely civilian targets within the United States, and seeks to acquire weapons of mass destruction for such attacks. Because of the secret nature of al Qaeda's operations, obtaining advance information about the identity of al Qaeda operatives and their plans may prove to be the only way to prevent direct attacks on the United States. Interrogation of captured al Qaeda operatives could provide that information; indeed, in many cases interrogation may be the only method to obtain it. Given the massive destruction and loss of life caused by the September 11 attacks, it is reasonable to believe that information gained from al Qaeda personnel could prevent attacks of a similar (if not greater) magnitude from occurring in the United States. . . .

One of the core functions of the Commander in Chief is that of capturing, detaining, and interrogating members of the enemy. . . . It is well settled that the President may seize and detain enemy combatants, at least for the duration of the conflict, and the laws of war make clear that prisoners may be interrogated for information concerning the enemy, its strength, and its plans. Numerous Presidents have ordered the capture, detention, and questioning of enemy combatants during virtually every major conflict in the Nation's history, including recent conflicts such as the Gulf, Vietnam, and Korean wars. Recognizing this authority, Congress has never attempted to restrict or interfere with the President's authority on this score. . . .

We conclude below that the Fifth Amendment Due Process Clause is inapplicable to the conduct of interrogations of alien enemy combatants held outside the United States for two independent reasons. First, the Fifth Amendment Due Process Clause does not apply to the President's conduct of a war. Second, even if the Fifth Amendment applied to the conduct of war, the Fifth Amendment does not apply extraterritorially to aliens who have no connection to the United States. We address each of these reasons in turn. . . .

Under traditional practice as expressed in the customary laws of war, the treatment of unlawful belligerents is left to the sovereign's discretion. . . . Under our Constitution, the sovereign right of the United States on the treatment of enemy combatants is reserved to the President as Commander-in-Chief. In light of the long history of discretion given to each nation to determine its treatment of unlawful combatants, to construe these statutes to regulate the conduct of the United States toward such combatants would interfere with a well-established prerogative of the sovereign. While the Geneva Convention (III) Relative to the Treatment of Prisoners of War, Aug. 12, 1949, . . . imposes restrictions on the interrogations of prisoners of war, it does not provide prisoner of war status to those who are unlawful combatants. . . . Those restrictions therefore would not apply to the interrogations of unlawful belligerents such as al Qaeda or Taliban members.

The second exception recognized by the Supreme Court arises where the application of general laws to a government official would create absurd results, such as effectively preventing the official from carrying out his duties. In Nardone, the Supreme Court pointed to "the application of a speed law to a policeman pursuing a criminal or the driver of a fire engine responding to an alarm" as examples of such absurd results. . . . For the reasons we explain above, the application of these general laws to the conduct of the military during the course of a war would create untenable results. . . .

In the context of interrogations, we believe that interrogation methods that do not involve physical contact will not support a charge of assault resulting in substantial injury or assault resulting in serious bodily injury or substantial bodily injury. Moreover, even minimal physical contact, such as poking, slapping, or shoving the detainee, is unlikely to produce the injury necessary to establish either one of these types of assault. . . .

[On Maiming]

Another criminal statute applicable in the special maritime and territorial jurisdiction is 18 U.S.C. § 114. Section 114 makes it a crime for an individual (1) "with the intent to torture (as defined in section 2340), maim, or disfigure" to (2) "cut, bite, or slit the nose, ear, or lip, or cut out or disable the tongue, or put out or destroy an eye, or cut off or disable a limb or any member of another person." . . . It further prohibits individuals from "throw[ing] or pour[ing] upon another person any scalding water, corrosive acid, or caustic substance" with like intent. . . .

The offense requires the specific intent to torture, maim or disfigure. . . . Moreover, the defendant's method of maiming must be one of the types the statute specifies—i.e., cutting, biting, slitting, cutting out, disabling, or putting out—and the injury must be to a body part the statute specifies—i.e., the nose, ear, lip, tongue, eye, or limb. . . . Similarly, the second set of acts applies to a very narrow band of conduct. It applies only to the throwing or pouring of some sort of scalding, corrosive, or caustic substance. . . .

Here, so long as the interrogation methods under contemplation do not involve the acts enumerated in section 114, the conduct of those interrogations will not fall within the purview of this statute. Because the statute requires specific intent, i.e., the intent to maim, disfigure or torture, the absence of such intent is a complete defense to a charge of maiming. . . .

[On Criminal Prohibitions Applicable to Conduct Occurring Outside the Jurisdiction of the United States]

There are two criminal prohibitions that apply to the conduct of U.S. persons outside the United States: the War Crimes Act, 18 U.S.C. § 2441, and the prohibition against torture, 18 U.S.C. §§ 2340–2340A. We conclude that the War Crimes Act does not apply to the interrogation of al Qaeda and Taliban detainees because, as illegal belligerents, they do not qualify for the legal protections under the Geneva or Hague Conventions that section 2441 enforces. In regard to section 2340, we conclude that the statute, by its terms, does not apply to interrogations conducted within the territorial United States or on permanent military bases outside the territory of the United States. Nonetheless, we identify the relevant substantive standards regarding the prohibition on torture should interrogations occur outside that jurisdictional limit. . . .

Section 2340A of Title 18 makes it a criminal offense for any person "outside the United States [to] commit or attempt to commit torture." The statute defines "the United States" as "all areas under the jurisdiction of the United States including any of the places described in" 18 U.S.C. § 5, and 18 U.S.C.A. § 7. 18 U.S.C. § 2340(3). Therefore, to the extent that interrogations take place within the special maritime and territorial jurisdiction, such as at a U.S. military base in a foreign state, the interrogations are not subject to sections 2340–2340A. If, however, the interrogations take place outside the special maritime and territorial jurisdiction and are otherwise outside the United States, the torture statute applies. Thus, for example, interrogations conducted at GTMO[3] would not be subject to this prohibition, but interrogations conducted at a non-U.S. base in Afghanistan would be subject to section 2340A. . . .

Thus, to establish the offense of torture, the prosecution must show that: (1) the torture occurred outside the United States; (2) the defendant acted under the color of law; (3) the victim was within the defendant's custody or physical control; (4) the defendant specifically intended to cause severe physical or mental pain or suffering; and (5) that the act inflicted severe physical or mental pain or suffering. . . .

To violate section 2340A, the statute requires that severe pain and suffering be inflicted with specific intent. . . . For a defendant to act with specific intent, he must expressly intend to achieve the forbidden act. . . .

Here, because section 2340 requires that a defendant act with the specific intent to inflict severe pain, the infliction of such pain must be the defendant's precise objective. . . .

[In Summary]

Section 2340's definition of torture must be read as a sum of these component parts. . . . Each component of the definition emphasizes that torture is not the mere infliction of pain or suffering on another, but is instead a step well removed. The victim must experience intense pain or suffering of the kind that is equivalent to the pain that would be associated with serious physical injury so severe that death, organ failure, or permanent damage resulting in a loss of significant body function will likely result. If that pain or suffering is psychological, that suffering must result from one of the acts set forth in the statute. In

---

[3] **GTMO:** The military abbreviation for the prison maintained by the U.S. government at Guantánamo Bay, Cuba.

addition, these acts must cause long-term mental harm. Indeed, this view of the criminal act of torture is consistent with the term's common meaning. Torture is generally understood to involve "intense pain" or "excruciating pain," or put another way, "extreme anguish of body or mind." . . . In short, reading the definition of torture as a whole, it is plain that the term encompasses only extreme acts. . . .

As we have made clear in other opinions involving the war against al Qaeda, the Nation's right to self-defense has been triggered by the events of September 11. If a government defendant were to harm an enemy combatant during an interrogation in a manner that might arguably violate a criminal prohibition, he would be doing so in order to prevent further attacks on the United States by the al Qaeda terrorist network. In that case, we believe that he could argue that the executive branch's constitutional authority to protect the nation from attack justified his actions. This national and international version of the right to self-defense could supplement and bolster the government defendant's individual right.

Conclusion

For the foregoing reasons, we conclude that the Fifth and Eighth Amendments do not extend to alien enemy combatants held abroad. Moreover, we conclude that different canons of construction indicate that generally applicable criminal laws do not apply to the military interrogation of alien unlawful combatants held abroad. Were it otherwise, the application of these statutes to the interrogation of enemy combatants undertaken by military personnel would conflict with the President's Commander-in-Chief power.

We further conclude that CAT[4] defines U.S. international law obligations with respect to torture and other cruel, inhuman, or degrading treatment or punishment. The standard of conduct regarding torture is the same as that which is found in the torture statute, 18 U.S.C. §§ 2340–2340A. Moreover, the scope of U.S. obligations under CAT regarding cruel, inhuman, or degrading treatment or punishment is limited to conduct prohibited by the Eighth, Fifth and Fourteenth Amendments. Customary international law does not supply any additional standards.

Finally, even if the criminal prohibitions outlined above applied, and an interrogation method might violate those prohibitions, necessity or self-defense could provide justifications for any criminal liability.

Please let us know if we can be of further assistance.

John C. Yoo
Deputy Assistant Attorney General

---

[4] **CAT:** The UN Convention Against Torture and Other Cruel, Inhumane, or Degrading Punishment, to which the United States is a signatory.

READING AND DISCUSSION QUESTIONS

1. How do these memos define torture?

2. What arguments does Yoo put forward concerning the power of the presidency?

3. These memos provide a legal framework for interrogations conducted by representatives of the U.S. government according to U.S. law. How does Yoo address international law? Judging by these memos, how does the United States balance international and domestic concerns?

VIEWPOINTS

Immigration and Assimilation in Postwar Germany

The migration of foreign workers to Germany in the decades following World War II began at the invitation of the German government. During the 1950s and 1960s, as Germany recovered from the devastation of the war, the key limiting factor in German economic growth was a shortage of labor. By the early 1960s, there were more unfilled jobs in Germany than there were Germans on the official unemployment lists. The government responded by signing agreements with a number of countries to allow the temporary migration of "guest workers." When those guest workers defied government expectations and sought to settle in Germany, it raised a host of unexpected questions. How would these "foreigners" fit into German society? What adjustments would Germans have to make as their country grew more diverse? How did the permanent presence of guest workers challenge prevailing notions of what it meant to be German?

33-2 | A Management Expert Explains How to Make Guest Workers Feel Welcome

GIACOMO MATURI, *The Integration of the Southern Labor Force and Its Specific Adaptation Problems* (1961)

As more and more guest workers made their way into the German labor force, German employers struggled to come to terms with their "differentness." When problems arose in the

---

integration of the new workers into existing production regimes, employers tended to explain those problems in cultural terms. From employers' point of view, German industrial norms reflected German culture and the German character. If Spanish, Portuguese, or Italian workers failed to fit in, it was, in essence, because they were not German. In this excerpt from a paper delivered at a 1961 convention of German employers, Giacomo Maturi, an industrial psychologist employed by the Ford Motor Company, presented his views on the cultural differences between southern European and German workers, as well as his suggestions for overcoming those differences.

Many of the difficulties in the integration of foreign labor power in the German economy originate in the *differentness* of these southern people. These are psychological difficulties, which cannot always be resolved by adapting these people to the German mentality and German forms. These difficulties can only be mastered by getting to know the eccentricities of these foreigners. They arise primarily when one tries to handle these people like Germans. It is only when one knows foreignness that a right-minded negotiation with them is possible, in which case the difficulties cease to exist, or are not that bad after all. They are only new manifestations that one must take into account; they can even be useful for the business milieu. . . .

The roots of these differences lie in the climate, in the landscape, in the historical development, in the culture and education, and in the societal structure of these peoples. The depth and momentousness of these factors show that it is impossible and irrational to demand a quick and total adaptation.

The Influence of the Climate on Life Rhythms

The southern climate demands and enables a different life rhythm than here in the north. Life is livelier; it is less strict and regulated. Without affecting actual productive potential, the climate has an effect on people and demands a different daily schedule, conditioning the distinct habits of these people, in private as well as in business life. Labor takes place in a different way than in the northern countries; it does not have the haste and the tempo that is common here. These people are no less willing to work or capable of work. This fact needs no further proof, because everyone praises the industriousness and the joy in working evident among the Italians. The legend of lazy Italians is, after all, a thing of the past. The overtly negative aspects can also be attributed to the climatic influences; it is also true, nonetheless, that southerners have another understanding of work.

The Southerner's Idea of Labor

Southerners are more conscious than others that they do not live to work but work to live. They are, after all, the heirs to the ancient Roman and Greek societies that regarded handiwork as slave labor and saw life's ideal as an *otium*—meaning liberation from material handiwork—in order to devote oneself to the greater values of life. They carry themselves with a distinct sense for the truly human aspects of life, because they do not really need to give themselves over to a hasty industriousness in order to drive away boredom. They value many things much more than financial affluence and the comfort of technology. Moreover, their deeply religious, sometimes fatalistic sense for life leads them to undervalue many external things.

The beauty of the landscape, the mild climate, the clear blue sky and sea on the heavenly coasts are not inconsequential for them, in that they encourage a more contemplative and nature-bound way of living.

The pressure of work and income has, however, become great among these people of late. This fact is evident in their desire for overtime and their thrifty intentions to send as much money back home as possible. But one may not forget the conventional attitude of these people toward material labor if one wants to understand this or that particular manifestation. Their lack of hardiness and reliability, which is cause for complaint here and there, can certainly be understood from this point of view. . . .

The Psychological Differences Between Germans and Southerners

The southerner wants to be dealt with in a very personal manner; he does not want to be a number. He needs warmth, sympathy, open and affectionate friendship, as well as recognition for work performed. Equality of rights and compensation is not sufficient for him; he is receptive and looks for a smile from his boss or employer.

The German, in contrast, is cold and objective; he is usually honest, just, and shies away from playing favorites, but he smiles too infrequently. For the southerner, he is not human enough. The tone one finds in the businesses here, particularly in construction work, is too tough and raw for southerners and sometimes appears almost brutal to them. These people are not exactly sensitive but they do tend to react more quickly. Even their voices sound different, particularly when they are fighting. They are impulsive and sometimes violent, but this behavior is only their passions coming to the surface. . . .

Most German employers are happy with the performance of these newly recruited foreigners, but the latter are too often conceived of only as labor power, as an economic factor, not as people. This perception does not mean that too little is being done for them; many firms even provide housing and supplies for them. But the human contact is missing. Coworkers also do not do much to foster intimacy with these people, to understand them. Foreign labor power is certainly not merely "foreign workers" anymore, but these people are still not perceived as full humans; they are isolated. Families living in the area also tend to avoid contact with these people as much as possible. There are no free rooms to rent for them; they are not wanted.

One should greet them, invite them in, receive them warmly, in order to introduce them into the new society. The economic problems of immigration should not overshadow the purely human problems. Inclusion in the economy demands inclusion in society.

READING AND DISCUSSION QUESTIONS

1. According to Maturi, what are the key differences between Germans and southern Europeans? How does he explain these differences?

2. What suggestions does Maturi offer employers seeking to facilitate the adaptation of foreign workers to German conditions? What does his advice suggest
   about German attitudes toward foreign workers in the early 1960s?

33-3 | German Academics Take a Stand Against Immigration

Heidelberg Manifesto (1982)

By the early 1970s, the unbridled economic growth that had accompanied the rebuilding of
Germany had come to a halt. Recession, inflation, and rising unemployment became the economic watchwords in Germany and, indeed, throughout the West. The guest workers who
had arrived in the previous decades did not leave when economic conditions changed. Despite
official policy to the contrary, many guest workers put down roots in Germany, starting families and building communities. This combination of economic hard times and the increasingly
apparent reality that former guest workers and their families intended to become permanent
residents fueled widespread anti-immigrant sentiment in Germany. This 1982 manifesto,
authored by a group of leading German academics, captures prevailing German attitudes
toward immigration in the 1970s and early 1980s.

We are observing a development with great concern, a development initiated by
a euphorically optimistic economic policy that has resulted in a state of affairs in
which approximately 5 million guest workers and their families are now living
and working in our country. Obviously, it has not been possible to halt the influx,
despite a moratorium on recruitment. In 1989 alone, the number of registered
foreigners rose by 309,000; 194,000 of those were Turks.

  The situation has been exacerbated by the fact that little more than half of the
necessary amount of children are being born in order to maintain zero growth of
the German population in West Germany. A renewal of the procreative function
of the German family is urgently needed.

  Many Germans already feel foreign in their own neighborhoods, work-
places, and homeland in general—just as foreign as the guest workers are in
their new surroundings.

  The government's decision to promote the influx of foreigners in an era of
unbridled economic growth is now widely recognized as questionable. Up to this
point, the German population has not been informed of the significance and consequences of this process. We believe that the establishment of a politically independent consortium is necessary, one that will work in dialogue with politicians

toward a (preferably) universal solution. This problem must be resolved if it is not to become a fateful impasse for guest workers as well as the host country.

One complication in the search for a solution to this problem is the fact that one can no longer pose the necessary questions in public debate without incurring accusations of Nazism. For this reason, we must stress that we stand firmly on the foundation of the Basic Law in all our efforts toward a solution. We emphatically oppose ideological nationalism, racism, right- and left-wing extremism.

The integration of large masses of non-German foreigners is not possible without threatening the German people, language, culture, and religion. Every people, including the Germans, has a natural right to preserve its identity and character in its residential areas. Respect for other peoples necessitates their preservation as well, not their assimilation ("Germanization"). We perceive Europe as an industrious community of peoples and nations that gives rise to a coherent higher order through culture and history. As Solzhenitsyn suggests, "Every nation is a one-time facet of a divine plan." On April 5, 1981, the voters of a multiracial nation, Switzerland, approved a model.

Although we know about the abuse of the word *Volk*, we must remind the reader that the Basic Law emanates from the term *Volk*, indeed from the German *Volk*, and that the federal president and the members of the government take this oath: "I swear that I will dedicate my energies to the good of the German *Volk*, further its interests, and prevent injury to it." Whoever understands this oath cannot deny that it is the German people whose "preservation" is at stake. And those who decide that there are no peoples worth preserving disregard the rules of scientific hermeneutics and grossly misinterpret our concerns.

We do not hesitate to remind you that the goal of reunification—an obligation established in the preamble of the Basic Law—could be most grievously endangered through the current foreigner policy.

How is reunification to remain a possibility when many regions of Germany are becoming ethnically foreign? What hope for the future do the hundreds of thousands of guest-worker children have if they are illiterate in both their native language and German? What hope do our own children have when they are being educated predominantly in classes with foreigners? Only active and viable German families can preserve our people for the future.

Technological advancement continues to offer various possibilities to make the employment of guest workers superfluous. The highest priority of economic management must be to bring machines to people, not people to machines. Solving this problem means improving the living conditions of the guest workers in their own countries through targeted development assistance—not here with us. Reuniting guest workers with their families in the ancestral homeland—on a voluntary basis, of course—will relieve the burden on our overindustrialized country, a country suffering from environmental destruction.

Almost none of the responsible persons or the functionaries from prominent social institutions have dared to face facts, let alone to propose a realistic concept for a long-term policy. To this end, we believe the formation of a politically independent consortium is necessary, one that will encourage organizations, associations, and individuals to collaboratively dedicate themselves to the preservation of our people—its language, culture, religion, and way of life.

We as university instructors, a profession with lofty tasks and responsibilities that compel us to ensure an appropriate and reasonable education for foreigners in our country (especially those from the so-called third world), must, on the grounds of our professional legitimacy, point out the seriousness of the current situation and the menacing consequences of a trend already under way.

READING AND DISCUSSION QUESTIONS

1. How do the authors define what it means to be a German? Why do they believe that immigrants threaten the survival of a distinct German identity?

2. How might the German experience under the Third Reich have shaped the debate about German cultural diversity in the early 1980s? Why do the authors of the Heidelberg Manifesto feel compelled to defend themselves against "accusations of Nazism"?

VIEWPOINTS COMPARATIVE QUESTIONS

1. What differences do Maturi and the authors of the Heidelberg Manifesto identify between native Germans and immigrants working and living in Germany? What importance do they attach to these differences?

2. How would you account for the very different attitudes toward immigrant workers revealed in these two documents? What had changed in Germany between 1961 and 1982?

3. On what, if anything, might Maturi and the authors of the Heidelberg Manifesto have agreed? What solutions might Maturi have suggested to the problems identified by the manifesto's authors?

33-4 | Second-Wave Feminists Define Their Objectives

BETTY FRIEDAN, *Statement of Purpose of the National Organization for Women* (1966)

Women's rights activists of the late nineteenth and early twentieth century focused their attention on obtaining for women the right to vote. The "second-wave" feminists of the

---

National Organization for Women, "Statement of Purpose," www.now.org/history/purpos66. html. Reprinted with permission. This is a historical document and may not reflect the current language or priorities of the organization.

1960s and 1970s pursued a much broader agenda. Rejecting biological determinism, second-wave feminists attacked both discrimination against women and the social structures and patterns that established and reinforced male dominance. This statement of purpose, written in 1966 for the National Organization for Women (NOW) by Betty Friedan (1921–2006), captures much of the outlook and objectives of this new generation of activists. As you read it, think about how it differs from earlier efforts to define and defend women's rights.

We, men and women who hereby constitute ourselves as the National Organization for Women, believe that the time has come for a new movement toward true equality for all women in America, and toward a fully equal partnership of the sexes, as part of the world-wide revolution of human rights now taking place within and beyond our national borders.

The purpose of NOW is to take action to bring women into full participation in the mainstream of American society now, exercising all the privileges and responsibilities thereof in truly equal partnership with men. . . .

NOW is dedicated to the proposition that women, first and foremost, are human beings, who, like all other people in our society, must have the chance to develop their fullest human potential. We believe that women can achieve such equality only by accepting to the full the challenges and responsibilities they share with all other people in our society, as part of the decision-making mainstream of American political, economic and social life. . . .

Enormous changes taking place in our society make it both possible and urgently necessary to advance the unfinished revolution of women toward true equality, now. With a life span lengthened to nearly 75 years it is no longer either necessary or possible for women to devote the greater part of their lives to child-rearing; yet childbearing and rearing which continues to be a most important part of most women's lives—still is used to justify barring women from equal professional and economic participation and advance.

Today's technology has reduced most of the productive chores which women once performed in the home and in mass-production industries based upon routine unskilled labor. This same technology has virtually eliminated the quality of muscular strength as a criterion for filling most jobs, while intensifying American industry's need for creative intelligence. In view of this new industrial revolution created by automation in the mid-twentieth century, women can and must participate in old and new fields of society in full equality—or become permanent outsiders.

Despite all the talk about the status of American women in recent years, the actual position of women in the United States has declined, and is declining, to an alarming degree throughout the 1950's and 60's. Although 46.4% of all American women between the ages of 18 and 65 now work outside the home, the overwhelming majority—75%—are in routine clerical, sales, or factory jobs, or they are household workers, cleaning women, hospital attendants. About two-thirds of Negro women workers are in the lowest paid service occupations. Working women are becoming increasingly—not less—concentrated on the bottom of the job ladder. As a consequence full-time women workers today earn on the average only 60% of what men earn, and that wage gap has been increasing over the past twenty-five years in every major industry group. In 1964, of all women with a yearly income, 89% earned under $5,000 a year; half of all full-time year round women workers earned less than $3,690; only 1.4% of full-time year round women workers had an annual income of $10,000 or more.

Further, with higher education increasingly essential in today's society, too few women are entering and finishing college or going on to graduate or professional school. Today, women earn only one in three of the B.A.'s and M.A.'s granted, and one in ten of the Ph.D.'s.

In all the professions considered of importance to society, and in the executive ranks of industry and government, women are losing ground. Where they are present it is only a token handful. Women comprise less than 1% of federal judges; less than 4% of all lawyers; 7% of doctors. Yet women represent 51% of the U.S. population. And, increasingly, men are replacing women in the top positions in secondary and elementary schools, in social work, and in libraries—once thought to be women's fields. . . .

WE BELIEVE that the power of American law, and the protection guaranteed by the U.S. Constitution to the civil rights of all individuals, must be effectively applied and enforced to isolate and remove patterns of sex discrimination, to ensure equality of opportunity in employment and education, and equality of civil and political rights and responsibilities on behalf of women, as well as for Negroes and other deprived groups.

We realize that women's problems are linked to many broader questions of social justice; their solution will require concerted action by many groups. Therefore, convinced that human rights for all are indivisible, we expect to give active support to the common cause of equal rights for all those who suffer discrimination and deprivation, and we call upon other organizations committed to such goals to support our efforts toward equality for women. . . .

WE BELIEVE that this nation has a capacity at least as great as other nations, to innovate new social institutions which will enable women to enjoy the true equality of opportunity and responsibility in society, without conflict with their responsibilities as mothers and homemakers. In such innovations, America does not lead the Western world, but lags by decades behind many European countries. We do not accept the traditional assumption that a woman has to choose between marriage and motherhood, on the one hand, and serious participation in industry or the professions on the other. We question the present expectation that all normal women will retire from job or profession for 10 or 15 years, to devote their full time to raising children, only to reenter the job market at a relatively minor level. This, in itself, is a deterrent to the aspirations of women, to their acceptance into management or professional training courses, and to the very possibility of equality of opportunity or real choice, for all but a few women. Above all, we reject the assumption that these problems are the unique responsibility of each individual woman, rather than a basic social dilemma which society must solve. True equality of opportunity and freedom of choice for women requires such practical, and possible innovations as a nationwide network of child-care centers, which will make it unnecessary for women to retire completely from society until their children are grown, and national programs to provide retraining for women who have chosen to care for their children full-time.

WE BELIEVE that it is as essential for every girl to be educated to her full potential of human ability as it is for every boy—with the knowledge that such education is the key to effective participation in today's economy and that, for a girl as for a boy, education can only be serious where there is expectation that it will be used in society. We believe that American educators are capable of devising means of imparting such expectations to girl students. Moreover, we consider the decline in the proportion of women receiving higher and professional education to be evidence of discrimination. This discrimination may take the form of quotas against the admission of women to colleges, and professional schools; lack of encouragement by parents, counselors and educators; denial of loans or fellowships; or the traditional or arbitrary procedures in graduate and professional training geared in terms of men, which inadvertently discriminate against women. We believe that the same serious attention must be given to high school dropouts who are girls as to boys.

WE REJECT the current assumptions that a man must carry the sole burden of supporting himself, his wife, and family, and that a woman is automatically entitled to lifelong support by a man upon her marriage, or that marriage, home and family are primarily woman's world and responsibility—hers, to dominate—his to support. We believe that a true partnership between the sexes demands a different concept of marriage, an equitable sharing of the responsibilities of home and children and of the economic burdens of their support. We believe that proper recognition should be given to the economic and social value of homemaking and child-care. To these ends, we will seek to open a reexamination of laws and mores governing marriage and divorce, for we believe that the current state of "half-equity" between the sexes discriminates against both men and women, and is the cause of much unnecessary hostility between the sexes.

WE BELIEVE that women must now exercise their political rights and responsibilities as American citizens. They must refuse to be segregated on the basis of sex into separate-and-not-equal ladies' auxiliaries in the political parties, and they must demand representation according to their numbers in the regularly constituted party committees—at local, state, and national levels—and in the informal power structure, participating fully in the selection of candidates and political decision-making, and running for office themselves.

IN THE INTERESTS OF THE HUMAN DIGNITY OF WOMEN, we will protest, and endeavor to change, the false image of women now prevalent in the
mass media, and in the texts, ceremonies, laws, and practices of our major social
institutions. Such images perpetuate contempt for women by society and by
women for themselves. We are similarly opposed to all policies and practices—in
church, state, college, factory, or office—which, in the guise of protectiveness,
not only deny opportunities but also foster in women self-denigration, dependence, and evasion of responsibility, undermine their confidence in their own
abilities and foster contempt for women. . . .

WE BELIEVE THAT women will do most to create a new image of women
by acting now, and by speaking out in behalf of their own equality, freedom,
and human dignity—not in pleas for special privilege, nor in enmity toward
men, who are also victims of the current, half-equality between the sexes—but
in an active, self-respecting partnership with men. By so doing, women will
develop confidence in their own ability to determine actively, in partnership
with men, the conditions of their life, their choices, their future and their
society.

READING AND DISCUSSION QUESTIONS

1. What was the purpose of NOW? How did its agenda differ from that of earlier
   women's rights organizations?

2. Why did NOW believe that a push for full equality was particularly urgent in
   1966? How was the statement of purpose shaped by the larger context of social
   and political change in the mid-1960s?

33-5 | Life at the Margins of the Modern City

JONAS BENDIKSEN, *"New Settlement": A Slum in Caracas, Venezuela* (ca. 2007)

In 2011, more than one billion people on earth lived in areas defined as slums. These often
massive clusters of makeshift housing sprung up around major urban centers in various world
regions to accommodate migrants, refugees, foreign workers, and others who are unable to
afford safer and more stable accommodations. While slums have been a feature of urban
environments throughout the modern era, contemporary slums are both much larger and
much less permanent than their historical counterparts. Slums in the twenty-first century
operate outside or on the margins of regular urban infrastructures; sanitation, health care,
crime prevention, and other services are usually absent, and slum populations are often only
informally connected to the networks of commerce and government that structure other
urban areas and populations. The photograph here shows a makeshift slum structure in
Caracas, Venezuela.

© Jonas Bendiksen, Magnum Photos.

READING AND DISCUSSION QUESTIONS

1. What buildings are featured in this photograph? What is the effect of presenting these buildings together?

2. What does the lack of walls and the visibility of furniture and other possessions imply about the lives of the people living in this dwelling?

3. The figures in the foreground appear to be playing or dancing. Are their actions or attitudes surprising, given the context? Explain.

■ COMPARATIVE QUESTIONS ■

1. What does John Yoo's memorandum suggest about the way the author saw the relationship between the United States and the rest of the world? In your opinion, does the memorandum reflect a significant departure from earlier U.S. viewpoints and policies? Why or why not?

2. Compare and contrast the postwar surge in immigration with the similar surge that occurred in the late nineteenth and early twentieth centuries (see Chapter 27). What similarities and differences do you note?

3. In what ways does the agenda articulated by the founders of the National Organization for Women differ from that of earlier women's rights advocates? How did second-wave feminists build on the ideas and accomplishments of their predecessors?

4. Each of the documents included in this chapter touches on a major global challenge: war and terrorism, the movement of peoples, racism, gender inequality, and poverty. What connections can you make between these challenges? How does each contribute to the others? What other contemporary challenges would you add to the ones noted here?